Studio Teaching in Education

Well-established in some fields and still emerging in others, the studio approach to design education is an increasingly attractive mode of teaching and learning, though its variety of definitions and its high demands can make this pedagogical form somewhat daunting. *Studio Teaching in Higher Education* provides narrative examples of studio education written by instructors who have engaged in it, both within and outside the instructional design field. These multidisciplinary design cases are enriched by the book's coverage of the studio concept in design education, heterogeneity of studio, commonalities in practice, and existing and emergent concerns about studio pedagogy. Prefaced by notes on how the design cases were curated and key perspectives from which the reader might view them, *Studio Teaching in Higher Education* is a supportive, exploratory resource for those considering or actively adapting a studio mode of teaching and learning to their own disciplines.

Elizabeth Boling is Professor of Instructional Systems Technology and Associate Dean for Graduate Studies at Indiana University, Bloomington, USA.

Richard A. Schwier is Emeritus Professor of Educational Technology and Design in the Department of Curriculum Studies at the University of Saskatchewan, Canada.

Colin M. Gray is Assistant Professor in the Department of Computer Graphics Technology at Purdue University, West Lafayette, Indiana, USA.

Kennon M. Smith is Associate Professor in the Department of Apparel Merchandising & Interior Design at Indiana University, Bloomington, USA.

Katy Campbell is Professor and Dean of the Faculty of Extension at the University of Alberta, Canada.

Studio Teaching in Higher Education

Selected Design Cases

Edited by Elizabeth Boling, Richard A. Schwier, Colin M. Gray, Kennon M. Smith, and Katy Campbell

NEW YORK AND LONDON

First published 2016
by Routledge
711 Third Avenue, New York, NY 10017

and by Routledge
2 Park Square, Milton Park, Abingdon, Oxon OX14 4RN

Routledge is an imprint of the Taylor & Francis Group, an informa business

Library of Congress Cataloging in Publication Data
A catalog record for this book has been requested

ISBN: 978-1-138-90241-1 (hbk)
ISBN: 978-1-138-90243-5 (pbk)
ISBN: 978-1-315-69742-0 (ebk)

Typeset in Galliard
by Cenveo Publisher Services

Printed and bound in the United States of America by Publishers Graphics, LLC on sustainably sourced paper.

Contents

List of Figures   viii

List of Tables   xii

1 Introduction   1
ELIZABETH BOLING

2 Curators' Notes   4
ELIZABETH BOLING AND RICHARD A. SCHWIER

Studio Design Cases

3 Hither and Yon: Learning ID in a Studio-Based
Authentic ID Context   21
RICHARD A. SCHWIER

4 The Studio Approach at the University of Georgia:
Always a Work in Progress   37
LLOYD P. RIEBER, GREGORY CLINTON, AND
THEODORE J. KOPCHA

5 Emergent Tensions in Teaching an Interior Design
Studio: Reflections and Opportunistic Redesign   60
KENNON M. SMITH

6 The Rapid (Interactive) Design Studio for Slow
(User and Learner) Change   73
MARTIN A. SIEGEL

7 How I Learned, Unlearned, and Learned
Studio Again   88
ELIZABETH BOLING

8 Constructing | Connecting | Conveying:
   A Beginning Studio Student and Instructor
   Journey of Meaning and Experience   101
   JILL B. PABLE

9 The Lake Course: A Studio Apart   123
   JAY WILSON

10 Evolving into Studio   137
   ANDREW S. GIBBONS

11 Orchestrating Learning   152
   KATHERINE S. CENNAMO

12 Reflective Practice: Educational Changes
   Based On Professional Expertise   164
   FRED M. DUER

13 The Creativity Habit   180
   BRAD HOKANSON AND MARIT MCCLUSKE

14 How I Gave Up ADDIE for Design Thinking,
   and So Did My Students   195
   MONICA W. TRACEY

15 A Case of User-Centered Design as
   Subversive Practice   206
   KATY CAMPBELL

16 Undisciplined and Out of Control: A Course
   in Systemic Design for First-year
   Undergraduate Students   222
   GORDON ROWLAND

17 Design Thinking in Action: Perspectives on
   Teaching and Redesigning a Learning Design Studio   235
   MICHAEL M. ROOK AND SIMON HOOPER

Studio Pedagogy

18 What is Studio? 248
KATHERINE S. CENNAMO

19 Critical Views of Studio 260
COLIN M. GRAY AND KENNON M. SMITH

20 Emergent Views of Studio 271
COLIN M. GRAY

About the Contributors 282
Index 289

Figures

2.1   Color-coded organization of design cases   6

3.1   Online studio spaces for ID teams in the LMS   22

3.2a-d Teams meet in mashed-up online and face-to-face
studio space   23

3.3a and b Students presenting high fidelity prototypes
to client groups   27

4.1   A graphic depicting the core studio courses and their
placement in the master's program at the University
of Georgia. The three studio courses are, respectively,
EDIT 6190 Design and Development Tools, EDIT 6200
Learning Environments Design I, and EDIT 6210 Learning
Environments Design II. Other departmental courses that
complement the studio courses are also shown. Graphic
adapted from Clinton and Rieber 2010, adaptation created
by students in the EDIT 6210 Studio class   41

4.2   Model desktop critique. Graphic by EDIT 6210 student
Sarah Ashton   45

4.3   The University of Georgia LDT Studio Showcase in
progress, Spring 2010   50

"Save the Shells" by Benjamin Rockwood   54

"Numbers All Around" by Sam Winward   55

"Fun for All!" by Michael Gardner   56

"Chuck Close: Off the Wall" by Michael Gardner   56

"Maternal Transgressions: Musings on Foucault, Power
and the Label Known as Disabled" by Teri Holbrook   57

"Are You Here to Cause Friction?" by Ben Rockwood,
David Clark, Denise Domizi, Kim Gibson, Bobby Mitchell,
and Akecia Mobley   58

"Georgia Flash Map" by Emily Pitts Ennis   58

6.1   Two interactive screens from Storyshare. Shankar
Balasubramanian, Evan Tank and Zhijian (Owen)
Shi (2015). Reprinted with permission   79

6.2   "The Man with the Dog" by Jared Forney (2013).
Reprinted with permission   86

7.1   Four stills from Nicole Hatch's documentary featuring
      the Newseum in Washington DC. This choice was
      challenging because of the scope of the project, the
      need to get permission for access, and the challenge
      of collecting photos and video footage within the
      museum guidelines. After a contact visit to the
      museum, the project looked more feasible   93
7.2   Documenting a weekend English language club, one
      student included text describing the informative bus
      driver who drove the members to meetings. Reviewing
      the documentary very close to the due date, she
      decided a photo was important to the story; she
      reworked a section of her documentary and
      returned to the field to collect the photo   98
7.3   The classroom available for studio is unprepossessing,
      but allows for tables to be placed so that students
      can talk while they work and listen in on consultations
      I am having with others nearby   99
8.1   This Poetry Project solution by Katharine Galvin shows
      a perspective rendering of the airport corridor.
      The poem *Who Said that Love was Fire?* by Patience
      Worth is interpreted here as a human relationship that
      begins as a brightly burning soul-engulfing experience
      and that later settles first into long-enduring embers
      and then, ultimately, into ash – the thing that remains
      when love is spent. The floor plan's series of rooms
      carry visitors through a corresponding series of
      visual experiences   107
8.2   The classroom layout of clustered individual drafting
      tables forms pods for a sense of community   108
8.3   Example of a concept board for a shrine for secular
      humanism by Katie Timmerman. Steps include
      deconstructing the concept idea of a puzzle piece, then
      reconstructing it using architectural expressions   116
8.4   In Timmerman's final model of the solution, the
      concept of puzzle pieces finds its outlet in an overhead
      trellis intended to reinforce the logical underpinnings
      of secular humanistic belief   117
8.5   Example of the resulting model from the Student
      Dormitory project – a residential room for a single
      person by Victoria Davis. Given the artistic movement
      of graffiti, Victoria chose the concept of a billboard
      (an all-too-often palette for these artists), expressed
      here in metal railings, catwalk-like metal flooring in

the second level and vertical orientation of the
space's circulation   119

8.6   Example of the model from the course's final shrine
project by Hae Jeong Hwang. Lighting and its effects
is a major part of the project along with functional
space planning and concept. This project expressed
the Wiccan religion as a paradigm of the natural
world echoed here through abstracted tree forms   120

9.1   As the instructor, I am able to connect deeply
with the students   124

9.2   Students collaborating in the close quarters
classroom environment   128

9.3   Images of the lake site   129

9.4   Students work in an environment they create and control 134

13.1   Idea capture form, from first day of class. Brad Hokanson 181

13.2   Wearing Something Different. Marit McCluske   183

13.3   A sketch depicting an Attribute Listing exercise.
In the exercise, attributes of an object or process are
listed, then changed to generate new ideas. Brad Hokanson   185

13.4   Wearing something different: clothes to read the
newspaper at the bus stop. Jude Michael   188

13.5   Eating something different – bagel with cream cheese,
via one's feet. Lindsay N. Smith   189

13.6   Something your "other" does. Annika Q. Yan   190

14.1   Google site for the course   198

14.2   Assignments from Week 1   199

14.3   Screenshot from video assigned Week 1. CBS News   200

14.4   Assignments from Week 5. Note: Reflection question #4
referred to a slide that addressed uncertainty in design,
so students were being asked to reflect on their
own thoughts about uncertainty in design   201

14.5   Instructional message for Weeks 14 and 15   203

14.6   Reflection questions for Weeks 14 and 15   204

15.1   Sample narrated PowerPoint slide Module 4: User
profiling. Slide 11 with narration text: For example, your
client wants to develop an online dating service. Your user
research strategy included a user segmentation process in
which you identified x key segments of the target user
population: singles 27-34, and older adults 44-67. The latter
segment contained several categories, including females who
were widowed, and males and females who were divorced
Here is a persona named Kelly (that's me, by the way)   210

15.2   First UCD Mindmap 2003   212

15.3   Table of contents for the revised handbook, 2005   218
15.4   Excerpt of the introduction to the course from the
       handbook, 2005   219
16.1   Cycle of learning events for each unit   226
17.1   The Spring 2014 LDS Homepage   237
17.2   The Krause Innovation Studio classroom at the
       Pennsylvania State University   240
17.3   The Breakout Area in the Krause Innovation Studio   241
18.1   Diagram of the Bauhaus curriculum, as designed by
       Walter Gropius   250

Tables

5.1   Example of a curriculum map for major requirements
in a four-year interior design degree   62

6.1   Three sample sprints with overlapping projects   83

8.1   First summer and fall semesters of the four-year
Interior Design undergraduate program of studies   102

8.2   Studio 1 course project names, order, length and
brief description   106

9.1   A timeline of the course with major themes and milestones   130

11.1   Excerpt from the syllabus   160

13.1   Percentile increases calculated from raw scores   193

15.1   Course description   213

15.2   Mini-case #1 rubric, 2005   215

15.3   Excerpt from student's self-assessment journal, 2006   217

16.1   Units and challenges   226

17.1   Individual perspectives on LDS   238

1 Introduction

Elizabeth Boling

Interest in studio forms of teaching and learning is growing outside the fields of design where it has traditionally been practiced, but studio can be challenging for those who have not previously taught in this mode or experienced it as a student. Instructors like these may be the majority of those either contemplating adaption of studio to their own courses, or facing the requirement to do so as programs shift focus. The editors of this volume saw the need to provide instructors who may be exploring studio pedagogy with a source for multiple and varied narratives describing studio courses and the experience of teaching them. Other readers who may find value in this volume include those with general interests in studio pedagogy, those studying this form of teaching and learning, and those studying design education.

Our intention from the beginning was to produce an integrated volume in which the chapters offered strongly individual stories but a similar level of detail and reflection. We feel we have accomplished this by using a process in which authors started their chapters in a similar way before taking them in the unique directions warranted by their individual practices of studio teaching.

The first group of eight authors invited to participate in writing design cases gathered on the campus of Indiana University to spend an intense day and a half hammering out first drafts of those cases. We worked in short bursts, 15–20 minutes, responding to a set of prompts covering the main elements of design cases and allowing the time pressure to promote a free flow of narrative onto the page. Between these short sessions we shared thoughts on how the writing was going and how our narratives might serve the purposes of the book. The prompts were as follows:

1. What is the context in which you have taught basic design? For how long? To what kind of students in what kind of program? Where did it come from? What is the general configuration of the "traditional" course you may have been teaching?
2. What is the genesis of any ideas you have had regarding problems, concerns, enthusiasms, and new directions in this teaching? When did you

start thinking, "I want to change this"? What is your remembrance of steps you took to act on these ideas? What were those steps and how did they work out early on?

3.   What are the specifics of the course you teach now? Time, interactions, activities, materials, physical facilities, technologies, experiences, grading? Tell this as if explaining how to teach it.

4.   What is it critical to remember in teaching this way? Common reactions of students? Common difficulties? High points? What has to be different in you to teach this way? What concerns do you have throwing a colleague into this class?

5.   How did you decide on the major features of the course? If theory – say so. If elsewhere – say so. What alternatives did you consider? Why did you reject them? What has just not worked?

6.   What changes are you considering? Why? What stresses does this course cause for you? Colleagues? Administrators? Students? What do you want to be doing that you cannot? Which have been overcome? How?

Another six authors and four co-authors were subsequently recruited to contribute chapters. We asked them to choose a period of time during which the prompts could be sent to them via email, one at a time, and they could spend 15-20 minutes responding to each one via the same rapid writing technique. When all the draft chapters had been generated, authors revisited them to pull each one together into a coherent form. These revised drafts were distributed between the authors for an initial review focused on readability and clarity, as well as for suggestions regarding which parts of each case struck the reviewer as especially interesting and worth further elaboration. Authors revised their drafts accordingly.

Subsequently the co-editors reviewed each draft again, providing the authors with specific feedback on what seemed to be the "heart" of each design case. We encouraged the final revision of each chapter to emphasize these distinctive elements of their narratives. This process has resulted in a series of design cases that offer readers a consistent level of detail in the cases together with a variety of vicarious experiences in studio teaching.

As the design case chapters came together, subsets of co-editors also produced three chapters addressing studio from an academic perspective. These appear after the design cases. The first presents a model of studio focused on its core features rather than surface appearance, encouraging readers to see that there is no single template for what constitutes studio pedagogy and to consider what the distinguishing features of studio are. A chapter detailing critical views of studio is provided next, illuminating well-known and emerging concerns regarding studio pedagogy. These concerns do not undermine the studio form of teaching and learning, but serve to counteract the assumption that studio is a panacea for the known problems of teaching design via lectures, structured projects and fixed models. Finally, we present a chapter surveying emergent studio pedagogy, or studio as it is being adapted into fields of design where it has not previously been the norm in teaching and learning. This is the context in which a majority of the design cases are situated.

Near the end of the process, two of us collaborated on producing the Curator's Notes. Of course you, the reader, can dive in and start reading anywhere you like, but this chapter is intended as a useful starting point, similar to the notes that may guide a viewer in a museum who are approaching a collection of artifacts. The notes only scratch the surface of how these design cases may be experienced, compared, mined for detail and simply enjoyed as experiences to be stored away until they surface later when you are designing or teaching a course yourself.

The editors recognize that contributing to this volume has been demanding for the authors who joined us in this project. We express our appreciation to them for all the work they have put in, for their willingness to tackle a somewhat unfamiliar form of representing knowledge, for their responsiveness to our feedback and for their patience with us as we have wound our way toward publication.

2   Curators' Notes

Elizabeth Boling and Richard A. Schwier

This volume comprises 15 design cases describing the experiences and reflections of educators who use various forms of studio teaching in their secondary education courses. Some of the cases came out of disciplines with a long history of studio teaching, where this approach is the dominant and default pedagogy. Others came from programs taking early steps into the studio or operating some years into adaptation of studio; in these cases the potential of studio has been seen as worth the pedagogical risks they might incur while introducing a novel way of approaching teaching and learning.

These are not case studies. The aim of a case study would be to examine a course or teaching practice using a structured method and to arrive at conclusions that may be applied to other, similar, situations. The author of a case study decides where its value lies, and discusses where the knowledge generated by such a study might be applicable. In contrast, design cases are carried out to give, as well as the authors are able, a rich experiential view to their readers of something that has been designed – in this case, studio courses and the teaching of them. They are descriptive rather than analytical, and the value of a design case is realized by the reader at the time that the knowledge it contains is actually used. This use is seldom linear; design cases do not present object lessons, lessons learned or propositions in the form of principles, and they are not generally used as templates for future design actions.

What is the reader who may be unused to design cases to make of the chapters in this book when they do not offer any explicit advice and the reader does not know at the time of reading when the stories they tell might be of use? As editors, our intent is to assist such readers. However, we do not do so by conducting any type of cross-case analysis or by drawing principles out of the cases ourselves. Rather, we emphasize the tentative and experimental nature of applying design knowledge, and respect the readers' role in drawing meaning from the work of these authors over time. We do so by adopting the role of curators.

A curator typically serves as an assembler, a caretaker and an interpreter of a collection of objects – in this situation, the design cases on studio teaching. A curator carefully selects or assembles related works, and organizes them appropriately to facilitate the reading of the viewer. Curators often provide narratives that help viewers understand themes that permeate a collection, as well as to envision the overarching view shown in the collection. A curator decides how to arrange the work so that commonality and contrast are heightened to the benefit of the viewer, with the aim of helping readers appreciate that work in more depth than would be possible when encountering each piece individually. This means the curator must appreciate the work and be immersed in it, and consider the work in relation to larger ideas.

This is a tall order, of course, but that's what we intend to do here. As curators, we will draw out some themes, similarities and contrasts, observations and interpretations that may be helpful in deepening the potential value of readers' investment of time and effort. But be warned: we cannot draw out everything to be found in the book. That is the job of the reader. Fortunately, it does not all have to be done at the time of reading. The nature of a design case is such that it will reveal its worth to you at an unspecified time in the future. We hope to help you engage with the cases deeply enough that they will be available to you effortlessly at the moment when you may need to draw upon them.

So, enough talk about it: let's get on with the job.

Assembling and Arranging the Collection

This collection was assembled, as described in the introduction, by selecting authors known to be teaching in studio or proto-studio formats. Several of these were invited from disciplines where studio is the signature pedagogy (Smith, Pable and Duer). Several more represent situations in which the forms of studio being practiced are established in the programs but are significantly dissimilar to traditional studios (Hokanson and McCluske, Rowland, Wilson, and Rieber, Clinton and Kopcha). Lastly, the bulk of the cases we will term *emergent*; in these, studio is being introduced in a fluid manner - either because its form has not yet become stable or because it is not firmly established within a curriculum. An original core of chapters was augmented several times through invitations to additional authors as we identified those whose contributions would enrich the set. In addition to their individuality as persons and the differences in their programs, the authors speak from their own educational backgrounds and their experiences in teaching. Some of them bring to the courses they are describing what we can call *received understanding* of studio, meaning that they have studied in higher education studio environments themselves. Others have observed studio teaching, studied it as a form of pedagogy, read about it and imagined it, but have not experienced it as students or taught in an environment where it is the unexamined norm. A few have direct experience of studio and have also taught in programs where lecture and project-based courses dominate. The perspective of each author is a useful lens for readers to keep in mind.

However, the chapters are not arranged by the type of studio practice they describe. We have ordered them by looking across the many characteristics of the design cases and using those we saw as salient to sequence them. Using a small card for each case (Figure 2.1), we represented the multiple characteristics of each as colored squares. We organized them visually so that each shared at least three characteristics with its neighbors on the left and right, and each differed from those neighbors by at least three characteristics. We hope the similarities and contrasts between chapters will be appreciable to readers, even if they are not always obvious. As curators of the 15 works in this collection - narratives of the experience of studio teaching - we see our arrangement of those narratives as a sixteenth work. For readers who decide to peruse every chapter in order, we anticipate that these salient dimensions will provide a pull through the volume from one story to the next. As an example, consider the Tracey, Campbell and Rowland chapters. They share with their neighbors a narrative about transforming curriculum, but differ in

Figure 2.1 Color-coded organization of design cases.

the domains where they are situated. The outcomes of their efforts differ, as do the formats of the classes that they design, with Tracey establishing her approach essentially in one swift move, and Campbell evolving hers in multiple, painful steps. Campbell and Rowland's stories share the dimension of struggle between institutional norms and their emerging course designs, whereas Rowland's narrative ends with a course well established on his campus and Campbell's does not. Tracey and Campbell's voices share a comparatively "hot" tone in expressing their interactions with students; compared with Campbell, Rowland's tone in describing interactions - while clearly involved and committed - is more "cool." A reader attending to these and many more similarities and differences will find their appreciation of the cases enhanced.

Readers are welcome to jump around the chapters, of course. It may also be fruitful to read adjacent chapters and consider them in the light of one another, or to read them end to end and allow the composition of them all to form a single, textured vicarious experience of teaching in the studio.

Studio is Often Emotional, in Both Painful and Pleasurable Ways

We address first a pervasive emotional dimension in these narratives. The authors describe how their courses are constructed, the activities that take place, the knowledge, skills and attitudes they hope to impart. Beyond this, though, they discuss their own and their students' feelings about the work, and their own feelings during teaching and learning, as an integral part of the studio experience - in some cases, as critical to both teaching and learning effectively. Readers may note this as a quality that sets these design cases apart from descriptions of courses and teaching approaches that consist primarily of lesson content or sequences of activities.

Almost every author talks about the deep immersion students experience in the studio. Such immersion is generally expressed as a positive feature of studio, and those in the field currently devoting themselves to creating immersive learning environments might attend to how often it seems to manifest in these settings. Readers should also note that this immersion is not necessarily pleasant. Pable's students are exhausted from the experience of the studio, as they are challenged to complete five design projects, juggling and applying technical and creative content from a cluster of preliminary courses that add up to a "collective high-stress event." Rieber explicitly encourages his students to create projects that follow their passions, and this fuels tension when students (and some faculty) question the legitimacy of studio learning compared with conventional classrooms. Students at the University of Saskatchewan have dubbed a studio class in ID "the widow(er) maker" because of its requirement that they deliver a completed team project "on time, on budget, and beyond expectations" to clients, regardless of the workload. More than one author describes acting as a counselor to students (wondering if it is appropriate to do so), or offering advice on balancing the work they are doing willingly in the studio with other school and life requirements – like sleep!

Some authors describe their own emotional investments as studio instructors as well, often those tied to their awareness of discomfort on the part of students in the studio. Studio instructors can be acutely aware of the discomfort they intentionally cause, and are sensitive to keeping it manageable for students. Boling feels doubts about herself as a teacher and she suspects her students do too, when she avoids giving her students the comfort of clarity as a core strategy in developing their faculties of judgment. Hokanson and McCluske talk about how comfort zones conflict with the creativity they're trying to nurture, and they underscore the importance of trust to learning. Smith reminds us of how difficult it is to know when to step in and when to let students struggle, meeting this difficulty by being honest and transparent with students about why they can't expect to have questions answered by the studio instructor.

Readers can consider the ways in which the authors express and resolve (or do not resolve) the question of causing anxiety, discomfort, confusion and even anger in students, and how most of them seem to consider this a necessary dilemma. Smith observes that students have become accustomed to the idea (almost a guarantee or social contract) that if they work hard they will be successful. This contract is often violated in studio, and that can cause some consternation. Far from being neutral, or even always nurturing, authors are intentionally causing their students pain and discomfort in these learning environments – at minimum these environments are not all completely comfortable places for their students. These narratives imply that the studio learning experience for students requires them to work at it and, while there are emotional and even social pressures to make the studio experience more comfortable, the studio instructor needs to balance the need for reassurance and clarity with the need to challenge students to learn by doing and struggle with messy challenges. Gray and Smith, in their Critical Views of Studio chapter (Chapter 19), raise the caution that the emotional dimension of studio can tip too far toward the negative if students' discomfort becomes an outcome in its own right, or if it is not carefully weighed for its value in this form of experiential learning.

The emotional dimension of studio environments involves, for more than one author, the *positive* stress of staying on one's toes. We hear Smith and Duer both talk about needing to respond differently in the moment to individual students depending on an appreciation of the students' efforts and their needs, and Cennamo gauging success differently for each student depending on appreciation of where that individual starts out. Smith and Boling describe studio teaching as walking into a situation where they cannot predict what will be demanded of them, and where they may be called on to help students work through problems they, the instructors, do not know immediately how to solve themselves. Wilson has to be "on," Tracey has to be "all in," and Rowland works to be "present, engaged [and] observant" in order to stimulate, match and sustain the excitement and commitment their students put forth. We also hear about positive responses from the students – Hokanson's colleagues ask whether he is teaching a class or leading a cult because of the enthusiasm his students demonstrate. Hooper speaks of joy and satisfaction; Gibbons includes "enjoyment in design" and "a sense of design as discovery" as intended outcomes for his students. The tone signals that these are not just charming expressions; the authors see these emotions as compelling, important, and hopeful requirements for preparing designers.

It bears noting that the emotional dimension of studio for students explored by these authors is discussed *as observed and understood by the instructors*. However concerned these instructors may be for their students, and however keenly they observe them (as many of these authors do), they are not speaking directly for them. As editors, we invited instructors to author the design cases speaking directly to other instructors – course designers speaking to course designers – rather than asking students to describe studio from their perspective. As curators, we encourage readers to attend as much to *how* the authors speak of their students as to what they say *about* them. They are concerned for the wellbeing of their students, speak about trust in them and respect for them.

Studio Tends to be Activity-Centric, and Those Activities Vary Across Studios

What do we mean by "activity-centric"? Many of these authors speak in the physical sense about activities - most report that they walk around the classroom a lot, in some cases using specialty analog tools or helping their students to use them, and many conduct critiques at the desk of each student. Wilson takes his entire studio group to a lakeside retreat for a week, which includes carting equipment and food to the location and hustling from one place to another while they are there, keeping everyone up and running. The striking sense in which *activity* characterizes studio experiences, however, is the way in which the students are engaged in action most of the time in most of these courses. Boling summarizes this aspect of her studio by saying "students follow a pattern that goes, roughly, panic, ruminate, plan, stumble, recover, plan, do, do, revise, do, revise, do." Design briefs or project assignments form the core of most of these studio classes, stimulating the action taking place there.

The size and number of projects in a studio experience can be seen to shape that experience profoundly. Gray and Smith, in this volume, caution that large projects, and their concomitant large investment of time and effort on the part of students, may play into a culture that "crosses the fine line between hard work and exploitation of students" (Fisher 1991, p. 9). However, we see authors discuss the pressure students face responding to small, fast-paced assignments as well. We see in these cases that the activity-intensive nature of studio requires individual instructors, or program designers, to make decisions about the contextual pressures they face, the learning benefits they value and the resources available to them when they elect a "Big Project" or a "Many Projects" studio approach.

The "Big Project" Studio

In the "Big Project" studio, a single design brief spans a semester, although there may be additional activities required along the way. Video projects for Wilson's students span an entire summer with individual work at the beginning and end, and a unique studio environment constructed at a lake in a summer camp-like format in the middle. Each student in Boling's class produces a documentary, video or interactive, describing a design in the world that they did not create themselves and requiring a full semester to complete. Schwier's students spend a full term working in teams on a project that is negotiated ahead of time with an external client. Smith's studio class is composed as a set of small, short projects that crescendo in a large design project carried out by each student. Each of the cases written by these instructors projects a kind of intensity that comes with carrying out a complex project and bringing it to completion, and with the intention to build a strong commitment in students to a product displaying design integrity built into it over time.

The Big Project experiences do vary. Wilson interjects a distinctive experience-within-an-experience into the summer term, providing unusual full-time absorption and proximity for himself and his students in a highly collaborative, supportive and intense learning environment that still allows for the continuity of individual students working on a single large project over a significant period of time. Boling allows considerable leeway for students to choose the target of their documentaries at the start of the term, eating up time students may need later, but also laying foundations for projects that will have "integrity as a designed communication," and for which students exhibit "palpable commitment" to carry them through the entire effort. Schwier's pre-negotiated projects save time that he considers to be precious for his students because it can be devoted to the design of the project, although this sacrifices some potential learning about how to whittle a contract and make good decisions. He discusses his desire to reduce the intensity of the experience for the students, recognizing the extreme time pressures they face in order to bring the project to completion successfully. Smith worries that the number of students and the number of projects reduces the opportunity for group critiques.

The investment for instructors in Big Project studios is described as centering on the effort to be fully present with their students throughout a sustained experience, and to facilitate growth through the single, rich vehicle that experience provides. It also allows for repeated versioning – iterating toward a product in a way that can be rewarding for learning but exhausting in process. Instructors in these studios reflect on how they manage the outlay of personal effort this requires.

The "Many Projects" Studio

Most of the authors here describe studio experiences in which activity is driven by several small projects, sometimes leading up to a larger (but still smallish) project at the end of the class. Duer assigns several projects rather than a single big one, explaining that students working on one larger project will inevitably put off work until later in the semester. He also gives his students considerable latitude and recognizes their limitations, presenting an interesting tension between being directive and permissive – negotiating the students' need for direction and the instructor's intention to help them grow independence. Pable also uses several projects where authenticity is a key thread that runs through the individual briefs. She emphasizes the importance of repetition in design learning, which she feels can be better achieved with a series of smaller projects than with larger projects that span a full term. Similarly, Hokanson, Rowland, and Siegel (although his course is titled "Slow Design") all use a cascade of small projects in their studios, explaining that the brisk pace they set injects a sense of urgency and keeps students moving. These instructors value a willingness to work iteratively, drafting and discarding versions of a project quickly. The investment for instructors of Many Projects studios is described as effort given to developing the projects, and to a high load of assessment and feedback on the part of the instructor. They discuss the strategies they use to meet this load, often involving peer review and the assistance of students senior in their programs.

Individual and Group Projects

Some studios employ group projects and some emphasize individual projects, depending on the context and intentions of the work. Some authors feel that group work and teamwork are typical of the work environments students will experience after they graduate, so they build activities that will mimic their professional experiences. This suggests that social engagement is a key element in the learning for those projects, and that the process of design should not be separated from the interactions among team members. Inevitably, group design influences the product(s) students produce, given that the products are negotiated and individuals must sometimes press an idea and other times capitulate. But other studios use individual projects, which seem to capitalize on the unique ideas and creative energy that individuals bring to the learning environment. Individual projects also yield a greater number of artifacts for critique, and a wider array of examples for other students to experience vicariously in the studio.

Signature Activities

With activity as a central feature of studio, readers may note that some instructors describe activities they consider especially compelling and productive. We are calling these *signature activities* – each seems to give the course being described a character unique to that course and that instructor. One of these, Boling's documentary, is the primary assignment for the course. It is unusual within an instructional design program and unusual as a production course because the students are not designing instruction directly, but are learning production skills in the service of documenting someone else's design. This activity places a signature on the course, shaping its timeline for each student and providing the opportunity for multiple episodes and types of learning.

Most of the other signature activities take place in parallel with either large or small primary projects. Duer has - after much thought about how to connect his students to past knowledge important to their future professional performance - incorporated into his studio an activity called *N2K* (*Need to Know*) in which his students research designers of note in their field from a list of 150 that he maintains; students are reinforced with a verbal "ding!" for discovering links between these designers. The activity carries over more than one semester and outside the classroom and can be imagined to serve as a signature element of studying in Duer's studio.

Rook and Hooper employ a popular activity titled *What's Hot* to keep their students current with new technology ideas in the field, requiring each student to post an idea each week and starting every session with a short discussion of these posts. Hokanson's signature activity, *Do Something Different (DSD or Differents)*, also establishes a thread running through the course, but the *Differents* evolve in complexity as the semester unfolds. *DSD* "becomes part of the learning process of the class" in multiple ways – affording discussion of what is original or creative, changing team relationships and building willingness in the students to take risks. In both these courses the activities are described as compelling, although for different reasons. Rook and Hooper's students see *What's Hot* as a useful addition to their knowledge, while Hokanson and McCluske discuss the nature of the *Differents* as sometimes very disconcerting but ultimately compelling.

Both Siegel and Schwier discuss activities that establish reflection as a key element of design performance. Drawing from the extensive *This I Believe* archive of statements from people in all walks of life, Siegel starts each class session with such a statement and builds to a point at the end of class when the students produce statements of their own. A more open-ended activity takes place in Schwier's studio, with students gathering at the end of work sessions (classes) to "step back from the projects and have an open discussion about what we are learning about instructional design." He does not structure the sessions, but illuminates their reflective nature by describing one group in which each member started these discussions with "I feel …" statements that "almost always led … into deeper conversations about the struggles and joys of doing ID."

   None of these activities is designed to teach content explicitly or directly. Duer's may look most like direct instruction of content, but the primary point of this activity is not to drill the facts of theater design history as much as to build the mental habit of noting and connecting significant precedents in theater design. Instructors are setting up circumstances that encourage habits of thought and action, promote reflection (instead of simply assigning it), and increase the identification students experience with their courses.

Pacing, Assignments and Sequencing are Variable Across Studios and Instructors

In traditional courses we (at least we who identify as instructional designers) expect certainty and clarity. We articulate the objectives; we clarify the expectations for our students; we outline and fuss over the sequence of content; and we are able to answer the inevitable question, "What do you want to see from me on this assignment?" Studios seem to complicate matters. In this collection, we see content and outcomes emerge from the experiences in the studio, both individual and group experiences, and from an intense engagement with design challenges. Content, outcomes, and even process to a certain extent, are shaped to fit the context, and that context is often in a state of flux. Hokanson and McCluske are explicit about discovering course elements as the course is in progress, and scaling up the course on the fly. Wilson's "lake studio" course involves a particular kind of community engagement, culminating in a public premiere of products. Cennamo, Campbell and Gibbons display confidence, tentative though it may be, as they work with students through ideas that are uncertain, vague or unclear at first, but trust that the process of design will bring them around. Similarly, Rowland intentionally downplays content and emphasizes action, setting up a learning context where messiness, chaos and things that don't work are wrestled into designs that will work. Program pressures also shape what is done in studio. For example, Smith worries that the expansion of content required for professional certification in her program means that lectures encroach significantly on studio time. All of this can seem like a violation of expectations to students who are used to lecture-based classrooms or regulated project-based courses – or to studio learning *without* lectures. Part of our responsibility as instructors in studio settings is to help students understand the learning environment, and to nudge them into trusting it. (Sometimes the same thing goes for our colleagues and administrators as we shall see in the sections on spaces and on the ingenuity required to maintain studios.)

The implementation of studio pedagogy has challenged instructors to rethink and sequence their content differently. The inclusion of core content is one example of how a studio disrupts the traditional relationship between what is learned and how it is learned. Consider how authors grappled with the issue of teaching theory and fundamentals first, concurrently, later, or not at all. Gibbons states explicitly that he leaves the two primary approaches to instructional design that he uses (core content material in a traditional course) in the background and lets "expediency reveal moments when one or the other could help if it were pulled into the foreground." He says this is because when he taught technical processes and language first the sequencing confined, and even interfered with, students' abilities to be creative and imaginative in their work. Rowland's approach is similar. He introduces design processes later, only after students experience design challenges. Interestingly, both still see utility in teaching some of the traditional process skills, but introduced them later or concurrently so students are not frozen by a process mindset.

Cennamo also encourages students to design relatively theory free, and then she asks them to reveal the underlying theoretical explanations for their decisions. Students are directed to identify a theory and apply it to the process of design. Tracey's experience "forced me to realize that the students I was teaching would not be able to do this work if I continued to teach [instructional] design the way I was taught and the way it was currently being taught in the classroom. Although I always knew that the step-by-step approach to teaching design did not apply outside of the safe confines of the classroom, I had not up to this point realized I was actually doing a disservice to my students." She understood design not as systematic, but rather a space where designers work with others to innovate solutions to constantly-changing complex problems. The boundaries of theory and the studio alike need to be permeable.

This issue appears to come up more often in the instructional design cases than it does in other disciplines, and this is understandable. Some would argue that instructional design is just now becoming a design area after a longish obsession with technical systems/process concerns. The freshness of this perspective may account for the attention paid by authors to the placement (or elimination) in their courses of the systematic approaches and language that characterized instructional design historically. Areas more firmly identified as fields of design also seem to have a longer experience with studio, which is a signature pedagogy for design rather than a pedagogy in the earlier stages of experimentation.

Studio Happens in a Place; it can be Tricky to Find and Hang On to Studio Spaces, and Virtual Spaces may not Provide a Complete Substitute

Studio learning is often based in physical settings that are resource-intensive for institutions. A large space can be required for specialty equipment, digital and otherwise, as well as to spread out analog work and to display it for critique. If that space is to be made available to a comparatively small group of students around the clock, or even for extended periods, costs go up further because other courses are not cycling through classrooms at the same rate as they would be for lecture-based courses. The ideal pedagogical demands of studio exacerbate the cost pressures, because students not only need space to work, but their work should be available at odd hours, and work-in-progress should remain on constant display.

As difficult as studio spaces can be to justify in the first place, given cost-benefit arguments, some authors *were* successful in obtaining space when they emphasized the need to match the pedagogy with emerging theory and needs. Gibbons spent several years lobbying his Dean for a dedicated studio space where projects in progress could be on continual display and available for repeated critique. His argument for dedicated studio space was based in the theoretical shift that demanded, in his view, a different form of pedagogy that was butting up against the current, unsuitable, teaching space. Tracey was also driven by the conflict between her theory and teaching approaches versus the space she occupied, and created a space where designers could work with others to innovate solutions to constantly-changing complex problems.

As difficult as studio spaces may be to set up, they may be even harder to hold on to once you have them. A dedicated space was available and already well-established in Smith's case, but there are continuing tensions around enrollment. Fifteen students are needed to run a course, with 20 the average target as her university leans toward pedagogies that allow high student/teacher ratios. In order to allow for individual attention to each student her program assigns an instructor for every 15 students, but pressure remains. She explains that her program has the space they need because they are located at the edge of campus in a building undesirable to most other programs and posing access concerns for their students.

Almost all of the design cases describe conventional studios, where students and instructors meet in physical spaces. Seldom mentioned, yet representing an interesting direction, are blended online and face-to-face groups in studio environments. Blended groups present unique opportunities and introduce severe limitations. Bringing some students into a studio via laptop connections can be accomplished relatively easily and effectively using video-based communication tools. The space to accommodate them is essentially free, and it affords a familiar communication channel among participants in the studio, whether for group work or for individual critiques. We see an example in Schwier's studio where online students join their classmates in the studio weekly to work on projects together, and to participate in three group reports to the clients to reveal the design plan, working prototype, and the final evaluation and delivery of the product. But the limitations are considerable. The online studio space is open only occasionally and for short bursts of time. Work in progress is available to the group, but not in a shared space that invites regular critique and conversation. The contact among face-to-face participants is more natural and intimate, so closer relationships seem to emerge in the physical studio groups. Also, of course, occasional technical problems or outages disrupt the communication patterns. Improvements in technology may mitigate the limitations experienced in blended settings but, currently, blended studios are difficult to handle pedagogically, whereas conventional studio spaces are hard to justify without a strong argument for pedagogy.

Studio Allows for Differential Responses to Students and Variable Goals for Their Achievements

In contrast to courses in which consistent feedback and consistent outcomes for each student are core values, these authors mention repeatedly the ways in which they adjust their responses to individual students and endorse differential outcomes for them. Smith is straightforward in describing her differential responses; "I tell different students different things, and I answer questions for some students that I might not for other students." Her constant contact with students in the studio, observations of their work in progress, and understanding of them across more than one semester makes it possible for her to gauge closely what response will be most appropriate for each one in that moment. Duer and Pable both mention their roles as quasi-therapists to their students, strongly suggesting that students' differing circumstances are salient to them as instructors. These three are instructors in traditional domains of design where the expectation that students will be following different paths through their projects (rather than following a strictly defined process) is common, as is the expectation that feedback will be responsive to a student's ability to receive and use that feedback.

Instructors in non-traditional and emergent forms of studio also discuss the differential nature of their feedback to students - and differences in the outcomes for students. Boling asks about each student, "have I usurped their position in our partnership?" and says, "the right balance is different for every student at every stage, so this equation has to be re-figured continuously." Rook and Hooper describe "guidance ... in the form of carefully timed nudges toward experiences or resources that ... help the students figure out answers to their problems," and it is logical to assume that these nudges have to be tailored to the problems each student presents in the moment. Tracey spends hours on feedback to individual students during the first weeks of her course, moving each of them forward until they "get it" (design thinking), and assessing which of them will need additional support during the second half of the course to reach that "get it" state. Pable's assessment is continual; she assigns "a written account of the grade" for each desk critique session she holds with each student all the way through her course making her assessment fully tailored to the situation and needs of each student. Cennamo keeps her syllabus flexible so that she can respond differentially to the entire class as a result of determining their progress in whole-class critique.

In all of these examples, careful attention is paid to what is happening with students, and the instructor's scrutiny is constant. The instructor's watchful eye is constantly scanning students – their work and their capacity – and instructors intervene regularly. In traditional classrooms these kinds of interventions might be considered bothersome, but it is an expectation carefully cultivated in most studio settings. We also see flexible, selective approaches. Not every student gets the same kind of feedback, or even the same amount of input on their work. Instructors hover and give input selectively, responding to their assessments of the students' needs and what will help them, without taking ownership of the design decisions by providing direction that is too... directive. In every case, it is clear that conversation and communication form a core strategy, and it is tailored to the learning situation and the individual or the working group.

Studio in an Emerging Design Field may Require Courage to Start and Ingenuity to Maintain - and Traditional Studios are Not Without Their Complications

In one way or another, every author talks about breaking rules or flying under the radar. Even the narratives from a traditional program like Pable's shows tension. In her case she says, "I feel the studio experience should probably be the lynchpin course around which other courses revolve (but I don't come out and say this to other instructors!)." She explains later that some degrees of freedom in her Studio I class were achieved when several colleagues retired.

More than one emergent studio was conceived in subterfuge and later moved out into the light, usually over a period of several years. Along the way, most instructors had to repurpose existing structures not originally intended to support studio in order to support studio. Rieber, Clinton and Kopcha describe the reconsideration of a program that had existed successfully for a long time. An organizational shift from a quarter to a semester system provided the opportunity to institute dramatic pedagogical change, and they used the common device of a course repeatable for credit to bracket the program with one course, essentially taken twice. Campbell, by contrast, discusses intrigue around needing to disguise her course design as something else as she attempted to try something new within a system not completely open to it.

Transformed practice in most stories required co-optation – of space, furniture, time, policies, personnel, and ritual. We already mentioned the several-years-long process Gibbons went through to persuade his administration of the need for changing a traditional classroom into a dedicated studio space. In Boling's case, we see how she nudged a deep and entrenched department culture and turned existing courses into something new. In the process, Boling took on the bigger job of reflecting and learning about an approach she had experienced for a long time, and probably took for granted, in order to build the case for what she knew she needed to do in a program that had little familiarity with it, and convince more established colleagues to go along with her judgment. Similarly, Campbell underscored the example of trying something new within a system that is not completely open to it, or being pushed to do something new when she or he is not personally 100 percent sold on the idea.

When he knew he had to move away from an established, and largely unsuccessful (at least for him and most of his students), systematic design class to create something more vibrant and authentic, Rowland encountered a dynamic tension between the university and the needs of the class. Everything from the name of the class to enrollment and teaching load presented issues that had to be navigated or negotiated. We also see how Duer journeyed through recruitment, course goals, outcomes and professional practice issues to sort out how to approach his teaching of scenic design. Ultimately he built three courses from a card sorting exercise, which he used to work out the curriculum and role of each course – a revelation for him, and one which undoubtedly sent shock waves through his program.

The effort does not always work out. Campbell wanted to introduce an instructional design course, but had to mask it as a course on user-centered design (UCD) in a communications program because the program in which she taught did not include educational technology and design. She invented and reinvented an instructional design course hidden in UCD, and its design and delivery was replete with big social issues such as gender, marginalization, vulnerable groups, and diversity, and she delivered it online through a learning management system. She attempted to design an elegant course, pedagogically and strategically (and subversively, as she puts it), but in every case ran into resistance, even from students, and ultimately decided to abandon the course. Her courage and tenacity are clear and compelling, even if it did not result in the successful introduction of a design course. The failure to introduce new content and pedagogy subversively, in an established program that emphasizes different content, demonstrated how difficult it is to introduce design courses in contexts that are ultimately hostile to the idea.

Studio can Raise Big Moral and Social Issues, But Does Not Do So Automatically

As curators, we look to relate these narratives to large concepts in design, specifically the moral and social dimensions of design. Designers practice in morally coherent *and* incoherent circumstances. Design is not a dry or technical process, nor is it practiced in an emotional vacuum. It is a process that involves choices, and the ways in which those choices line up with the designers' personal and professional values can determine how happy and satisfied they will be in the long run. When we work on projects, we continually confront decisions about what we value and what others value, how we are required to act, and how we feel about ourselves when we do. As designers, we feel more comfortable, more purposeful and more powerful when our values are aligned with the projects and organizations we work with, and we feel disenchanted or maybe even hypocritical when we work at cross purposes to our own values. This alignment is referred to elsewhere as moral coherence (Campbell *et al.* 2006). Designers are regularly confronted by – and need to resolve – ethical dilemmas and moral conundrums in their daily practice (for example, an instructional designer works on a training program about fracking in the oil industry, but personally opposes the use of fossil fuels). This suggests that, although the initial presentation of a project may imply that the designer has no choice but to provide exactly what the client or project manager has requested, most designers have powerful tools with which to exert moral force.

Similarly, how we teach can introduce a hidden curriculum that influences the professional identities of students and even broadens a perspective of the larger influence of a profession that is seldom confronted or even mentioned. We can talk with our students about the larger institutional and societal influences of our disciplines, and how their actions can have large consequences. But smaller, subtle actions can also be important. For example, a designer is taking a moral stance and communicating a social message when she models the use of gender neutral language in products. Whether grand or miniscule, this tension influences professional identities and it deserves the attention of those of us teaching design.

There are hints of a moral and social overlay in this volume. Katy Campbell expresses deep concerns about big social issues such as gender, marginalization, vulnerable groups, and diversity. She addressed her concerns and breathed life into her approach to instructional design by using user-centred design. Similarly, Schwier deliberately exploits social agency by finding and serving not-for-profit agencies who are charged with a social mission (for example, Fetal Alcohol Spectrum Disorder Network; Community Living; Red Cross). Socially targeted projects go beyond doing something beneficial for a deserving but underserved group; they remind students that they can do things that benefit communities and society, and that their professional identities can include a dimension of public service and social agency.

The issue was qualified by Kathy Cennamo, who observed that a designer can do things for the "right reasons" – the loftier ones we prefer to admit, like "preparing instructional designers for the realities and variances of professional practice, my immersion in the literature on case studies and other constructivist methodologies," but studio also allows for the grittier, more intimate reasons that drive us ("my desire to never lecture again!").

Teaching in the Studio is a Personal and Complex Enterprise

The reader looking here for a template or guidebook on studio teaching will be disappointed – by intent. There is no single, generalizable set of guidelines that we can, or want to, offer. As we laid these cases out side by side, it was clear to us that even those instructors who teach traditional forms of studio shape this general form around their own characters to fit the circumstances within which they work. Those teaching studio in emergent contexts innovate the form in multiple ways, also reflecting individual identities and values, and how they are related to the larger context of teaching. The day-to-day practice of studio teaching is also dependent on the nature of each instructor. As many characteristics as their studios share, they diverge in many others. Facing a class in which each student is at a different, unpredictable place in a project unique to that student, or small team, and knowing that this place might not be one in which the instructor knows exactly what to do, is a complex enterprise that requires some courage and an adventurous spirit. As the authors attest, this enterprise cannot be scripted, only prepared for, and each prepares in an individual way. These preparations result in distinctly different performances of studio teaching from one instructor to the next. Each of these authors has told a story that may help you in that preparation and we hope that our arrangement of those stories, as well as these curator's notes, may increase the value of the individual chapters.

References

Campbell, K., Schwier, R. A. and Kenny, R. (2006) 'Conversation as inquiry: a conversation with instructional designers'. *Journal of Learning Design*, 1(3), pp. 1–18
Fisher, T. R. (1991) 'Patterns of exploitation'. *Progressive Architecture*, 9

3 Hither and Yon

Learning ID in a Studio-Based Authentic ID Context

Richard A. Schwier

In this chapter you are going to hear a story about the second course in a two-course sequence of instructional design courses. Both courses emphasize studio approaches conducted partly or entirely in online settings, but we will focus on the second course where students are expected to go beyond the fundamentals and start doing real design work for a client in a team setting. This is my own look at what we do and why we do it, complete with a magnifying glass hovering over my uncertainties and prideful accomplishments in roughly equal parts. I don't presume to dispense advice or speak for other instructors, but I invite you on a journey of opportunities taken and opportunities neglected, failures and victories, regrets and hopes. I ask you to keep a few big themes in mind – themes that will surface in a few different places and in a few different ways.

- You will encounter the tension between the tidy, structured, traditional content of instructional design and the dynamic, messy learning that happens in our studios. I worry out loud, and I hope you will tolerate the uncertainty and relentless change that accompanies our growth as a program.
- You may notice how important social agency is in our program. I take it seriously, and it provides a strong sense of purpose for our students.
- You will no doubt appreciate the various pressures that working on authentic projects in an online setting places on students and instructors alike.
- Also I hope, I dearly hope, you sense the deep and profound connections our students feel to each other, to their instructors, and to the program, despite the fact that most of what we do (entirely for some of our students) happens online.

Where Do Students Fit In?

Most of the students in our program are educators but they have no background in instructional design; ID is a mystery to them and many come to us hoping for some kind of conversion experience. Students are looking for a new career path, or they want to find a new direction within the careers

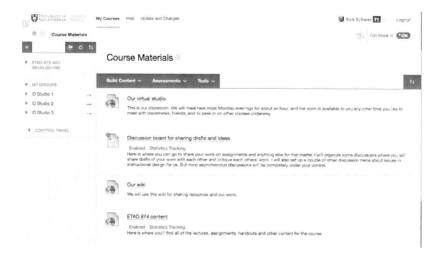

Figure 3.1 Online studio spaces for ID teams in the LMS.

they've already chosen, and instructional design offers tangible opportunities. Most are K-12 teachers, and they have fairly strong disciplinary identities in subject areas such as mathematics, science, or language arts.

Armed with some of the basic concepts and language of instructional design from the introductory course, our students arrive in this second course as members of an ID team working under my guidance in the role of Project Manager. The advanced ID class is designed as a studio-based, service-learning course. It is also a blended online and face-to-face group. Some students meet regularly in the classroom; an equal or greater number meet online. Everyone joins class meetings (usually three hours weekly) in an online studio environment, whether they are originating from the physical classroom space or the online space. We typically use BlackBoard Collaborate™ as the tool for the online studio because it includes chat, video, audio, whiteboards, a chat room, and file transfer. But students regularly jump out and add other communication tools – a class wiki, Skype®, Google Hangouts™, Google Drive™. They hop from space to space, and it creates a dynamic, if a little chaotic and unpredictable, studio space.

As I write this, I am wishing I had spent more time taking screenshots of the variety of spaces that were mashed together by students. I hope you can close your eyes and imagine some of them.

On Time, On Budget, Beyond Expectations, and Without a Net

Groups of four or five students carry out each instructional design project. Early on, I try to match the projects and skills of the students and assemble teams.

(a)

(b)

Figure 3.2 a-d Teams meet in mashed-up online and face-to-face studio space.

(c)

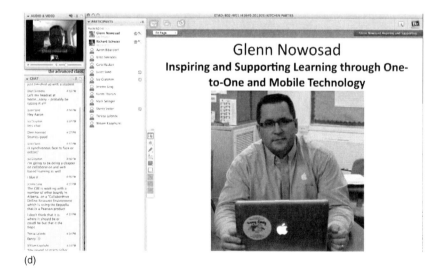

(d)

Figure 3.2 a-d (Continued)

Teams are assigned to one of the contracts with an actual client, and they are expected to deliver a professional quality product that meets or exceeds the expectations of the contract. My expectations have evolved over time. Originally, we were explicit with clients and with students that while we intended to complete projects, there were no guarantees. I sensed this lowered the intensity and authenticity of the class. Now I ask students to commit to completing the project with no safety net, and I ask students to transfer to a different course if they are unable to make the commitment. This increases the urgency in the class, and also mimics the pressures our students will feel when they take on their first positions as instructional designers.

When I prepare to teach the course, typically several months before startup, I find a project and sign a contract or agreement with a local non-profit agency. I negotiate a memorandum of understanding (MOU) with the responsible officer of the organization. In addition to the social criteria mentioned earlier, I look for ambitious projects that can be completed within a 13-week period. In early meetings with potential clients, I try to emphasize that the primary purpose of the class is to provide a rich learning environment for the students, and the client must fulfill their obligations to the project. The MOU is used to articulate the terms of the agreement and also to provide a clear understanding of what is expected of both groups. It takes several weeks or months to locate and negotiate the right kind of contract, but it is essential to the success of the project. I want clients who have a real need, but who appreciate the context. They must realize that students will be under pressure to deliver a completed project, but they also know the project may require follow-up and additional revisions following the completion of the class. I typically meet with a potential client two or three times before I understand the demands of the project and have confidence we can work together. Unfortunately, all of this happens before our students are available to experience it. Wherever possible, I ask students who will take the course to accompany me to the advance meetings so they can experience the process of negotiation, and then share their observations with other students once the class begins. But, otherwise, this largely happens behind the curtain.

This presents a significant challenge. I want to bring students into the process earlier, but the timing of university registration does not promote it. One possibility I want to try in the future is to carry out this part of the process during the first course as an activity for those students who intend to move on to the advanced course. Students who attend from a distance could join meetings virtually.

At the first class meeting (sometimes shortly before the class officially begins) the entire design team meets with the client(s). Again, some attend in person and others join via online video-conferencing. The purpose of the meeting is to introduce all of the participants, and to share and clarify all of the decisions that have taken place previously.

Immediately following the meeting, the instructional design teams revise the plan and timeline based on the meeting with client. The members of the teams decide individual roles and make recommendations, subject to my approval (as PM). This oversight is important, and not inconsistent with what our students will experience as professional instructional designers. I review the decisions to determine whether there is good alignment of skills and responsibilities, and also check for equity of workload.

For the duration of the project the group meets with me weekly for team meetings, and I meet regularly with individuals as they work on their parts of the larger project. The team meetings include a review of readings that design team members found to inform their work, round-table reports where each team member reports on individual progress since the last meeting and lays out plans for the coming week, the identification of support required by individuals and the team, and an open discussion of difficulties and opportunities.

Facing the Beast: Client Meetings and Deliverables

There are three formal meetings with each client. At these meetings, the principal client and any other members of the organization are invited to receive a report by the instructional design team(s). The three reports delivered include:

1. Front-end analysis report (including a needs assessment, context analysis, content analysis, and user/learner analysis);
2. Prototype (a high fidelity draft of the product);
3. Evaluation report and final product (usability and formative evaluation results, revisions and delivery of the final product).

At each meeting, business clothing and a professional attitude are required, and the instructor emphasizes how important it is to act professionally, yet personably. Each deliverable is signed off by the project manager and the client. During the development of the MOU with the client, we explain that we require one representative of the client to act as a signing officer with complete authority to make judgments for the client. This is necessary, I learned, because if clients need to obtain authorizations from others in their organizations (for example, to obtain approval from a Board of Directors) it can stall the development process and interfere with the completion of projects. Following each meeting, and regularly throughout the course, the team's performance is reviewed, and the students discuss what they learned about the project, and also what they learned about the process of instructional design, a kind of meta-studio critique.

(a)

(b)

Figure 3.3 a and b Students presenting high fidelity prototypes to client groups.

Assessment and Critique in the Studio

In early iterations of the course, assessment included several formal layers including weekly peer assessments of individual contributions by team members, weekly summaries of two readings, peer and instructor evaluations following each deliverable, reviews of the product and the performance of the team by clients, and my final evaluation of the products, teams and individuals. Part of the final assessment was (and still is) performed by the client, who provides a report that comments on the performance of the team and the quality of the product. I provide a similar report, written independently, and both comprise the major portion of the grade that students receive in the course. Students were also required to maintain a professional journal, in which they recorded and considered their challenges, learning and growth as instructional designers.

After offering the class twice, it was clear to me that the assessment pieces were too numerous and some were being treated as annoying tasks rather than as essential learning opportunities. I needed to streamline the processes so I jettisoned the reading summaries and journals, given how cumbersome they had become. It seems to be much more productive to keep the group's focus on the project and propel the activities of the groups. Students are still required to do additional reading and encouraged to keep a private journal, but these items are no longer assessed.

I also eliminated the formal peer assessments, at least in their original form. Originally, team members filed a peer evaluation that identified their own contributions and the contributions of each other team member to the process. These were formative assessments. Disagreements among team members about relative contributions surfaced, and disagreements were brought to me to resolve. I found that a monitoring function was important to the success of the projects, and the process helped identify problems before they became unmanageable. It was also consistent with the intention of using studio spaces as locations for the critique of processes, individuals, and teams, not just products.

Currently, every class meeting is a working meeting. We toss what we have on the screen and we critique what is being developed, and argue about decisions. The teaching and learning environment feels about right, full of critical analysis and careful conversation, but I am not tracking performance or what they are learning about ID in a standardized way. The assessment is narrative and iterative, and students' learning about ID depends to a great extent on shared trust – I trust them to be working hard and learning things of value; the students trust me to guide them faithfully and to help them learn important lessons about ID, not just survive the experience and create a decent product. Most class meetings feature generous amounts of time to work in studio, with some students joining their teams online and some meeting in the classroom. At the end of each class we step back from the projects and have an open discussion about what we are learning about instructional design. One group even created a tradition of having each person completing an "I feel…" statement, which opened us to discussing the challenges, hopes, fears, and sometimes-hilarious emotions we encountered. Statements could range from "I feel like this project will never end" to "I feel like punching the client in the head", and almost always led us into deeper conversations about the struggles and joys of doing ID.

Sometimes I worry I have gone too far in dismantling the traditional academic features of the course. Where should the fulcrum be set between academic prescriptions versus trusting the learning to emerge from the experience? All work happens in the open, typically in an online space, and iterations of work by each participant are on full display for other team members to see and critique. And they do criticize, but not necessarily formally or well. If, for example, four people are working on the design of a visual historical database, they will give each other feedback while work is being done together. Designers might be building in one online space and discussing it through a Twitter feed at the same time. This seems to be an effective and natural way to support the product development, but it is informal and dependent on who happens to be in the studio and working on the project simultaneously. We use the studio space less frequently for formal critique, and I think this is a feature that needs to be bolstered. Why? Because I miss doing more of it, and because I think it offers an opportunity to inject larger lessons about ID into the flow of the class.

Authentic and Self-Directed Learning Values

The key features of the class were drawn from a value framework that grew over time in our entire program based on authenticity and self-directed learning. We messed around with the course with these things in mind and, based on what we learned over time, we articulated a framework for our program. It was reciprocal design, values feeding the features of the class, and experiences shaping the values.

As features evolved – I hesitate to say "matured" – the authentic approach was fleshed out to include a set of program-wide intentions: problem-based learning; situated (or real-world) learning activities; authentic assessment; project management; scaffolding; and social agency. We have fallen short, I think, of balancing these intentions or even addressing some of them in any meaningful way in the course I'm describing, but these items inform the program, and the course emphasizes at least three of them: problem based learning, situated learning activities, and social agency. It is much weaker in the areas of authentic assessment, project management, and scaffolding, although they are dealt with to some extent.

Getting Real – the Authenticity Piece

My bottom line is that it makes practical sense to offer students an authentic learning opportunity. An effectively implemented authentic experience will realize benefits for both the students and the clients. While there are many smaller considerations, I decided that any authentic learning environment should include a few basic elements:

- Select a project that can be completed in one semester. Ambitious but focused projects seem to be best as they allow for sufficient time to reflect, review, discard, and revise the process and products of learning.
- Choose a client who is flexible, and who accepts the primary goal of the experience is the students' learning, not the finished product.
- In writing and verbally, share a clear understanding of what is expected of the students, the instructor, and the client.
- Expect to deal with unexpected events and put contingency plans in place before beginning the project.
- Establish and maintain clear and regular communication among the instructor, client and students.
- Ensure the deliverables are delivered, and that they meet the expectations of the client and the demands of the learning context.
- Promote and regularly focus on what is being learned about ID.

Now the truth is that I seldom, if ever, actually achieve all of these things. But I do try, and the list still serves as a useful set of checkpoints.

In addition, I created and live by the mantra: "on time, on budget, and beyond expectations" to focus on the authenticity of the experience. Instructional designers everywhere live within time and budget constraints, and so these are essentially elements of survival. But I also want new instructional designers to understand that their success depends on exceeding minimal expectations; the best instructional designers consistently deliver products that are better than contracts require.

I Should Have Known Better

The largest practical problem we faced initially was that I slavishly followed a design I borrowed from Elizabeth Boling at Indiana University during the first offering of the advanced class at my university, and I soon discovered this was a mistake. Our programs are different; the students are different (students at Indiana University have a much stronger background in instructional design by the time they take this class); and of course the instructors and projects are different. I asked my teams in the first iteration to take on the role of project management. They did not have enough background to manage their own projects, so I was setting them up for problems and failure.

An important consequence was that I knew less about the workings of the teams and projects, and students felt they needed to solve all of the problems they faced without guidance. They were hiding some of their experiences from me (especially the bad ones) thinking they had to fight their way through them. That resulted in one case of a team being drawn by the client into a host of unnecessary activities, and it destroyed my summer as I took over that bloated and moribund project and brought it to completion for the client myself after the course was done. That was a mistake I never again want to make, and it convinced me to anoint myself project manager with oversight on all decisions the design teams make. I do assign team coordinators to provide some exposure to project management (along with some additional readings), but I am the final arbiter.

Designing Messy and Socially Significant Projects

I want the experience to be really difficult, really complex, and a little frightening. I also want students to discover that even seemingly easy tasks are complex. I want the problems to be messy, and I want to bludgeon the myth that good design can happen the way students thought it could – linearly and predictably. I want to require them to reinvent their own processes, including the ADDIE (Analysis, Design, Development, Implementation, Evaluation) processes they learned in the traditional class, to respond to the demands of their projects.

As mentioned previously, one of the unusual features of the course design is our explicit desire for our students to develop a sense of social agency. Some of the students who come to us are motivated financially, hoping to leave the relative obscurity and poverty of the teaching profession behind and walk toward what they see as the glowing and abundant horizon of corporate life. I do not mean to suggest our students should not be motivated to improve their financial position or career path, but I worry they might overlook aspects of their work that can give them a larger sense of purpose. I want them to do something that is socially important, something that will help an organization or an agency that needs help, but that could never afford to hire an instructional design team to complete the work. Hidden in this agenda, I want the team to find out how much solid, team-based instructional design efforts cost.

So I deliberately added a social sensitivity criterion to the selection of class projects. I intentionally identify potential clients who could not otherwise afford professional instructional design services. These are typically community-based non-profit agencies and organizations (for example, Fetal Alcohol Spectrum Disorder Network, Saskatchewan Council on Ageing, Red Cross, Saskatchewan History and Folklore Society).

There was another more pragmatic reason for focusing on these clients. In our program we want to avoid competing for contracts with the private sector and avoid potential interference with the business community in our own region. The university is accused of leveraging university resources and public funding to gain an unfair competitive advantage in the marketplace. This issue may be more sensitive for us, given the relative intimacy of our market in a city with a population of only 300,000. Our university is seen as both an economic engine and as a privileged recipient of subsidies from the government when we "take work away" from the private sector.

Another constraint is the time frame for projects. The University of Saskatchewan has semesters that run 13 weeks, shorter than many other North American universities. As described earlier, this results in the difficult but necessary decision to negotiate the terms of client contracts ahead of the actual offering of the course. Our courses do not offer enough time to allow students to participate in this important part of most every instructional design project.

I have also noticed that the self-directed, team-based design of the course, and my emphasis on creating a context-sensitive approach (not model-based systematic design), causes students to feel disoriented at first, and suspicious about what they learned in the introductory course. The question of "where do we start" occupies the first class meetings, and I find the teams need that time together to clarify their roles and decide on clear tasks. I suspect it feels like some kind of dirty trick I am playing on them in their first class. I think I need to confront this issue explicitly in the first meeting of the group and to sort out their misgivings. I also think it would be useful to work with the teams at the first meeting to identify the things we *don't* need to do, or to which we can give cursory attention, essentially giving permission to step away from a model-based approach. But this also suggests a larger program issue and, as we migrate the program to studio approaches, we need to revisit how we teach our beginning ID tool skills course.

The Haunted Life of the Instructor

I continue to struggle with the balance between academic learning and the practical demands of the projects in the class. I wonder how much my students are learning about ID given the overwhelming demands of completing the project. I require readings and we devote time weekly in studio to what we are learning from the project and to readings, but spontaneous conversations are seldom as deep as I would like. In one offering of the course, I experimented with regular asynchronous online discussions on readings and instructional design topics, but the workload associated with the course grew considerably and students recoiled. I have not yet found a satisfactory solution to this challenge. I have come to appreciate that in this kind of class there will always be an important tension between meeting the contractual needs of the client and the learning needs of the students, and sometimes these issues will be in direct conflict. As a result, one thing I have done is to reach explicit agreements with clients that acknowledge the primacy of learning, that clearly state that projects may not achieve the standards they (or I) hope, and that explicitly mention that learning trumps product delivery if there is ever a need to choose. This is, however, not a message I share as clearly with my students; I want them to be completely devoted to delivering a superb project and share the exquisite, authentic uncertainties with me.

What is Real Teaching?

One of my personal challenges with this approach was abandoning some of my own assumptions about teaching and learning, and my fixation on delivering content. I'm pretty sure that if an instructor is married to particular content, this approach to a course will be difficult to implement. With a studio approach and project focus some things are fairly predictable, typically related to project management, but pinning the learning to specific concepts or literature in ID, and relying on prescribed content, is folly. At the same time, the students learn all kinds of things they would never have encountered any other way: how to work with teams and how *not* to work in teams; how to manage client expectations; how to face the black hole of anxiety over whether something is good enough; how to become hardened but not brittle to others' vocal opinions about their work; how to listen to, and even invite, honest criticism. When learning is calibrated to content, we can find the answers to questions through simple inquiry. But some terribly valuable lessons in ID are subtle and unpredictable, and can only be learned by doing the work. These are important things to learn, they are seldom confronted in traditional courses, and I value them. Still, as a teacher of many years and students, I still struggle with the loss of control when I abandon prescribed learning outcomes. Of course, if I'm honest with myself, my students have never reliably learned those things I intended, but somehow it felt like it was more their fault and less mine when I could articulate what the intended learning outcomes actually were. I concluded that if I required firm footing, and was unwilling or unable to move with the flow of the experience and draw out the learning from the experience, then this would not be a comfortable experience for me. I'm guessing it will be similar for you.

I also learned this is a very difficult way to teach, and it requires a different kind of preparation and confidence. The instructor needs to be well versed in design knowledge and literature, and needs to be able to draw on a deep well of experience to respond to opportunities as they present themselves in the class. I find I have to confront my "imposter" fears and acknowledge the confidence and experience I have. I need to read broadly and deeply while the course is happening, following up on leads my students give me, often in the form of problems they are facing.

Students are terrified when they enter this class and with good reason. It has developed a reputation as a time thief and students dubbed it "the widow(er) maker". The high student anxiety results in a number of different reactions. Some students are challenged by it and invest deeply. Some get bossy and try to organize everyone else on their team to comply with their way of approaching the project. Some look for easy answers and convenient solutions. Some become paralyzed. We need to spend time in the class talking about each of these things and how teams come together (and fly apart).

In asking a colleague to teach this class I find my biggest hesitation is to convince myself that it will be acceptable if she does not approach it exactly as I do, and my second hesitation is that she will teach it the way I do and see all of the holes in the approach I use. But, regardless of these concerns, all of us agree that we need to first attend carefully to the selection of projects and clients. If a new instructor does not start identifying the projects and clients early, we fear we will introduce our students to a project they can't finish or will do badly. The gestation period for good projects is protracted, so we require any instructor interested in teaching this course to spend a lengthy period of time, usually a few months prior to the start of the class, negotiating a project that will mutually benefit the client and the students.

Next Time, I Really Must...

A feature I have not yet fully implemented, but intend to employ in coming years, is to include meetings with practicing instructional designers to test ID team ideas and to get advice on the projects (professional critique panels). These meetings will combine face-to-face and video-conferencing, and the goal is to inject another dose of authenticity into the work our students do - to allow established instructional designers to critique their work and provide advice on projects. It will also help me deal with what I think is insufficient attention to authentic assessment.

Another feature I am considering is more frequent instructor-led studio critiques and building an online environment that will allow for deep engagement and a feeling of intimacy in the group. We need a more reliable online space where work can be displayed easily and more naturally, and where students can study the work the other students are creating. Given that so many of our students are online and joining team members who are meeting face-to-face, we need a digital space that will accommodate both groups seamlessly. To my surprise, this has created very few practical or technical problems to date. The infrastructure and tools exist to make it relatively easy for our students to interact. But it does mean that the studio display space also needs to be online. While there are tools that allow for this, I haven't found anything to date that meets our need to easily draft and post material in common areas, and that also allows for shared marking up and commenting on those items in real time and asynchronously. Google Docs™ imported into a Google Hangout™ is as close as we have found for the environment we would like to see. We have been pleased to see that students seem to enjoy the process of negotiating their work together, and they have been remarkably resourceful in cobbling together the tools they need to accomplish their work. But I want something that is more seamless and that we can replicate from year to year and from course to course. I feel a need for a common area that we can make our own.

I would also like to implement a more reliable approach to client feedback. Clients, for the most part, have been thrilled with the products they have received. Our deliverables are free, after all, and they are much better than their organizations could have accomplished without our support. This leads to glowing, puffy and generous assessments that make our students feel very good, but that probably do not provide the level of criticism they would face if the clients were paying for the projects. For example, clients are always impressed to find out how many person hours are devoted to the work; I suspect they would be less impressed if they were paying an hourly rate for the work.

One key stressor already mentioned is the workload for students and the instructor associated with this kind of work. Students devote considerably more time and effort to this course than to their typical graduate courses, and the amount of personal investment is very difficult to predict or control. Similarly, the instructors must invest heavily in the course and take responsibility for managing student learning in a unique and unpredictable way. I need to attend more carefully and more frequently to the work the students are doing. Teaching in this environment requires energy, patience and flexibility, and a large amount of tolerance for ambiguity. Not everyone can, or wants to, take on this kind of messy, heavy teaching.

Another stressor is individual assessment. I believe that traditional grading does not make sense with this kind of approach to teaching and learning, but I live in an academic setting that requires it. Students work in groups, so a large part of their final marks is comprised of group marks. I go to some lengths to inject some individual marking into the system, adding assignments and activities where I can reasonably observe individual performance. But, in the end, it is the most artificial part of the course, and my cries for authenticity ring a little hollow when I turn my attention to handing out grades. Also, there is occasional free-riding (students letting others in the team carry a heavier load of work) and, while it is rare, I still do not know how to fix it should it become a larger problem.

A final component I would like to add to the program (probably not specifically in this course) is project management. Our master's program includes a capstone project that is individually defined by students and supervised by faculty that could offer the venue for additional experience with project management. Our program does include this as part of the introductory ID course, and it is also a feature of an advanced course on program evaluation, where students are expected to manage their own projects for individual clients. But students do not manage design teams and we do not yet deal explicitly with program management as a content area in the program; it is integrated and treated as an artifact of the other things we teach.

In the final analysis, this course has been one key part of a larger shift in our graduate program. We have intentionally moved design to be the center-piece of all of our work, and we have experimented with studio pedagogy throughout and embedded everything in a context of authenticity. One of our biggest challenges, and also one of our most important contributions, is our attempt to build blended face-to-face and online learning studios. The teaching/learning challenges have been as authentic as the projects we've carried out. We don't have confidence that we have found the answer but we are enjoying the process of trying to find new approaches that excite our students, and us, and that lead to deeper levels of appreciation for design as a fluid and creative process that goes far beyond the technical/systematic models that defined our field until recently.

4 The Studio Approach at the University of Georgia

Always a Work in Progress

Lloyd P. Rieber, Gregory Clinton, and Theodore J. Kopcha

Origins of the Studio Approach at UGA

We teach the design of educational multimedia at the University of Georgia (UGA) in a special group of four courses that we collectively call the Studio curriculum, or just simply the Studio (Clinton and Rieber 2010). This Studio began in 1998 after about two years of planning. The catalyst for creating the Studio was the conversion of a quarter-based calendar to a semester-based calendar at the University of Georgia in 1998. University of Georgia administration strongly encouraged programs not to simply "convert" all 5-quarter courses to 3-semester courses. Instead, programs were asked to engage in reflection on our curricula and to consider ways to revise and improve our teaching. Programs had several years to plan for and implement this conversion.

Our program's faculty took full advantage of this opportunity. At that time in our program's history our faculty went on a yearly retreat to Sapelo Island, a barrier island off the Georgia coast reachable only by ferry. Partly because of its remoteness, retreats at Sapelo offered unique, fresh and reflective thinking and conversations. Our master's curriculum at that time had three computer-based instruction or multimedia courses with a progression of skills - design and technical - that was typical for a program, like ours, that was considered fairly strong in teaching multimedia development. The first two of these courses required students to develop an individual project, whereas the third and final course required a team-based project.

Theoretical Influences on the EDIT Design Studio: A Personal Reflection by Lloyd Rieber

I had been strongly influenced in my own thinking about learning, design and technology by the constructionist writing of Seymour Papert and his students and colleagues. I was a public school teacher at the time that Papert's (Papert 1980) book *Mindstorms* was published. I was quite captivated by the idea that technology should not be used to create things that are given to students (for example, computer-based tutorials) but, instead, that the technology should be turned over to students for them to create artifacts that would be publicly shared and critiqued. In the mid-1990s the principles of situated cognition were also very influential in our field, as were many other constructivist ideas. Although we were generally pleased with our individual teaching efforts, we saw an opportunity to redesign our curriculum so that we would "practice what we preached" as it related to these constructivist ideas.

I think it is important to point out that many of us were already trying to practice the constructivist principles in our individual courses. For example, I had long used the "project-based approach" to teaching multimedia and had long ago abandoned the use of tests or quizzes. I was, and remain, rather uncomfortable with "grading" student projects on the basis of some objective criteria. Yet, at the same time, students were eager for my feedback, at least as it related to their progress - and eventual grade - in the course. Despite my efforts, it all still felt as though I was teaching in a way that contradicted my own personal teaching philosophy. I yearned to teach as part of a curriculum that was likewise based on these constructivist principles with like-minded faculty.

Another important influence on my thinking about a design studio was my own experience in the early 1980s learning to program educational games on the Apple II family of computers. I became a public school teacher at exactly the time when the Apple computer was introduced to K-12 schools. Although I had been introduced to programming during the few years I spent as an undergraduate engineering student, those experiences were unsuccessful and frustrating. I was introduced to programming using a main-frame computer and punch cards. I distinctly remember my first programming experience as a freshman at Georgia Tech. One had to go to one building to punch cards, then to another to deliver and submit the cards for processing. Finally, one had to return to this second building some time later when the computer finally got round to running the code. I remember my output just showed errors (I'm guessing I simply misspelled a word, such as "print," on one of my cards).

In contrast, I found myself quickly learning to program in Applesoft BASIC on the Apple IIe. I then found myself designing simple educational games that dealt with some of the content I was teaching to my fifth graders. I didn't know it at the time, but I was practicing a form of rapid prototyping (Tripp and Bichelmeyer 1990) where I designed a small working prototype of the game and then brought it to school to show my students. To my delight, they were very interested in the game and offered many creative suggestions, which I tried to incorporate into my next draft. None of this learning on my part was done as part of a graduate class; it was all self-directed. I remember the feeling of being in the flow state (although I didn't know it was called this then). It was a very satisfying experience to design and develop something and bring it out for public scrutiny as I was building it, while also at the same time learning the technology.

My first direct experience with the studio approach occurred while I was an assistant professor at Texas A&M University. There was a studio in the College of Architecture and its director was previously a colleague in the college of education at Ohio State University (OSU). At the time, I was very involved in an organization called Association for the Development of Computer-based Instructional Systems - ADCIS - that had a strong OSU connection. Although I never experienced the studio model as a student, I visited this studio frequently and soaked up the ambience of a group of people intensely working on various projects over a long period of time in a shared space. I sat in on one of the introductory courses and got to know the instructor and some of the students. Of course, I was familiar with the term "studio" before that, but this was the first time I had seen it used in a college setting. As we developed our new approach at the University of Georgia, the term "studio" was used from its earliest conception.

During our season of planning at UGA, leading up to the big conversion from quarters to semesters in the fall of 1998, we had formed a student advisory panel to inform the faculty and offer advice. The three students on the panel all came originally from fields with a history of studio teaching. One was from art, the second from graphic design, and the third from architecture. I also want to point out that my own daughter had started college and eventually majored in art, so I also became very informed about studio teaching from her.

At UGA most, but not all, of the faculty were supportive of moving to this studio approach. The three people who were the core teaching faculty of our existing three multimedia courses were solidly behind the idea (Dr. Michael Orey, Dr. James King and myself).

One of the most exciting aspects of our early designs for the Studio was the idea that all students would work together regardless of where they were in their learning trajectories. That is, students who were just beginning the Studio would work beside students who were in their last semester. However, we still had to make all this work within the constraints of the university system. Students in the Studio would be enrolled in one of three distinct courses, with an individual faculty member as the instructor of record for each course. But the day-to-day experience of the Studio would be one collective space and collective experience. This meant that the respective instructors would truly have to team teach. Consequently, the instructors would also have to plan together for the weekly formal Studio class time. This was a very new experience for us. Mike, Jim and I took to it without any difficulty, but it is important to note that other faculty who have participated in the Studio since then have varied in their acceptance of team planning and teaching.

It is important to understand the need for a team-teaching approach within a studio curriculum. Although each instructor assumed the management of one of the Studio courses being offered in a semester, there was a need to coordinate the overall Studio experience. For example, each week began with a large group meeting attended by all students, followed by a series of concurrent events that were attended potentially by any of the students. There was also a large and continual assortment of tasks of a general nature that applied to students in all of the Studio courses. The decision was made early to "appoint" one of the instructors as basically the Studio Project Manager to coordinate the weekly schedule of events and to communicate these to all Studio students. Information or tasks specific to one of the Studio courses would still be the responsibility of that respective instructor. Studio faculty would meet at least once a week for one to two hours to discuss and prepare for the coming week. These meetings also helped instructors bring to the forefront areas of the respective courses in need of attention, based on their experiences with students. The idea was to keep the plan for the Studio - both near (i.e., the next Studio class) and far (i.e., the semester plan) - flexible and responsive to ongoing needs and issues. Each semester would begin and end with extended Studio instructor meetings. The beginning meeting would organize the effort to launch the Studio that semester and was often dominated by updating the stylized, combined syllabus document we called the Studio Handbook. The ending meeting was dominated by discussing strengths, weaknesses, successes, and failures of the previous semester with decisions often made to improve the Studio for the subsequent semester.

EDIT 6190: The Constructionist Course

Since its inception, the course sequence of the Studio has been refined. The course sequence currently consists of three courses, which we refer to here simply as the first, second and third Studio course. In the first course students self-select a project that challenges them to advance their technical skills with any of a number of appropriate media development tools. In the second course, students work independently with a client to use the skills gained in the first course to complete an applied instructional design project. The third course is similar to the second course in that the students complete a project that is instructional in nature for a client; however, students work in teams instead of individually. Clients in the third course have proposed an applied instructional design project based on current needs in business and industry or higher education. Figure 4.1 contains a graphic that represents the course sequence for our master's program and the core studio courses (i.e., EDIT 6190, EDIT 6200 and EDIT 6210) within that sequence. As the graphic notes, the courses are sequenced such that students assume greater responsibility for their learning experience as the program progresses.

Of the three Studio courses, the first represents both a conceptual advancement in our curriculum and a closer embodiment of the constructionist principles discussed above. For that reason, we now focus on the first

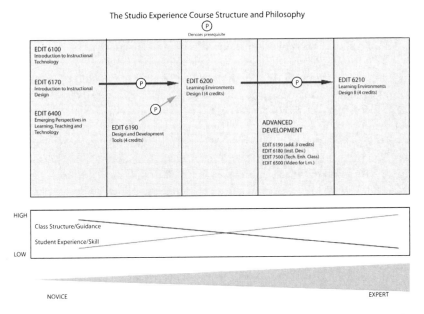

Figure 4.1 A graphic depicting the core studio courses and their placement in the master's program at the University of Georgia. The three studio courses are, respectively, EDIT 6190 Design and Development Tools, EDIT 6200 Learning Environments Design I, and EDIT 6210 Learning Environments Design II. Other departmental courses that complement the studio courses are also shown. Graphic adapted from Clinton and Rieber 2010, adaptation created by students in the EDIT 6210 Studio class.

Studio course and the students' experience in this course. Students in our master's program are required to take this course twice – once early in their program and once near the end of their program. We simply refer to these students as "first-timers" and "second-timers." Both first- and second-timers meet together in the fall semester. The experiences of both first- and second-timers are presented below to illustrate the Studio experience at two different points in our program.

The First-Timer Experience

Being responsible for the first-timer section of the first course is a challenge given that this is the students' first experience with the studio approach while, at the same time, also being one of their first experiences in the graduate program. This can be an uncomfortable learning experience at first for many people simply because it does not meet their expectations of what "school" should be like. Indeed, the fact that these students find themselves sitting in this graduate course is proof enough that they have "figured out" this thing called school and have been successful at it. But now, they are being asked to put aside what they know about "school" and learn in a different way.

We hold class discussions about this in order to help students confront and deal with this discomfort. For example, we talk about how the kind of learning they will be doing in the Studio actually resembles the kind of learning they experience in their everyday life. That is, they are constantly needing to learn new things yet rarely do they sign up for formal education or training to learn it. The task of deciding what kind of car to buy, or how to decide what new cell phone and usage plan to purchase, are good examples. Instead of enrolling in formal instruction to help make these sorts of decisions, we learn how to find, evaluate, and use a variety of guides and resources, including asking "experts" for their experience and advice (for example, family and friends who previously faced such decisions and seemed to make good choices). The list of everyday needs that depend on this kind of self-directed learning goes on and on. Of course, sometimes we do choose to review more

---

Getting the Right Metaphor: Greg's Perspective as a Student

It was my first semester in the Ph.D. program at UGA, Fall 2002. As a new student, I had only the late registration period available to me, which meant that many of the classes I needed were already full. But I had heard from Dr. Rob Branch about this thing called "The Studio" that could be a viable elective for doctoral students. I was intrigued, and signed up for the first-level course. Little did I know that in my imagination about a studio I was making the same mistake that many of my own incoming students would make later - I was conjuring up a mental image of a production studio, a space filled with people and electronics and production equipment (either for film or for music - these are the examples I was most familiar with). And since I was entering a technology-oriented program, this was an easy leap – why wouldn't there be serious media production in something called "The Studio"?

But the production studio idea was the wrong metaphor. Not entirely wrong, since learning multimedia development tools and putting them to use was woven into the fabric of the concept. Media production was definitely part of the picture. Nonetheless, the imagery associated with music or film studios – light trees, microphone stands, sound-absorbing materials on the walls, engineers behind cameras or consoles, cables going everywhere – was not to be seen in the environment I found myself in. Essentially we were in a classroom with students seated at tables, and some of the time we would migrate to a computer lab down the hall.

Fortunately, I didn't embarrass myself by complaining about this unmet expectation. Perhaps it was the shared energy and enthusiasm for "all things Studio" projected by Dr. Rieber and the team of instructors that carried me along. Or perhaps it was that the idea of a design studio was not at all foreign to me. I knew what an art studio was and I had been an art student many times in grade school. I was also busy making the same adjustment to self-directedness that other students were making. In any case, what emerged, and was fully explained by the second class meeting ("be sure to read the Studio Handbook by next week"), was the intended design studio metaphor.

By the end of that semester I knew I had been a part of something extraordinary. I had experienced a very meaningful, well-scaffolded, personal and professional learning process and, at the same time among the student projects, I watched some captivatingly creative designs unfolding. The memory of these stuck with me until, ultimately, the design studio curriculum would become the choice of a research setting for my dissertation study. To say the Studio was a life-changing experience would not be overstating the case.

formal educational materials, such as those found on the Internet or in books we can check out of our local library.

A constructionist approach

The first Studio course requires students to decide on what software tools they will choose to learn to create an independent project due at the end of the course. We refer to the first Studio course as the "constructionist" course because it was overtly designed to follow a constructionist approach as put forward by Seymour Papert and his colleagues at MIT (Papert 1991; Kafai and Resnick 1996).

Following the constructionist approach, we allow each student to select any topic of their choice for their project. We go to great lengths to explain that it *does not* have to be an instructional project. Instead, it should be a topic about which the student is genuinely passionate. We emphasize that the first Studio course focuses on "Design with a capital D." We want students to explore the general nature of design without worrying about specific criteria that others may give them (such as would be the case in an instructional design project). Instead, we expect students to identify their own design criteria for the project they select.

Project selection

Surprisingly, many students find the opportunity of selecting a highly personal and motivating project difficult. It is unclear why this is, but we suspect it is at least partially related to the fact that we rarely ask students to consider their passions when in school. Also, many students feel compelled to do something that will have utility in their work lives, though usually these project topics are not ones about which they are passionate. We encourage people to choose their project topic as soon as they can, but we require them to declare their project at least by the mid-point of the semester. The majority wait until the due date to make this declaration. Starting with the first class meeting, we point out that the real learning begins when they start to work on a project that they are passionate about and are intrinsically motivated to work on. Our motto has been "The Project Rules" when it comes to what tools to learn and why.

Software skills

Given that most students do not choose their project topics early on, we make it clear that they need to begin learning software skills immediately. This is an awkward time. In order to work on a project, one needs multimedia skills, but how can one begin work on a project without these skills? So we provide much scaffolding during this process. We require students to learn at least one "authoring" tool (for example, Articulate Storyline or Captivate) and at least one "multimedia" tool (for example, Photoshop), while trying to help them see the difference between these two general categories. In the past we have recommended various software books, though in the last few years we have used video courses available at Lynda.com. We make it clear that they do not all need to learn the same tools and that they will not learn the tools adequately just by coming to class. Instead, the tool learning will occur outside of the weekly class. However, in the spirit of scaffolding, we do provide a variety of introductory workshops on some of the main tools (for example, Storyline, Captivate, Photoshop or GIMP). More importantly, we try to create a mindset and expectations that the weekly class for the first half of the semester is a time to come to get help and resolve problems. The instructors manage the process by setting up deliberate opportunities for first-timers and second-timers to interact, with the second-timers taking on the explicit role of mentors.

In the second half of the semester the focus is squarely on the design and development of students' individual projects, with class time structured to provide opportunities for critiquing. It's not that students are no longer learning software skills – rather, they are learning them in the specific context of their own personal project. Since this learning is embedded within their project work, we require everyone to provide a minimum of four desktop critiques or "desk crits" for short. These desk crits must be given verbally and in writing and are designed to provide substantial suggestions for project improvement. That is, just providing compliments is discouraged. To facilitate effective desk crits, the instructors give advice and preparation to students on how to conduct an effective desk crit. A model desk crit is provided in Figure 4.2.

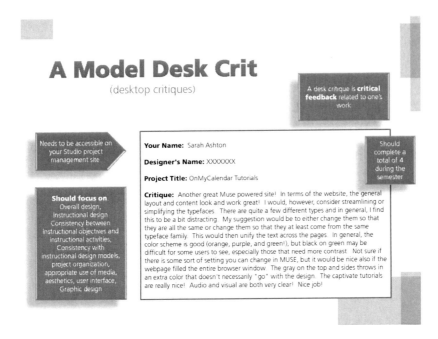

A Model Desk Crit
(desktop critiques)

A desk critique is **critical feedback** related to one's work

Needs to be accessible on your Studio project management site

Should complete a total of 4 during the semester

Should focus on: Overall design, Instructional design, Consistency between instructional objectives and instructional activities, Consistency with instructional design models, project organization, appropriate use of media, aesthetics, user interface, Graphic design

Your Name: Sarah Ashton

Designer's Name: XXXXXXX

Project Title: OnMyCalendar Tutorials

Critique: Another great Muse powered site! In terms of the website, the general layout and content look and work great! I would, however, consider streamlining or simplifying the typefaces. There are quite a few different types and in general, I find this to be a bit distracting. My suggestion would be to either change them so that they are all the same or change them so that they at least come from the same typeface family. This would then unify the text across the pages. In general, the color scheme is good (orange, purple, and green!), but black on green may be difficult for some users to see, especially those that need more contrast. Not sure if there is some sort of setting you can change in MUSE, but it would be nice also if the webpage filled the entire browser window. The gray on the top and sides throws in an extra color that doesn't necessarily "go" with the design. The captivate tutorials are really nice! Audio and visual are both very clear! Nice job!

Figure 4.2 Model desktop critique. Graphic by EDIT 6210 student Sarah Ashton.

Second-timer Experience

As mentioned above, students in our master's program take the first Studio course twice in their coursework – once early in their program (first-timers) and once near the end of the program (second-timers). The rationale is that one never learns any single development tool adequately in a semester and also that there are so many viable software tools to learn. We wanted our students to have the opportunity to return to the constructionist environment to tackle new tools or learn previous tools with greater depth. Because our program is now a cohort model, first- and second-timers take this course in the same semester and share class meeting sessions. This creates a pedagogical challenge. Second-timers are adept with many web development tools at this point in their coursework and have had multiple experiences with design and development in real contexts. As a result, they have little need to revisit the basics (i.e., basic design principles, software skills, server-side management, etc.) that occupy much of the first-timer coursework. They are looking for more from this Studio course than the first-timer experience offers, yet need to fit in the course structure and meeting sessions that are associated with the first Studio course.

For the last few years, TJ Kopcha has been responsible for leading the second-timers in their Studio experience. During this same period, Lloyd Rieber has been the instructor for the first-timers. TJ addressed the challenge of designing a unique experience for second-timers, in collaboration with Lloyd. A simple, but important, change was giving second-timers a different set of course readings. Collectively, the readings have been selected to encourage second-timers to become more reflective practitioners. These readings focus on helping students apply the concepts of design introduced by experts such as Moggridge (2007) (*People and Prototyping*), Gibbons (2003; 2011) (see Gibbons' ideas about "Layers and Centrisms" and "Young's Levels of Design"), Wilson (2005) ("Four pillars of practice"), and Parrish (2006) ("Design as storytelling") into a variety of contexts.

Moving Beyond Models - TJ's Approach to the Studio

When I came to teach the studio course to second timers, I had previously taught instructional design as a *model*. Don't get me wrong – models are powerful tools, both conceptually and practically speaking. But I had met with several limitations to this approach – chief among them that students often produced unexciting, unengaging projects. This had me concerned. As second timers, my students already had a good deal of design experience, including exposure to models. I wanted my teaching in the studio to move students beyond models, where they experienced design with excitement, creativity, and passion.

The question was, how do I make that happen, pedagogically speaking?

At a recent conference, Andy Gibbons and I enjoyed a lunch where he explained what is now known as his architectural approach to design. In the course of an hour (and with sketches on the back of several napkins) he presented what was perhaps my first introduction into design as something other than a model. Conversations with Elizabeth Boling similarly expanded my understanding. She talked about cultivating *design elegance* - that is, moving designers from *design as a model* to a more sophisticated approach, one that accounts for multiple considerations at various times within a project. Aesthetics. User experience. Organization of content. Each consideration as something that *emerges* in a project at different times and in different ways, often unpredictably and in ways that conflict with our models.

It was these perspectives that informed my first foray into the studio. In my very first class, I explained that we would cultivate *design elegance*. This led to a series of very challenging questions – questions to which, initially, I had no concrete answers. How do you know if something is *elegant*? What does *elegance* look like, and how do I know if I'm cultivating it? And my favorite: Is there a rubric we can have to make sure we're being elegant? (The answer to this last question was and still is a resounding 'no.')

This environment was highly challenging for me, but the challenge was motivating. I needed to develop my own *elegance* in designing the course and course experiences, and I enjoyed that process. I've gotten much better at teaching students about *design elegance* – I've culled a set of readings, resources, and activities that take students on an incredible journey in which they critically look at themselves, their skills as a designer, and their learning. For those students who are interested in cultivating their *design elegance* (and not everyone is, I've learned), this critical lens becomes as important a tool for design as models ever will be.

In addition, second-timers participate in *group* desk crits. Like the desk crits that first-timers participate in, the group desk crit is an opportunity to have focused and formative discussion about student projects. Unlike the first-timer desk crits, the group desk crit is conducted with a small group of students who share prototypes of their projects. In addition, group desk crits include the second-timer instructor. Thus, students not only offer critical advice on each other's projects but also see an expert modeling the critique of a project.

Finally, second-timers take a mentoring role with first-timers. This takes two forms. The first is one-to-one mentoring, where each first-timer selects a second-timer as a design mentor. As part of the mentoring relationship, the mentor helps the first-timer negotiate the demands within the Studio such as selecting software tools, deciding on a project, and improving their design work. The second type of mentoring that occurs is in second-timer panel discussions. Each panel consists of a small group of second-timers who show-case their own project work on topics such as web design, graphic design and media creation. The panels encourage rich discussion about making better use of tools and acquiring key design skills.

Managing the Studio

The Studio presents a number of challenges for instructors. These are not exclusive to issues with students – the Studio makes demands of instructors that are simply not present in courses that take a teacher-centered approach to instruction. Below are several common challenges that we have learned to manage over the life of the Studio.

Managing Expectations

One of the biggest challenges associated with the Studio is managing both student and instructor expectations for the course. With first-timers, it is particularly important to manage expectations early in the course. Unfortunately, those students who strongly resist the constructionist approach choose to see the experience as a way for the instructor to "get out" of actually teaching the course. By expecting a very instructor-directed experience, they expect to come to each class to learn exactly what tools or skills they need to learn. On the one hand, this is not an unreasonable expectation, assuming that the course is being conducted with a teacher-centered philosophy. However, on the other hand, this expectation is not valid within a course using a learner-centered and learner-directed philosophy. Therefore, we take time to deliberately confront these expectations and to discuss the role and value of self-directed learning approaches. We talk about how successful professional adults can easily slip into the mental model of "school" when they enter the UGA building in which we meet. It's as though some students cast off the persona of "highly successful adult professional" and take on the persona of "student" as they cross the school building's threshold. Teaching the first-timer section of the first Studio course requires an instructor who enjoys the challenge of working with students who are clearly outside their comfort zone during at least the first half of the semester.

There is also an uncomfortable reality that the first-timer instructor has to accept. For many students, it simply is not possible to "explain" the Studio experience in a way that prepares them fully for it. We have learned over the past 17 years of teaching the Studio that it simply takes students time to make a shift in their thinking about learning. At the end of the master's program the overwhelming majority of students report to us that the Studio courses were the most important and most valuable part of their master's experience, but that they did not start out with this attitude. For many students it is difficult (if not impossible) to get them to this point of realization sooner than when they are ready. It is important to point out that a small number of students also state that one of the reasons they chose our program was because of the Studio approach. Even if a student eventually decides that the Studio approach is "not for them," we feel it is a valuable experience for them to have, at least, experienced a different form of "school" for the first time.

Student Support

When we first started the Studio, we had a few students who were either unable to manage their time effectively or who were not willing to devote the necessary time to getting an initial software skill set. To address this we implemented a "performance review" that occurs right before the midpoint of the semester. The performance review is conducted in a one-on-one fashion with each student. During the performance review, the student is evaluated on their tool learning and essentially must prove to the instructor that they have acquired sufficient initial learning. Since the studio was first implemented in 1998 we have only had to counsel a handful of students, who didn't seem to have any evidence of learning, that they should withdraw from the course because we felt they would not be able to successfully complete a project with the time remaining. Students usually get a little anxious or nervous about this performance review meeting, which we think is actually a good thing in order to give some extrinsic motivation, should they need it.

Now that we have revised the Studio curriculum to accommodate a cohort model, for the first time we have a group of second-timers about equal to the number of first-timers taking the first Studio course each fall semester. We have experimented with ways for the second-timer mentors to help first-timers with the need to be self-directed in their software learning during the first half of the course. While this has been successful overall, we made several mistakes in our first implementation. When we first introduced mentoring to second-year students, we encouraged them to review first-timer performance. Second-timers, however, felt as if they were being asked to "grade" their first-timer peers. This is clearly not a role they wanted any part of, and rightly so. We've clarified since that their role is one of support, which is one they seem to enjoy taking on. Obviously, there is a fine line here that needs to be recognized and respected.

Teaching Philosophies

Of the many faculty who have tried the Studio approach, a few have not done well with it or within the Studio environment. Those who have not done well in the Studio are very uncomfortable with the feeling of not being "in total control." One has to be comfortable with a learning environment that appears much more messy (or "organic," as some might label it) than is usually found in a typical course based on direct instruction.

Another aspect of this relates to team teaching, which we discussed in the Theoretical Influences section above. For instructors to lead a successful Studio experience they need to participate in a true team-teaching process. Students in the Studio respond to the cohesion (or lack thereof) among the instructors who share the responsibilities associated with a given semester's Studio courses. Some faculty who have participated in the Studio simply were not interested in team teaching but, instead, want to "do their own thing, their own way." This can create inconsistencies regarding the role of the instructor that creates confusion among students and diminishes the value of the constructionist approach to learning.

We were very motivated at the beginning to design a studio approach in order for our teaching practices to be aligned with the major theoretical influences at the time. As already discussed, Papert's constructionism was among the most prominent theories. Another was situated cognition (Brown *et al.* 1989) and the closely related concepts of cognitive apprenticeship, situated learning, and legitimate peripheral participation (LPP) (Lave and Wenger 1991). Based on these theories, we designed a studio showcase to be held at the end of each semester. We advertise the showcase with much fanfare and as widely as we can in order to both emphasize its importance to students and, of course, to attract visitors. During the showcase, students share their projects with the professional community in order to demonstrate their design abilities and skills. Similar to someone playing a sport who practices for the "big game" or a musician who practices in order to perform at a concert, the showcase provides an authentic, social and purposeful event for investing such hard work over the duration of the semester (see Anderson *et al.* 1996). Figure 4.3 shows a scene from a recent showcase.

We also wanted less experienced students to "apprentice" with the most experienced students, so we used LPP to guide our design of the role that students in the second Studio course would play toward the teams in the third Studio course. That is, we wanted the students in the second Studio course to participate in the teams comprised by students in the third course, but not have any direct responsibility for how the teams were set up or run. Instead, each student was given the role of "consultant" for a team, each student had to provide a certain number of hours of work for the team, and to be under the direction of the team's project manager (similar to how a paid consultant would work with a group in the business world). So, a student "consultant" might work on generating a certain graphic for the project or help in editing a video that the team had made. They would do their jobs while at the same time being a witness to how the team was operating. The student consultants

Figure 4.3 The University of Georgia LDT Studio Showcase in progress, Spring 2010.

are told explicitly to look for ways in which teams work effectively and ineffectively so as to learn these lessons, and then to apply them when they assume full-fledged team responsibilities when they take the third Studio course in a subsequent semester.

In practice, the project teams find it very challenging to identify work assignments for consultants early enough in the semester to make good use of the consultants' availability. Moreover, the final two weeks of the semester are reserved for students' own project completion, so the window of opportunity for consulting work is somewhat limited. Nonetheless, via the consulting activity first-year students gain insight into what will later be expected of them, at a level that could not be afforded to them by any other means.

Striking a Balance between Freedom and Required Experiences

Many things have not worked out in the Studio, but we will focus on one of the most interesting failures. When we started the Studio we wanted to design a place where students would be influenced more by their intrinsic motivation to learn multimedia design than on the extrinsic motivators that we as the instructors might provide. Consequently, we designed the first Studio experience in 1998 with very few required meetings - basically just the Studio orientation, a mid-semester meeting, the "showcase dress rehearsal," and the all-important Studio showcase during the last class session of the semester. All other activities and meetings were organized into "workshops" (i.e., skill outcomes) and "design seminars" (i.e., design ideas). Students could attend any, some, or none depending on their interest and need. We wanted a place where students never felt they were being "held hostage" by an instructor to sit through something that they felt they already knew or didn't need to know. We had assumed everything would attain a natural balance. We would offer those workshops and seminars that people felt were important - those that people did not attend would be reworked or deleted. An interesting thing happened: the students rebelled, though in a good-natured way. Yes, instead of students embracing the idea that most of the Studio attendance was voluntary, most wanted the instructors to require attendance *more often*. Also, the very same students who demanded that we require attendance were often the ones who would not come of their own volition - an interesting contradictory stance that we have never fully understood. Over a period of some years at the beginning of the Studio, we slowly found a balance between required and optional classes. It has been an interesting dynamic. We now have very few classes that are truly optional, though we have several classes in each semester that are termed "project nights" where there is nothing on the agenda except to work on projects, give and get help, and give and get design critiques. But because everyone is required to be there, these sessions have been full of wonderful energy.

Recent Challenges

A few years ago we moved our Instructional Design and Development (IDD) program (which includes the Studio curriculum) from the UGA Athens campus to an "extended campus" located halfway between Athens and Atlanta in Gwinnett County (and thereby called the UGA Gwinnett campus). In combination with this move was the decision to modify the admission procedures from allowing admission in any semester during the year to a once-only admission with matriculation beginning in the summer term. A third and related alteration was moving to a cohort model in which students move through the sequence of courses as a group and the group takes two courses per semester (usually one is offered online and the other – a Studio course – is offered face-to-face). These changes to the IDD curriculum were made for two reasons: a slow, but steady decline in enrollments and the attrition of program faculty (i.e., faculty moving on from the program but few new hires due to budgetary constraints). The implications of these changes are discussed below.

One implication of the cohort model was that it would be impossible to continue offering all three Studio courses each fall and spring semesters. We considered this a fairly major blow to our studio philosophy because it meant that those students in their first semester in the Studio would no longer have the immediate opportunity to interact with our most veteran Studio students (those taking the third course and organized into project teams for that semester). Despite this disappointing implication, there simply was no way around making this change.

However, there were some positives associated with the cohort for the Studio curriculum. One of these was the social cohesion that the cohort experience brought to the Studio and to the IDD program as a whole. The intent of the Studio from the very beginning was to create a learning community, but the unpredictable change in the mix of students from one semester to the next was a limiting factor in the bonds that could be formed between students. The cohort model has certainly tended to deepen these relationships.

Also, as previously mentioned, the cohort model allowed us to redesign the Studio so that in the fall we would have a combination of first-timers and second-timers taking the first Studio course. We were now more or less guaranteed a balance of first- and second-timers taking the first Studio course at the same time. This had never been the case before. In fact, the time when students took the first course for the second time varied widely, with a significant number taking it in the summer (it was the only Studio course offered in the summer). Consequently, we usually only had a handful of first course second-timers in any given fall or spring semester; and they were assumed to be able to work more or less independently.

With the cohort approach, we now had an opportunity to redesign the second-timer experience in this constructionist course and to do so in such a way that they would become important mentors to the first-timers. (The second-timers would have already taken the second Studio course, so they were well seasoned Studio participants by the time they took the first Studio course for the second time.) So the fall semester experience now became a focus just on the constructionist learning experience with its heavy emphasis on principles of design and on tool learning.

In the subsequent spring semester, the first-timers and second-timers then take, respectively, the second and third Studio courses. This results in the spring semester being focused on instructional design projects for clients among a group of people who know each other very well given that they all worked together in the fall semester.

Another change, one we believe is also positive, is that the public Studio showcase is now only a once-per-year event (instead of every semester) and it occurs at the end of the spring semester. Students are free to show their work from the previous fall at that time as well. In the fall we hold an "in-house" showcase amounting to a showing of projects just among the participants with few or no outside guests invited. In the spring the showcase is a very public event where we invite everyone we can who are part of our professional networks (this was in keeping with the original design of the showcase). One reason we believe this is a positive change is that it had proved difficult to muster a large audience for the showcase each semester during the year. Now, with the showcase coming just once per year, it has been viewed with increased importance – both by the students and by our professional networks – so that its attendance by guests has increased.

Conclusion

While the Studio approach is not without challenges, students in our Studio community have developed web-based media that are, at times, in our view, stunning and highly creative. Along with the more conventional projects, we've had students learn to program 3-D gaming environments with Unity, create visually stunning apps, and develop rich case-based learning or situated-cognition environments (see the Appendix, page 54). Both the students and the instructors are amazed at times with the quality of work that emerges from this environment. Some of these outstanding projects reflect a degree of multimedia development background that students have brought with them into the Studio, but many others represent considerable learning that started at the beginner level. The Studio model accepts and builds on the skill level of the student when they begin. As we look back at the development of our own Studio coursework, we have accumulated and shared a number of "lessons learned," such as those described in this chapter, that have led to strategies for success. Also, as we move forward with the studio approach, we recognize that these strategies are, like the studio itself, flexible and constantly changing to meet a variety of demands, needs and interests. We offer our own studio experiences as tools for others to adapt, adopt and customize as they consider integrating studio approaches in their coursework.

Postscript

This book chapter has taken about three years to go from idea to published form. Given that the studio is "always a work in progress," it should not be surprising that much has transpired in these three years. The most notable change has been the moving of the IDD master's curriculum to an all-online format, anchored each year by an on-campus professional conference (titled "IDD@UGA"). At the time of writing, we are in our second year of the all-online curriculum serving two cohorts. A second major change has been initiating a face-to-face Studio experience at the main campus in Athens to meet the design expectations of our doctoral and research masters students. As Clinton and Rieber (2010) first reported, "the Studio continues to evolve in response to the needs of students" (p. 755).

Appendix: Sample Studio Projects

"Save the Shells" by Benjamin Rockwood.

This project is a role-playing game in which the player assumes the role of an environmental architect. The player learns that a roadway is going to be built across a gopher tortoise's habitat. The player is given the task to minimize the damage done to the tortoises by building tunnels and bridges to connect those parts of the habitat bisected by the road to enable the tortoises to continue to roam the habitat.

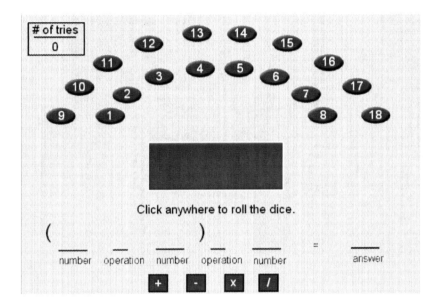

"Numbers All Around" by Sam Winward.

This project is a mathematics game. The player rolls the dice and is given three random numbers. The player places those numbers and their choice of math operations (add, subtract, multiply, and divide), strategically in the available spots at the bottom of the screen to "target" one of the numbers above. The targeted number is deleted from the group. The challenge is to remove all of the numbers in the fewest number of turns.

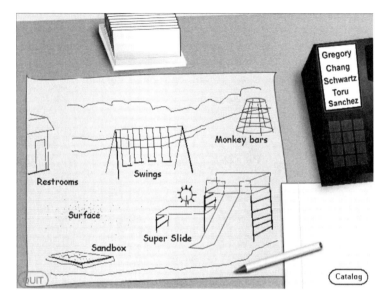

"Fun for All!" by Michael Gardner.

This project is a role-playing game in which the player assumes the role of a newly hired community director. The goal is to build a playground in a local park that will be as inclusive as possible for all children, particularly those with physical disabilities. However, you have a limited budget to work with so difficult decisions must be made.

"Chuck Close: Off the Wall" by Michael Gardner.

This project explored the life and work of the artist Chuck Close. This was an early example of a "second-timer" project that took full advantage of the design opportunities afforded students taking EDIT 6190 – labeled as "the first studio course" in the chapter - for the second time.

"Maternal Transgressions: Musings on Foucault, Power and the Label Known as Disabled" by Teri Holbrook.

This was a hypermedia project involving text and images. Teri was pursuing her doctorate in Language and Literacy Education when she decided to enroll in the UGA Design Studio. The project is extremely detailed and thought-provoking. Interestingly, the authoring tool Teri used was PowerPoint. We often show this project as an example to other students that tools may enable one's design, but they do not define the design.

"Are You Here to Cause Friction?" by Ben Rockwood, David Clark, Denise Domizi, Kim Gibson, Bobby Mitchell, and Akecia Mobley.

This project involved a variety of media, including video, simulations and gaming to teach fundamental physics concepts and principles.

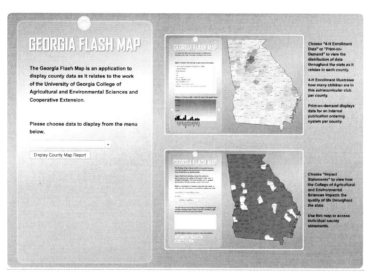

"Georgia Flash Map" by Emily Pitts Ennis.

This project used innovative visualization techniques to display various agricultural education information from an online database.

References

Anderson, J. R., Reder, L. M. and Simon, H. A. (1996) 'Situated learning and education'. *Educational Researcher*, 25(4), pp. 5–11

Brown, J. S., Collins, A. and Duguid, P. (1989) 'Situated cognition and the culture of learning'. *Educational Researcher*, 18(1), pp. 32–42

Clinton, G. and Rieber, L. P. (2010) 'The studio experience at the University of Georgia: An example of constructionist learning for adults'. *Educational Technology Research and Development*, 58(6), pp. 755–780

Gibbons, A. S. (2003) 'What and how do designers design?' *TechTrends*, 47(5), pp. 22–25

Gibbons, A. S. (2011) 'Contexts of instructional design'. *The Journal of Applied Instructional Design*, 1(1)

Kafai, Y. and Resnick, M. (Eds) (1996) *Constructionism in Practice: Designing, Thinking, and Learning in a Digital World*. Mahwah, NJ: Lawrence Erlbaum Associates

Lave, J. and Wenger, E. (1991) *Situated Learning: Legitimate Peripheral Participation*. New York: Cambridge University Press

Moggridge, B. (2007) *Designing Interactions*. Cambridge, MA: MIT Press

Papert, S. (1980) *Mindstorms: Children, Computers, and Powerful Ideas*. New York: BasicBooks

Papert, S. (1991) 'Situating constructionism' in I. Harel and S. Papert (Eds) *Constructionism* (pp. 1-11). Norwood, NJ: Ablex

Parrish, P. E. (2006) 'Design as storytelling'. *TechTrends*, 50(4), pp. 72–82

Tripp, S. and Bichelmeyer, B. (1990) 'Rapid prototyping: An alternative instructional design strategy'. *Educational Technology Research and Development*, 38(1), pp. 31–44

Wilson, B. G. (2005) 'Broadening our foundation for instructional design: Four pillars of practice'. *Educational Technology*, 45(2), pp. 10–15

5 Emergent Tensions in Teaching an Interior Design Studio
Reflections and Opportunistic Redesign

Kennon M. Smith

Several years ago I had the chance to transition my primary, full-time focus from the field of instructional technology, in which I had just completed my doctoral work, to the field of interior design as a faculty member in a professionally accredited, undergraduate degree program. This unexpected opportunity allowed me to blend the instructional design approaches I had come to know during my graduate work with the subject matter knowledge and professional experiences I had acquired during and after an undergraduate course of study in architecture. Teaching studio has been a major responsibility in my current position and in this chapter I will focus on a studio that is typically taken by students during their third year in the program. I will first provide some background information on the studio, and then discuss key issues that have shaped my experiences as a studio instructor: thinking about design studio as a signature pedagogy, grappling with the physical studio space, formulating the projects around which we build studio, and managing project feedback.

Background Context of Studio

As seems to be common among programs in visual arts and design fields, the interior design program at Indiana University has been structured around a series of design studio courses. Each of these seven required sequential studios is a semester long, and students take a studio every semester of the program with the exception of one of their first-year semesters (during which they are often expected to be taking visual arts courses to enhance their drawing skills). Each successive studio involves completing projects of increasing specificity and complexity. The earliest studios are intended to acquaint students with general design principles (such as symmetry, balance and proportion), expectations for the quality of finished projects (such as high levels of craft), and general tools for structuring design processes (such as the importance of conducting research upon which to base design decisions, or using diagrams to organize information from a project description).

These very early projects sometimes don't look much like interior design - they might instead involve designing a logo, packaging or a piece of furniture. I did not design these projects and don't usually teach these courses, but I believe that the projects are purposely broad in the actual types of design they involve, with the intention of helping students learn design principles apart from any misconceptions they might have about what interior design is or how designers behave. Perhaps more than most fields, introductory interior design courses must battle widespread misconceptions of the field that are propagated in popular "Do It Yourself" or "Home Improvement" type television shows. This disconnect between what some students expect to be doing in an intro- ductory studio (drawing floor plans) and what they might actually be doing (building chairs) can be jarring and it is my impression that some students do not see the links between principles they are learning in these early projects and how they might be applied to interior design. It seems that the instructors of these early studios find themselves going back and forth between more disci- pline specific projects and more general projects in an effort to help the students see relevancy, while also encouraging them to think about design and its opportunities more broadly than what they might have originally imagined.

Description of Studio

All of this hard work on the part of instructors and students in the introduc- tory studio courses usually pays off in a couple of big ways by the time students reach me in their third year of the program. First, the students are typically much more comfortable thinking about design in its broader context (instead of having a very specific disciplinary focus). Second, the students usually have a much better understanding of the role and work of interior designers, and are primed to jump into the more discipline-specific projects we often focus on in the upper division studios.

One of the studios I have often taught is the fourth of the seven studio sequence distributed across the four-year curriculum. It falls during the first semester of the third (junior) year. (See Table 5.1 for an example of a curriculum map.)

I have taught this course four times over five years and each time it has been team-taught in order to meet required teacher/student ratios. The program standard is to have at least one faculty member for every 15 students (though the ideal is to have one instructor for every 12 students). Depending on the number of students in a given cohort (typically between 25 and 35), the number of faculty tends to fluctuate between two and three. Most of the students are young, traditionally aged undergraduates when they enroll in this class. Each cohort has been overwhelmingly female and predominantly from the United States though, in recent years, there appear to be much more diverse cohorts advancing through the program. Students often know each other fairly well by the time they enroll in this class because they have taken other required courses together over the previous two years.

The studio meets twice a week, for three hours each session. Students are expected to work in the studio all three hours even if there is not a lecture

Table 5.1 Example of a curriculum map for major requirements in a four-year interior design degree.

The following table is an example of how a student might progress through interior design major requirements. It is important to note that, unlike some design programs which are housed in professional schools, this interior design program is located within a College of Art & Sciences. Students take a wide range of classes related to General Education and liberal arts requirements in addition to the major courses listed below.

Year	Semester 1	Semester 2
1	Design Studio 1.	Fine Arts Studios (e.g., drawing, color theory, 3-dimensional art).
2	Design Studio 2. Digital Communications (e.g., AutoCAD), Twentieth-century Design History & Theory.	Design Studio 3. Design Methods, Materials and Components of Design.
3	Design Studio 4 (Residential Emphasis). Design History Survey, Lighting Part 1.	Design Studio 5 (Commercial Emphasis). Lighting Part 2.
4	Design Studio 6 (Education Emphasis), Professional Practices.	Design Studio 7 (Healthcare Emphasis).

going on and even if they have already met with an instructor that day. Students sit next to each other at long flat tables and spread out their work in progress – typically including sketchbooks, sample materials, precedent images, and laptop computers. As projects progress, these materials tend to spill onto floors and along walls. As it gets down to the last days before a major deadline, it is common to see students stay beyond the conclusion of class and work until the building closes. Unfortunately, they do have to pack up their work before leaving, as a different class will be using the same studio space the next day. There has been some dissatisfaction on the part of students who would like to stay and work in the studio much later into the night (or even through the entire night), but personal safety and property security concerns have led to policies that preclude this opportunity.

The structure of this class follows many of the features found in traditional studio design courses: organizing the course around extended, complex projects; providing frequent feedback through desk critiques; and culminating major projects with public presentations of student work. Desk critiques usually last 10 to 15 minutes each, and involve myself or another instructor talking to each student one-on-one for individual projects or with a group of students if it is a group project. When students are not meeting with an instructor they are expected to be working on their projects – sketching, conducting research, gathering material samples, creating construction drawings or presentation renderings using specialized software, or informally collaborating with each other to share resources or provide peer feedback.

During some projects students present their work-in-progress to peers, visiting critics, or clients for interim feedback. Nearly every project is concluded with a formal presentation in which students display their completed projects (usually in the form of floor plans, 2-D and 3-D drawings of the completed designs, samples of materials, and documentation supporting and communicating design decisions). Students enter the class expecting this kind of experience (even though it is quite different from the way in which many of their other college courses are structured) because they have already been through several other studios by the time they reach their third year in the program.

One fundamental difference between this course and many of the studios I took when I was a student is that in this class more time is given over to lecture and demonstration than I believe would be ideal. There is a real tension within the program's overall curriculum because there seems to be an ever-increasing body of content that students need to know, and which is necessary to meet accreditation standards. For example, trying to keep current with changing technologies (including new computer modeling programs used for visual communication, or techniques and materials introduced as we become ever more aware of sustainability concerns) can eat up a significant number of credit hours in a student's schedule, but this does not mean the student can simply drop the more traditional disciplinary content (such as regulatory codes, materials, lighting, and accessibility standards) to accommodate the new.

Furthermore, university policies limit the number of credit hours that can be required in the program. As a consequence, and in order to squeeze more in, some of the content that would more ideally be situated in non-studio courses ends up getting offloaded into studio. Our responses as instructors have come in the shape of trying to re-evaluate what is a reasonable workload to put on students and to prioritize content that necessitates classroom instruction over that which might be acquired by students on their own if they are pointed in the direction of suitable resources. This is an on-going, largely unresolved tension at this time.

Because so much scheduled studio time gets eaten up by lectures (probably averaging about one hour per three-hour session), we do less interim whole-class critique than I think has often been the case in traditional design studios and I am concerned that this presents some limitations. However, the students have compensated for this in part by communicating between themselves and asking for informal feedback and critique from their peers. In addition to the feedback and critique received and shared in the actual studio, I know that they communicate a great deal in online environments, utilizing various social media tools as they work together towards clarified understandings and share insights, resources and encouragement.

The studio environment, which combines time-intensive projects with close physical proximity among students over the course of several years, seems to lend itself to students forming close-knit, strongly integrated cohorts each year. These social structures seem to have both benefits and drawbacks - they can be supportive to some students while being alienating to others. I worry sometimes that we lose students who may be great designers, simply because the social structure and personality of their particular cohort has not been consistent with their needs and they have self-selected out of the program by the time they reach the junior studio.

Making and Defending a Studio Environment

Finding the Physical Space

One of the perennial challenges in teaching these long studios has been in securing and protecting the physical studio rooms for student use during both scheduled and unscheduled blocks of time. These spaces need to have large work surfaces for students' use, and ideally provide room to display interim and finished work. The junior studio is accommodated in two large adjoining rooms. One of these is slightly larger than the other and permits the entire studio group to meet together at the beginning of class for announcements and for any lecture material that might be delivered, but it is not large enough to permit students to spread out the resources and reference materials needed during their design work. Consequently, after full-class announcements, approximately half of the students move into the adjoining studio, permitting students in both rooms to spread out their work on the large, flat work tables.

Protecting these large studio rooms as exclusive-use spaces can be difficult. As the university community is stretched thin with respect to the use of classrooms, it may appear indulgent to reserve these large rooms for lengthy studio sessions, and then to leave them unscheduled during many early morning and evening hours so that students are able to use the space to work before and after studio. The current studio spaces are probably in part available only because they are in a building located approximately a mile from the center of campus. The building was previously used as a laboratory elementary school affiliated with the university and, in more recent years, it has housed a wide range of functions, including document services and the ROTC. It is not considered a prime location for classroom space. This has made it easier to protect the studio spaces, but has also presented some difficulties for students who do not have their own forms of transportation to reach the building.

Justifying the Student/Teacher Ratio

In addition to protecting the large studio spaces, there occasionally arise questions about whether the relatively low student/teacher ratio is really necessary. Organizations such as the National Association of Schools of Art and Design (NASAD) set standards for student-faculty ratios in art and design studios. The 2014-2015 *NASAD Handbook* states, "When individual faculty attention to individual student work is required during class, class size shall be such that students can receive regular critiques of meaningful duration during the regular class period" (NASAD 2014, p. 61). In more detailed guidelines, it is recommended that class sizes for creative work should not exceed 25, are more effective when capped at 20 or fewer, and in some cases should be limited to 15 (ibid, p. 61). Even with 15 students per instructor, it can be challenging to get to all students in a three-hour window when some desk critiques extend beyond 10 to 15 minutes a piece. While the department has been successful in maintaining student-faculty ratios by demonstrating parity with peer institutions, there is a real sense that the day may come where it will be more difficult to keep these ratios from creeping upward.

Choosing the Best Tools

Students are required to have and maintain their own laptop computers for work both in and out of studio. Prior to the laptop requirement, upper-division studios were held in traditional, campus-supported computer labs. While this ensured that students were all working on consistent versions of the software and facilitated easier maintenance of the programs and computers, the work surfaces in these labs were taken up almost completely by large desktop computer monitors, and the overall room design was not conducive to any aspects of design work other than those tied directly to the computers. The advantage of implementing the laptop requirement has been that studio could be moved to large, multi-purpose workrooms.

When the laptop requirement was put in place in 2008 many students already had laptops, and this is even more the case today. However, there have been some significant challenges to overcome in specifying and supporting these individually-owned laptops. In order to remain current with professional standards, students need to use ever more powerful and sophisticated modeling and drawing programs. The processing power required to support these programs can far outstrip the basic entry-level laptops that some students initially bring with them to college. This can present a financial difficulty for students if they do not contact an interior design advisor for advice before acquiring a laptop. Even more common is the computer platform issue we sometimes confront. Because many students are under the impression that Macintosh computers are more desired in design industries, many of them specifically select these machines with the assumption they will best support their interior design coursework. However, some of the industry-standard drafting and modeling software was developed specifically for Windows operating systems and has typically required special machine configuration if they are going to be installed and maintained on Macs. While these might seem like trivial inconveniences, for some students these are stressful, and financially difficult, obstacles that seem overwhelming when also trying to balance entry into a very time-consuming, and relatively expensive, course of study. This platform issue is likely to be resolved as platforms and programs appear to be ever-more interchangeable in the design world, but I suspect there will be plenty of future technology-related challenges to replace any of those resolved today.

Crafting the Projects

This studio has been a part of the department's curriculum for many years – it started long before I arrived and the projects we run in the studio have been strongly influenced by the work done by faculty members before me, by collaboration with co-instructors, and by the accrediting standards that have been apportioned to this specific studio.

Ramping Up to the Major Project

The class lasts approximately 16 weeks and has been configured in many different ways over the years. In one configuration, the semester is divided into three sections, reflecting three main projects. The first is a short warm-up project that requires students to develop a small-scale residential living space design for a specific client. They are given an existing floor plan and a short narrative describing their clients (including client backgrounds, preferences and hopes for the new space). From this they generate a loose presentation within about a week and a half. These presentations are typically sketches, inspirational images, and sample finish materials that could be used in the space.

The next three to four weeks are devoted to an intensive unit on residential construction. This unit is very lecture-intensive, covering the basic process and materials in use in typical wood-frame residential construction. Lectures are supplemented by videos and, when possible, by a field trip to a home under construction. The students then work in teams to build scale models corresponding to an assigned set of construction drawings. These completed models are often used in fund-raising efforts for the local chapter of Habitat for Humanity.

At the completion of the construction project the students begin their major project, which runs for the remaining months of the semester. We have adjusted the details of this project over the years to accommodate different opportunities, but it is essentially an existing residential or commercial space that is radically redesigned to serve as a home for an assigned or student-selected client. Students work individually and the project is structured and submitted in pre-design, schematic design, and design development stages, aligning with industry standards for design services (which, in a professional setting, would also include construction documentation and contract administration).

The learning outcomes for the class are very specific, and have been determined as part of an overall curriculum design strategy to ensure that required competencies are demonstrated for accreditation purposes. As a result, the major project is designed with these competencies in mind and sometimes it begins to feel that project briefs become unreasonably inflated in an attempt to check off all the needed competencies. In most years, these issues have been included by emphasizing them in the client profiles assigned to the students. These profiles have varied over time and have included scenarios that raise issues such as universal design (including accessibility), alternative mechanical technologies (such as non-traditional heating systems) or greater cultural awareness (as in the case of designing for clients with cultural backgrounds substantially different from that of the student).

Deciding Who the Client Should Be

As faculty, we have sometimes struggled with the question of whether or not to include a "real" client. We typically find more opportunities to work with clients in some of the other upper-division studios (such as projects related to retail, office or restaurant spaces), but have less often found good fits for residential design (which has been the focus of the first junior studio). I personally have been quite concerned that students get too little experience interacting with and trying to communicate with clients. It seems to me that, in many cases, they begin to think of the professor as the client because, after all, they know they will be getting a grade and so they aim to uncover and satisfy the priorities of the faculty member in the same way that a professional might seek to clarify and understand the needs of a client.

In a recent iteration of the studio, all of the students in the class were given the same base floor plan (including a basic shell and structural components that had to remain), but each student was responsible for finding their own client and for radically redesigning the space to suit their client's needs. This seemed like it would be a good compromise because, with a consistent base plan, the studio instructors could have a basic understanding of the physical constraints and conditions that characterized the pre-design structure, but students would be able to select real people to interview and with whom to negotiate throughout the design process.

In reality, a number of issues arose in this project design. First, it was difficult to help students understand the scope of work that would be appropriate given the time and space constraints of the project. For example, some students ended up selecting a client who essentially would only need to house one or two people, while other students selected clients who might need to house far more people than could be reasonably accommodated in the given square footage. Some clients wanted extensive amenities and support spaces in the home (multiple offices, workout rooms, specialized studio spaces) and students working with these clients struggled to negotiate between their clients' dreams and the constraints of the available space. While this was a good learning experience from the standpoint of resolving conflicting goals, it also drained a great deal of time from other learning objectives that had been of importance in the class, while also diminishing our ability as instructors to assure that all students had experience grappling with some of the topics necessitated in our assigned competencies.

Becoming a Studio Teacher

Meeting Students Where They Are

While the over-arching studio structure, the physical studio spaces and (to some degree) the types of projects we will tackle during the semester are designed ahead of my intervention, the one aspect of studio that I and each of my colleagues designs for ourselves (and often re-designs on a daily basis) is our personal interactions with students. I personally find it a challenge to come prepared to respond spontaneously and flexibly to students during one-on-one desk critique. It is often impossible to prepare for these critiques in the same way I might prepare for a lecture or a demonstration. It is unpredictable and sometimes difficult to respond in the moment to the design challenges students present in their work. This is especially the case when I am moving from desk to desk, meeting with each student to review work in process. While there are some common patterns that seem to arise (such as space planning challenges that often come up early in the process), there are other times when students are at different places in their process, or where they are pursuing different kinds of goals (such as, for example, having a student choose to incorporate sustainable technologies in a building, while the next student is very interested in puzzling out how to apply historical precedents without mimicking traditional forms). Meeting each student where she or he is – that can be tough.

I have sometimes taught students in non-studio lecture courses in their sophomore or freshman years before teaching them in the junior studio. In such a case, I often know the student fairly well at the beginning of the semester and this can be helpful in trying to adjust on-the-fly to students' individual needs and interests. Other times, students change so quickly that I can't assume previous strengths and weaknesses will carry over from one semester to the next.

To me, the student-teacher relationship is a major factor in my studio teaching. I tell different students different things, and I answer questions for some students that I might not for other students. I try to be as transparent as possible with my students as to why I do or do not answer questions. This honesty and transparency seems to make it OK. Without this transparency, I think they would interpret my differential behaviors as evidence of favoritism or of distrust. I find that the better my rapport with the class, the more effective I can be in tailoring my feedback to them, and the more quickly they progress. I don't know at this time how I would do this if I were teaching a studio of 40 or 50 students, or even how I would do this online. Such a change of context would take considerable thought and reflection to figure out how this interaction, which I see as being one of the key components of studio education, might be translated into a different setting.

Figuring Out When to Intervene and When to Stay Out of the Way

Despite the considerable reflection I have given to issues of feedback and guidance, I find that I still sometimes struggle to determine the best way to provide feedback, especially when work is in process. For many students, the scope of the major project during their first junior studio far exceeds anything they have previously done in design and some are rapidly overwhelmed by this complexity. These students sometimes appear to get "stuck." I do have a hard time knowing when to intervene and when to let the student continue to struggle with the concepts or problems that are troubling them.

Perhaps the most concrete example of this kind of experience is in the space planning students do as part of most studio projects. Typically students are provided with a building shell – essentially the outer walls of the building – and they then need to develop all of the interior architecture (walls, floor heights, ceiling heights and articulations) in such a way as to meet certain square footage specifications for each of the necessary spaces or functions. At the same time, they need to be considering issues of privacy, access, functional adjacencies, privacy, views, acoustics, legal building code requirements, and a host of other related issues. For some students this is an engaging, puzzle-solving activity and they kind of dive in right away. Other students become overwhelmed, almost paralyzed, by the complexity and do not make much progress from one class session to the next. Another group (though I think usually a small number in each class) simply don't find the time to work on the project much from one class to the next. It is sometimes hard to tell the difference between these last two profiles and whether the student needs help getting "unstuck," or if they are assuming that they don't need to spend a lot of time on the project or grapple with those complexities because they know that at the next desk critique they will get advice that will help resolve the issues. In other words, it's hard to know if a student has gone as far as they can on their own and really needs assistance to progress or if assistance is going to cut short their learning opportunity. Similarly, I believe that the development, within the student, of design judgment and confidence is paramount and I am wary of looking like I have "the answer." First, such a stance might lead the student to distrust their own process and to constantly consult me. I believe it is necessary for students to learn to live with the uncertainties of each project long enough to learn who they are as a designer and what they can do. Second, for me such a stance would be patently dishonest – I know there are plenty of answers I simply don't have. In the long run, the students would "find me out" or catch me in a mistake if I tried to convince them otherwise. I share with students stories from my own educational and professional experiences in order to help them understand that becoming a designer is a life-long process. I am further along in my process than they are in their own. I can help them successfully complete their projects, but I am still often stumped by the projects I do – projects of ever-increasing complexity – and even find holes in my own knowledge when students bring me questions about changing technologies or contexts that I have not encountered. For me personally, this level of honesty with my studio students is much more comfortable than trying to keep up a charade of having all the answers.

Issues regarding how to design or shape feedback can also arise in studios where I am collaborating with one or two other instructors. While we might have shared curricular goals and believe in the value of the studio experience, we often have different views of the best approaches to help students mature as design thinkers. For example, we might disagree on whether it better to "correct" a student's design so that the student has a great-looking final project (that will feed into their portfolio), or if it is better to hold off and let the student discover some of these issues on their own, thus learning to judge their own work and that of their peers, even if it means the final project doesn't get as far or look as polished. For me this is a paradox in design studios. Sometimes a great final product might be evidence of great learning – at other times it might be evidence of great collaboration with the instructor. Sometimes a less-polished project might be the outcome of a tremendously successful learning process.

Helping Students Discover a New Way to Learn

Though students in the junior studio are in their third year of design coursework, the patterns of learning and thinking they adopted in high school, and which often still prove successful in their non-project-based courses, sometimes prove resistant to change in a design studio setting. This is challenging for me as an instructor and often for the students because there are not the kinds of guarantees to which they have become accustomed in much of their non-design coursework. For example, some expect that, because we have had desk critiques while the project is in process, I should have "corrected" any missteps along the way and that the final project grade should therefore always be an A. Similarly, most of the students have been successful in past non-design work as long as they have put in the time. It seems counterintuitive to them that design is not always like that and that, at times, you actually have to step away and spend a little less time to see things in a new way. These underlying assumptions are ones that I watch for as I work with students, and which I find myself needing to challenge on a regular basis as I try to help students develop more nuanced understandings of how learning might be facilitated, both by me and by themselves, in a studio setting.

Acknowledging the Boundaries of My Own Expertise

Teaching in the studio is challenging for me because it often forces me to confront my own limitations - as a teacher and as a designer. While I have a strong general design background and certain areas of individual design expertise, I am certainly not an expert in every condition that will arise in every project. As time goes on, individual students may surpass me in specific areas of expertise (this happens especially frequently as technologies change and students gravitate towards different modeling software), and my colleagues often have strengths in areas I do not. As noted above, I have to be honest with students about where and how I can help them and when I will need to send them somewhere else. In the bigger scheme of things, this is great because it is closer to what they will experience in practice (where they need to go to multiple sources of expertise to get their answers) but it can be unsettling in a classroom. As a beginning studio instructor I had to figure out how to lose a little ego, but still maintain my students' trust and respect so they would listen to me and consider my feedback.

Conclusion

Teaching in a design studio setting has proven a simultaneously challenging and rewarding endeavor. As a studio instructor, I have found that some of the major challenges I face come in the form of protecting studio spaces, time, and student/teacher ratios, trying to keep up with the rapidly changing tools of the discipline, crafting projects that meet curricular demands and mirror authentic design problems without placing unreasonable complexity on students, and in evaluating what it means to teach well in a studio setting. In the studio, students find themselves struggling not only to learn content matter, but also to learn a new way of learning. As their instructor I find myself working to be more comfortable with uncertainty, not only in terms of realizing I cannot predict what challenges students might bring to class on any given day, but also in terms of trying to shape my work as a teacher to the specific needs and developing design judgment each student might bring to those challenges.

It is my belief that design, in general, is an unpredictable endeavor. In spite of all the theory and evidence we might bring to bear on design decisions and products, the contextual complexities caught up in a proposed design's lived experience make outcomes exceptionally hard to forecast. Perhaps, in this way, design studios mirror the disciplines and ways of knowing of which they are a part. The challenges and tensions that emerge in the studio become opportunities to challenge preconceptions and to redesign the studio experience. Studio never seems to be quite the same from one class period to the next, let alone from one year to the next. This makes studio both challenging and compelling. As a studio instructor, I ask my students to embrace and tolerate a great deal of unpredictability, of uncertainty, and most come to believe that the outcomes of their studio journey have been well worth the effort. As their teacher, I suppose I should ask no less of myself, with the confidence that the journey will have enriched my own life - as a student, a teacher and a designer – as well.

Reference

NASAD (2014) *NASAD Handbook 2014-2015.* National Association of Schools of Art and Design. Available at: http://nasad.arts-accredit.org/site/docs/Handbook/ NASAD_HANDBOOK_2014-15.pdf

6   The Rapid (Interactive) Design Studio for Slow (User and Learner) Change

Martin A. Siegel

Origins

Since 1984, first at the University of Illinois and later at Indiana University, I taught the introductory graduate course in human-computer interaction design - Interaction Design Practice (IDP). For a long time I had felt that there was a need to have a "part 2" of the course. At the end of IDP students have a sense of how the "whole game" of interaction design is played, but they don't have sufficient practice of exploring a range of design challenges within varying contexts.

When some of my administrative responsibilities at the school concluded, my teaching requirement increased from two courses to three courses per year. This was my opportunity to create an IDP2, but I was uncertain of its content and form. At the same time, in spring 2011, I went on sabbatical for the semester. While it was not my sabbatical plan to design a new studio course, I used my time away from the university to think about its structure.

I initially called the IDP2 course "Rapid Interaction (Design) Practice" (RIP); I liked that acronym because it reminded me of Rest In Peace. I knew that at the end of the course the students would be dead tired and may feel that way at the conclusion of each project. I wanted the students to experience what it's like to perform rapidly in pressurized environments, not unlike the environments in which they will work as professional designers. I knew from experience and interviews with designers in software companies and design firms that time was critical; there wasn't much of it and often projects overlapped. Also, engaging in such activities as "research" was difficult. As one manager of a design agency told me, "the clients don't want to pay for research, so we have to squeeze it in the best we can." That attitude differs from the methodological practices taught in the academy, so I wanted to interject this authentic element of pressure and client response into the design studio.

Time would become an important design element of the class. Each project, from Monday to Friday, needed to be completed during that five-day period, but sometimes I would shorten the timeline to 24 hours or less. The students both loved this and hated it! They would finish the week's project on time, but they would have to be accountable for their results – a measure of authentic, if sometimes unwelcomed, pressure.

When I first floated the idea of an advanced studio course to my colleagues, I received pushback from them. While no one directly said this to me (I was on sabbatical at the time, visiting high tech companies on the west coast), they worried that my class would siphon too many students from their elective courses. An email to me from the program director summarized this concern; he suggested using my current research topic as the theme for my new course, thereby attracting fewer students.

I called my new research area "slow change interaction design." Whether it's diet, exercise, disease prevention, addiction recovery, or financial planning, appropriate behaviors in these and similar domains are particularly challenging to *initiate* and *sustain*. Moreover, websites, apps, and digital artifacts that support these behaviors are unsuccessful for many people beyond an initial period of compliance. With new research emerging in the fields of brain science and persuasive technologies, might there be new design principles and processes that could be applied to these "wicked" slow change problems? See Siegel and Beck (2014) for a more complete description of slow change interaction design.

So I decided, cleverly I thought, to combine the two ideas - rapid interaction design practice with slow change interaction design: Rapid Design for Slow Change (RDSC). There was little room to complain.

Students

RDSC students were second-year master's students in the Human Computer Interaction Design Program at Indiana University. The number of students in the studio increased from 24 students in 2011 to 39 students in 2015; project teams varied from two-person to three-person teams. As students entered the course they were a bit full of themselves, having just spent the summer in a successful internship receiving praise for their work. Moreover, many of the RDSC students were IDP mentors for the inexperienced first-year students and they received adulation from these newcomers during orientation. I needed to remind the RDSC students that they were only half-done with their master's program and that there was more to learn. To emphasize this point, I gave them an in-class 30-minute rapid design exercise. They failed. This woke them up.

Studio Mechanics

The course was structured, when first introduced in fall 2011, as a series of 11 design challenges, most of them spanning a range of well-established companies (for example, Microsoft, Adobe, Autodesk and HP) as well as a few lesser-known startups and nonprofits. Each project lasted one week – assigned on Monday at 9 a.m. and due on Friday at 5 p.m. – and completed by two-person teams, randomly paired. The studio course met on Tuesdays and Thursdays. On the first Tuesday, one day following the new design challenge, the students connected to representatives of the company via Google Hangout or Skype and asked any questions they wished; they were given 30 minutes to do so. On the Thursday following the project's completion, the company reconnected with the class to provide team-by-team feedback and to select the best team design according to their criteria; the top team would win some reward such as an invite to interview with the company, design books, gift cards, or a one-on-one portfolio review.

While most of the projects emphasized the rapid design theme, the last project or two represented slow change design, also completed in one week. The final design challenge was a three-week slow change problem solved by a four-person student team, self-selected.

As students engaged with the 11 projects, four aspects of the course required closer examination and improvement.

Evaluation and Feedback

Unlike the prior course, Interaction Design Practice (IDP), RDSC had no mentors; in fact, most of the IDP mentors were enrolled in RDSC. The only teaching assistant for the course was a doctoral HCI design student. To grade a dozen team projects in less than a week's time, and repeating that 11 times, was not feasible. Therefore, I devised a peer evaluation process: each team was paired with another team and they would present their projects to each other and provide feedback. Then one or two teams would be selected at random to present to the entire class for a group critique. Nevertheless, students complained that they didn't get to view the work of other students. In the second year of the course's implementation, this evaluation procedure was modified somewhat. Instead of pairwise reviews, we simply group-critiqued more of the projects, but not all of them. However, all projects were stored on a course server whereby any project could be reviewed at a later time. The students appreciated this process more, but I think we can improve this further.

Corporate Partners

In the first year I didn't have time to find many corporate partners; during the second year, however, it became easier. The students very much wanted to work on real projects; these projects not only provided challenges that existed in the workplace, but the projects afforded opportunities to make contact with potential future employers. From the company's perspective, their project created opportunities to see how student-designers addressed challenges in which they struggled.

Other Project Participants

Design teams rarely include just designers; they often include engineers, marketing people, graphic designers, etc. In the second year I implemented a project that included graphic design students from Fine Arts with our HCI design students. This project was two-weeks' long versus the typical one-week project. The design was to create "The Eames Store" in one of the larger Crate & Barrel stores. The experience was well-received by both the HCI students and the Fine Arts students, some of whom were undergraduates. A few of these students subsequently applied to the HCI design master's program.

Slow Change Design Versus Standard Design

After completing ten rapid design projects, the students found it difficult to work on a multi-week project, particularly one that contained slow-change elements. A crucial difference between these project types, other than the time to complete them, is that the slow change project required complex behavioral change. The students quickly realized that they could not achieve complete behavioral change with one project. Rather than moving the user from behavior A (for example, sedentary, desk-bound activity) to behavior B (an active daily runner), a better strategy would be to move the user from behavior A to behavior A' (a person who walks 4,000 steps each day), then to behavior A'' (4,750 steps), and so on. This led to a different kind of design thinking and important insights for the students - that is, a slow change intervention is likely to require a system of change processes, each building on the other. These interventions might employ quantitative and qualitative feedback as well as strategies that account for slips (failures to comply with the program). One normally doesn't think about slips in traditional designs; the designer assumes that the user will comply with the design's directions. But in a behavioral change program it's reasonable to assume that slips will occur such as, for example, walking only 2,000 steps on a given day rather than the expected 4,750 steps. In subsequent iterations of the RDSC course, strategies for slow change were discussed earlier in the semester and incorporated into some of the one-week projects.

Projects

Each project was conceived by the company and approved (and sometimes modified) by me. The projects varied in size and scope, and often took a few weeks to formulate the brief. One project from a team at Blackbaud, a leading provider of nonprofit software and services, is presented here in part:

Problem Statement
Nonprofit organizations rely on donations to help them achieve their goals, and major gifts (large donations) are a significant part of this.

A rule-of-thumb is that 80% of a nonprofit's funding will come from 20% of their prospects. To help identify major gift opportunities, nonprofits conduct prospect research. This is more than just identifying wealthy individuals. Andresen, Stepno, *et al.* advise that good prospect research "takes a more sophisticated look at donors and focuses on finding the right combination of factors including the: Right donor, Right purpose, Right amount, Right solicitor, [and] Right time." In other words, nonprofits need to connect with major gift prospects who have a combination of capacity and propensity.

Considering the sheer number of potential prospects and the variety of nonprofits competing for donations, relationships can be the difference between a successful gift and a missed opportunity. There are many types of relationships that could play into fundraising: personal, professional, organizational, educational, interest-based, geographical, etc. Recognizing particularly relevant relationships can help identify or make connections with potential major gift prospects.

Prospect researchers work to uncover relevant information that will help identify these individuals. The information includes both internal data (personal connections to the nonprofit, past gift or volunteer to the nonprofit, event attendance, etc.) and external sources (news articles, social media, etc.).

Your challenge is to design a solution that will help nonprofits achieve their fundraising goals by identifying and visualizing potentially important relationships.

Things to Consider

- Your solution must be ethical. The APRA Ethics and Professional Standards site can help guide you.
- Not all information is trustworthy or relevant.
- Too much information will become noise. How can you provide a beneficial service without overwhelming prospect researchers?
- Highlight actionable connections. We know that Bill Gates and Satya Nadella have a close connection. That doesn't help my small children's health center in Kentucky. Now if Bill Gates had a close connection to one of our biggest donors, this would be nice to know.
- In order to get a major gift, you need one-on-one time with a prospect. You cannot do this with all of your prospects. How can relationships help with this?

In this project, the solution required the team to design a system to leverage social media and other resources to identify "friends of donors" who might also donate to the donor's cause. One team proposed a design they called "Storyshare," fostering relationships through storytelling. Two of their interactive screens appear in Figure 6.1. The system included posting a story about why the cause is important to the donor as well as tools to reach out to the donor's network. Other parts of the system allowed fundraising researchers to filter through the list of generated future donors to focus on the ones that would be most valuable to the organization. Four senior designers at Blackbaud, including their lead UX designer and lead UX researcher, judged this project to be among the two best team designs, fulfilling the requirements of the brief.

Other project briefs explored different areas of design: new and advanced technology – Intel's RealSense R200 3D Camera to sense what's in a space to create a better user experience (for example, creating navigational aids for blind people); traditional e-commerce spaces (for example, redesigning eBay's checkout and shopping cart experience); or new kinds of UX services (for example, expanding Zoosk's online dating software to include life-long relationship services - a form of slow change design). These varied and short-term projects both heightened and intensified the students' studio experiences, yet tended to shift their focus from design processes to design outcomes.

Perhaps it was a function of providing first, second and third place "winners" to teams with the best design solutions, perhaps it was simply the nature of doing projects at all, but students continued to think of the brief's solution as the goal rather than learning from each project's process as an opportunity to build one's design repertoire and insights. I needed to make this point at the conclusion of each project. I would ask them, "What do you know now about the design process or being a designer that you didn't know before? What do you know now about working on a team?" These questions elicited many new observations from the students such as, for example: "It's very hard to refute a design proposed by a team member. Just saying 'I don't like this' is not fair… If one refuses another team-mate's idea, it is important to support it with a compelling rationale;" "Ironing out the details early in a project is important; discussing important details of the project just before the deadline is unnerving;" "Diving head-first helps. We had some excess time and we decided to video prototype the interactions; I learned the tool *Principle* in a matter of a few hours and was able to get a good working prototype out;" or "The team needs to get together and generate as many ideas as possible. Settling for a solution because the brief is challenging will lead to a very mediocre design if not a terrible one."

However, come the next project, their behaviors and thoughts substantially shifted back to goal-seeking and winning the prize, admittedly an honor that would bring distinction to their résumé. Admonishing them with statements like "you'll never be asked again to design a nonprofit donor system" did not seem to matter. Or perhaps I'm not fully detecting their slow change as a designer-learner.

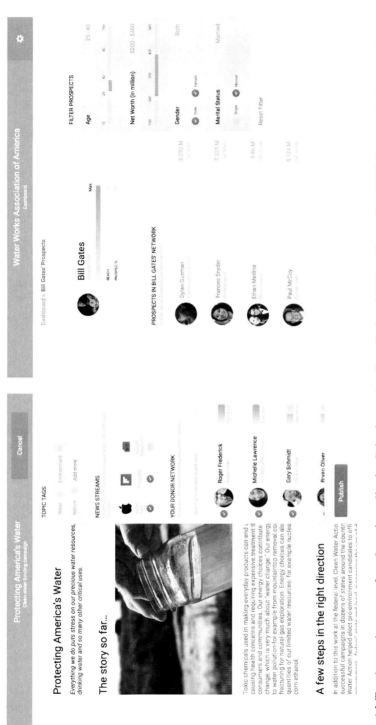

Figure 6.1 Two interactive screens from Storyshare. Shankar Balasubramanian, Evan Tank and Zhijian (Owen) Shi (2015). Reprinted with permission.

Other Project Issues

Some student issues were a function of early learning. For example, during their first project they quickly learned that time is precious and it can't be wasted on long discussions and debates. "[Expletive deleted!] The project is due in less than two days!" In short order, students learned to get organized quickly and focus. Other challenges needed to be experienced to improve on student execution. For example, with most projects a "curve ball" was introduced. Curve balls included such challenges as: changing design specs mid-stream; adding an impossible array of requirements (so the students would learn to appropriately push back); telling two teams that they would need to coordinate their designs and offer a single design, but one team pretends it is in Bangalore, India, so only Skype or email may be used to communicate between them, and having to schedule meetings at convenient times for both; or requiring the students to examine their design from a business perspective, specifying a minimally viable product solution. Each of these curve balls required discussion of best practices to overcome the challenge.

Also, some issues were characteristic of the projects themselves. For example, the project briefs varied from being narrow and specific to large and vague. Each required learning different design strategies. The narrow and specific briefs required a detailed analysis of the problem space with the opportunity to explore multiple iterations, whereas the broad and vague briefs required placing constraints on the problem's scope, creating a specific problem space within an ocean of possibilities. Other issues centered on the project's degree of "sexiness." Often design students work on "cool" projects in graduate school but, when they enter the workforce, they often encounter more mundane assignments. To increase project realism, the companies and I provided a mix of project types. What the students learned, however, is that professionalism is orthogonal to coolness; *all* projects require full attention and quality work.

The Reflective Practitioner

To help the students focus more on the process than the design's outcome, I set up an online forum where students posted weekly reflections. I quickly learned that to require students to post each week resulted in forced or banal reflections from some of the students. Once I removed this weekly requirement and made postings a voluntary activity, more thoughtful reflections ensued. This is a sample reflection from the dozens posted:

> This week, Whirlpool is our client. They asked us to explore the meaning of "Daily Care," and imagine future products for Whirlpool. We asked them during our client interview what "care" means to them; they reminded us that "care" can mean thousands of different things to

different people, that's why we should focus on the persona and user group we chose to design for.

However, they did mention that "the mission of other design teams is to make people fall in love with the products in the store. The UX team has another mission which is to make people stay in love with the product." Personally, I think this is the general meaning of "care" in the UX world.

New products pop out in the market every day to look for its potential owner, to fill our lives with possibilities, and that is the bright side of design. However, many products fail our expectations and curb our enthusiasm towards digital products. As a responsible designer for the industry, we need to reflect on how to retain users by keeping them in love with what we design.

Slow change is an important topic for today's digital designers who shape the future of digital experiences, and persuade people into the habit of living with these digital designs. In order to keep people in love with these experiences, we need to think about what changes are necessary, desirable, helpful, sustainable, all in all, beneficial to the user, environment, and other people in the long run.

In the US, people throw away 40% of the food, and restaurants throw away 60% of the food. It's not the food that is rotten, it's the food that can be repurposed, such as bananas that are a little old but can be perfect for banana pies or cakes. People in the US are getting into the habit of wasting. If we only use "User-Centered-Design" principles, we can surely design products that help people clean up "bad" food easily and quickly, but is that really what we want for the environment, the community, and the world?

Coming back to the topic of designing a new washing machine for Whirlpool. We need to think about the slow changes we can make on people's perspectives on consumerism. If your new washing machine can help you wash your clothes with ease, but also help you save water and energy, and even send a "thank you" note to your mom who has been washing your clothes for years, wouldn't that be pleasant?

The reflections tended to range from the philosophical and strategic (about 85 percent of the posts) to the very personal or "other" category (about 15 percent). Sometimes, but not often, students commented on each other's posts. Still, there were some students who posted no reflections; this was unfortunate for the learning is in the reflection as much as in the doing.

My Role

My traditional role of lecturer shifted dramatically in the RDSC studio. Aside from having negotiated and set up the 11 projects for the students, about half of them decided upon prior to the start of the semester, I saw myself as the studio mentor, providing just-in-time mini-lectures when needed, but mostly allowing the studio to run itself. There were key moments when I played more critical roles. The first came early in the semester. Before the students began their first project, I led them in a lively discussion on what they learned in the prior year and over their summer internships about good design process. They surprised themselves with how much they had learned, but this gave them a sense of false assurance moving into their first project; by the end of the first week they were disabused of that notion after my negative feedback followed their Skype interview with the company's designers, the ones who created the first design brief.

Many of the students' questions were naive: "What kind of solution do you have in mind?" or "Do you think we should design X or Y?" My feedback after their first interview was direct - "If the company knew the solution to their design brief, they would have built it already. The reason they hired us as their design agency is because they don't know the solution. Your questions sounded like the silly moves of a young child playing the '20 questions' game, asking 'Is it a horse?' [No.] 'Is it a ring?' [No.] as your first questions! You've got to be strategic in your questioning. It's your job to understand more deeply what is being asked of you. What have they tried in the past that didn't work? What would a successful project look like to them? Engage in a conversation with them. Discover what's important but didn't make its way into the brief." The students clearly understood I was not happy with their performance.

Of course I knew this would happen because it happens every year. During their first interview it sounded like a Q and A session, not a conversation. My reaction was swift and forceful. My goal was to wake them up from their overly confident selves. Throughout the semester, I helped the students refine their interview skills. Some of the more subtle interactions occurred over gender: "Did you notice that the three people you interviewed included a woman who rarely spoke. The men did not introduce her to us and they answered most of the questions. Next time, begin by asking each person to identify themselves and their role in the company. And regardless of who is doing all of the talking, make sure you include everyone in the conversation. No one should be marginalized. How might you have done this?" This always led to interesting conversations about power relationships and our role as their "design agency" in addressing these issues during an interview.

My role throughout the semester was opportunistic – adding to the company's feedback and providing intermediate feedback before the teams submitted their solutions. When new ideas were introduced in the studio, such as slow change design, I engaged the students in a mini-lecture or I would ask them to use their improved interviewing skills to interview me. The first time I did this the result was good; their questions were incisive and revealed critically important issues of design. I continued with this format in succeeding years; my mini-lecture came as a response to well-thought-out interview questions from the students.

Evolution

As the course evolved over the last two years, I added or modified some features to the RDSC studio experience. I was uncertain about their effect, but was pleased overall by their positive reception. Among the significant changes were the following.

Multi-Week and Overlapping Projects

Instead of 11 mostly one-week projects, the 2015 version of the course divided projects into three five-week segments or "sprints" with three to four projects each. The fifth week of each sprint did not include project work but was used for deep reflection - individually and as a group. In any given week during the prior four weeks of the sprint, the students were engaged in one to two simultaneous projects. As illustrated in Table 6.1 below, projects may be rapid *and* overlapping, each with a different team and some with a slow change theme. It's not unlike how designers will work in a real company.

This latest iteration of the class may have been "a bridge too far." In previous iterations of the course, no project overlapped with another. However, this version required students to manage two different teams and two different projects simultaneously throughout most of the semester. The fifth, tenth and fifteenth weeks were non-project and reflection weeks, which likely saved me from studio mutiny! Much of the discussion centered on managing

Table 6.1 Three sample sprints with overlapping projects.

WEEK 1	WEEK 2	WEEK 3	WEEK 4	WEEK 5
Project 1				Reflection!
	Project 2			
	Project 3			
		Project 4		

WEEK 6	WEEK 7	WEEK 8	WEEK 9	WEEK 10
Project 5				Reflection!
Project 6				
		Project 7		
			Project 8	

WEEK 11	WEEK 12	WEEK 13	WEEK 14	WEEK 15
Project 9				Reflection!
Project 10				
		Project 11		

simultaneous projects, and included interviews with designers at Google and Apple to determine their strategies and tools for simultaneous and overlapping project teams. Not surprisingly, the students learned that "over-communication" was key to their success - ensuring that all team members were well informed of timelines and expectations. During the reflection weeks we also discussed the need for rigorously honest conversations or what Susan Scott (2004) referred to as "fierce conversations." During the reflective week sessions, students hand wrote individual notes to each teammate, providing this kind of feedback. "No slacking" and clear communication quickly became the studio norm.

A team and project communications tool, *Slack,* was used "24/7" and synched on smartphones, tablets and laptops. Each project had its own channel: #p5-blackbaud, #p6-intel, #p7-ebay, #p8-microsoft, and so on. In addition, private channels were used for each team, for example, #7-ebay-team-b. The studio's teaching assistant and I had our own private channel, #instructors, and there were general channels for announcements and random thoughts.

For me executing the course required stamina, and every year I questioned my own sanity in requiring the considerable effort to plan the 11 projects with 11 companies. This process commenced months before the semester began and included negotiating the project's scope and pedagogical benefit. Why would a company such as GE or Microsoft devote senior designer and management time to understanding the RDSC studio mechanics, develop an appropriate brief, allow themselves to be interviewed by students, evaluate in a week's time as many as 13 different team submissions, and provide detailed feedback to each team while awarding first place honors and prizes? While demanding for these companies too, they recognized the value of the RDSC studio for training future designers and for possibly identifying future employees for their company. As one executive put it, "We all benefit when each of us excels." Several companies re-upped for succeeding years. One company, Whirlpool, did this three years in a row.

This I Believe

Each class began with a short story from the series *This I Believe* - "an international organization engaging people in writing and sharing essays describing the core values that guide their daily lives" (http://thisibelieve. org/). My reasoning behind using these stories – each about four minutes long and played at the start of each class without any discussion – was to help the students identify with "the human condition;" those life challenges and core values that guide action. One of my core beliefs as a design educator is that designers can't identify the deeper needs of others beyond what they have explored and identified in their own, but different, needs. It's arrogant to design for other people's needs without understanding one's own.

At the end of the semester, I asked the students to write their own "This I Believe" (about design) essay. Here is a sample from Jared Forney from fall 2013, reprinted with permission. His essay is titled "The Man with the Dog." This thoughtful essay, perhaps one of the best, was not unusual in its depth and personal exploration.

I believe in the power of perspective. My design education thus far has been characterized by how it has changed me as a person, both through my outlook on the world, and how others shape that outlook. My source of energy and inspiration has always been through other people; building on their ideas or internalizing and reflecting upon the feedback I receive from them as I posit my own. I cannot design in a vacuum; inasmuch as design serves to the aid of the People, so too do I see myself as a facilitator for my team's success. In the past, I've always found cohesion with the image of the stagehand; the person behind the scenes making sure everything runs smoothly, taking pleasure not in the limelight, but rather in the fact that the performance is smooth and seamless.

But perspective is prone to shifts, particularly when immersed in an environment that is wholly foreign from what is familiar to you. I found that paradigm shift in Paris. While presenting for SIGCHI 2013, my team and I had taken the opportunity in between sessions to tour the city, and we were on our way to see Notre Dame. On the way, we encountered a magnificent fountain, the Fontaine Saint-Michel, and stopped to take pictures. My eyes were slowly being opened to all that was around me, taking in the centuries of French reconstruction, when I saw him. The Man With the Dog.

Without realizing it, I felt the tactile click of the aperture wheel, the snap of the focus ring as I turned the shot into clear relief by hand. The report of the shutter. Pop, pop, pop. In an instant, the moment was past, and I heard what could have been a swear in French sent in my direction as I crossed the street, absorbed in my own world of exploration in hopes of greater understanding.

I casually glossed over my previous photos after taking a few more at the fountain, and when I scrolled back to the Man With the Dog, I froze. His expression is unfathomable, his eyes piercing and accusatory. "Do you really know me?" He seems to ask. His dress contrasts from what we might assume would be typical from the homeless, jarring perspective and norm. But the care and trust placed in him by his companion underscores what I believe to be the most important tenet of life: we must trust in one another, because when everything else is stripped away, all we have is each other.

This single image woke me on that street corner from the warm, dark desiderata of my sleeping mind. It woke me to the subtle language the

Figure 6.2 "The Man with the Dog" by Jared Forney (2013). Reprinted with permission.

world is always whispering, at first so tenuous and delicate it is too tremulous for talk. A spark so faint that even the most careful breath might snuff it out.

But over time, like timid lovers, we slowly learn the secret meanings of the conversation between ourselves and the world we live in. As designers we learn to communicate with subtle meaning through our designs, creating an unspoken dialogue of mutual understanding for those we serve.

I keep a framed version of this image in my home to remind me that as a designer, it is not about who **I** am, but **who** I am, all of the people whom I represent when I design.

And it is through them that I find strength in myself: sought, wrought and moved to purpose. This I believe.

At the conclusion of each year I vow that this will be the last time I teach this studio class. I have said this each time for the last four years. And I will say it again this year – this will be my last! Yet, I've already lined up my first company for next year. I continue with RDSC because each year I witness the transformation of young designers, from relatively over-confident and somewhat naive individuals to capable, self-assured designers ready to enter the profession – "sought, wrought, and moved to purpose."

References

Scott, S. (2004) *Fierce Conversations: Achieving Success at Work and in Life, One Conversation at a Time*. New York, NY: Berkley Books

Siegel, M. A. and Beck, J. (2014) 'Slow change interaction design'. *Interactions*, 21(1), pp. 28–35

7   How I Learned, Unlearned, and Learned Studio Again

Elizabeth Boling

As a BFA student in printmaking I remember the utter certainty with which my instructors moved through the studio spaces in which we toiled. They set perplexing and seemingly impossible problems for us, expected us to use unfamiliar and dangerous equipment, spoke – when they spoke – a nearly incomprehensible language, and didn't seem to notice or care that the environment, and the activities demanded of us within it, were foreign to most of us.

For our part, we watched them and the advanced students with the peculiar intensity that accompanies a complete shift in culture – a sort of hyper-awareness that fuses observation and imitation into rapid, involuntary changes in one's self. This was a familiar process to me because I had grown up in a military family and experienced such shifts every few years through-out my childhood. Other students may or may not have been able to relate this experience to others in their lives; no one discussed the strangeness of the experience directly with anyone else. You changed or you didn't, and if you stayed then how you managed the transition was your own business. Some didn't manage it and they didn't stay. The ones who stayed probably never noticed the moment at which they assimilated into the studio culture. Most of us only noticed, a little surprised, that next year's new students were not yet "part of the studio," whereas we now were.

When I moved on to take an MFA in printmaking at another institution, there were adjustments – a new town, new mix of people – but the studio spaces, activities and language were all completely familiar. When I taught lithography myself as a graduate student I was so nervous about possibly fumbling the demonstrations that I printed every stone in the print shop the summer before classes began. I was also anxious enough about accidents that I printed up a small booklet of procedures and cautions for my students. But I did not worry over what I was supposed to *do*. I set problems, demon-strated basic technique, led critique and ran the lab. This was studio. That's how it works.

After ten years in the field of instructional design practice (which I slipped into accidentally right out of graduate school by taking a job illustrating computer-based educational software), I was recruited to join the faculty of a venerable and well-respected program in instructional design. One hall-mark of this program is its roots in audio-visual education and its continuing commitment to media design experiences as an integral component of the curriculum. Just prior to my arrival, the media track in the program had been housed in a separate building and the courses comprising it had involved intensive hands-on experiences. There had also been a media production center in which most students worked at one time or another on projects for clients inside and outside the university. That center was closing and, based on input from alumni of the program, among others, the master's curriculum was being completely revised so that students would complete a core set of courses in which instructional design was treated as an integrated experience versus a set of topics treated separately in one course after another. Part of the integration was also to bring the "design track" (largely principles and theory-based) and "media track" (direct practice and craft-based) closer together so that they did not seem to the students to represent two entirely distinct domains of concern.

When I joined the faculty, having brought with me no degree in the field, I sat in as an auditor to the traditional basic courses still being taught. The new curriculum was not yet launched, so these were lecture courses for the most part - at least those in which I participated. Some lectures were more give-and-take than others, but this was a sit-and-absorb situation with propositional knowledge at its heart. Students practiced carrying out analyses and writing design plans, but these were individual tasks and discrete ones - that is, there was no explicit connection between one assignment and the next, let alone between courses. Students did their work outside class, handed it in for some comments and a grade, then moved on to the next assignment. Courses in which they used media were separate electives, not taken by everyone and not integrated with other courses.

I learned, along with the students, that instructional design was a system-atic, scientific endeavor - if you used the right methods problems were fully knowable in advance of making design decisions, and a fully known problem was as good as solved. Once a problem was analyzed, you chose an instruc-tional strategy linked to the appropriate theory or principle, tried to keep the artists and programmers from goofing up your nice design while they did whatever it is they do to make media materials, and *voila!* – an efficient and effective module of instruction would appear, ready for repeatable use with consistent results. It was conceded that there were areas of the field in which the full map of theory and principles was as yet incomplete, but building that map was the proper business of research in the field and a lot of people were busy doing just that. In the meantime, anything an instructional designer did rested on the best base of scientific knowledge obtainable from wherever it could be gotten (psychology, systems, computer science), and when there was no such base – well, those actions and decisions simply did not get a lot of discussion.

While I may sound dismissive of this view, I was not dismissive of it then, and am not wholly dismissive of it now. The underlying aspiration toward rigor in designing – the idea that there should be reasons for design decisions and that those reasons can be articulated – was, and still is, appealing and appropriate. But from where I stand now, I understand the sources of rigor and of design decisions to be more varied, more reliable, and often considerably less scientific, than those implied above. At the time, though, the systematic design process was presented to me confidently and with the support of multiple authorities (colleagues, journals, textbooks, conference presentations) as the unique basis for value in instructional design. Looking back, I realize that, as with my earlier BFA experience, during this period I was watching my colleagues and the students around me with the peculiar intensity that accompanies a complete shift in culture. And shift I did; it was not until later that I realized just how much!

Inching Back Toward Studio – The Course We Started From

In my first year on the faculty the entire group of us worked together on the design of the core courses we would put into place the following year. I was expected, together with Bob Appelman, a colleague, to develop the course that emphasized media design and then to team-teach it, which I did. Bob had a fine arts background in graphic design and had worked professionally in video production; between us we came up with a media production course that, after a few early iterations, settled into place as the follow-on to the basic ID course. Both courses were hands-on, although they were not directly coordinated with each other.

In the basic ID course (which I have also taught many times), students worked in teams of four or five to carry out two instructional design projects, which we termed "realistic." They identified a real context and audience, then carried out their analyses and their formative evaluations in those contexts, although they did not form client relationships or promise outcomes to anyone outside the class. Following this course they came to the production class - and all but a few dreaded it. Those few with a robust background in media development either relished it or were allowed to skip it, but the rest were typical instructional design students of their day. They came to our program from a variety of backgrounds, almost none of them including any form of design, and they expected in the future to design, or specify, instruction - but not to produce it. The prospect of learning end-user development tools like HyperCard™, Authorware™, Photoshop™, or Dreamweaver™, or – in the early days – analog tools for creating instructional posters, was daunting for them. Cramming both technology skills and design principles into the same one-semester course was daunting for us.

Consequently, Bob and I tinkered with the format of this course repeatedly. We spent one semester giving dozens of mini-workshops on tools, using several classrooms and volunteers to run them simultaneously, and giving the students a big menu of options for which ones they would take based on their project needs. In another instance we recruited advanced students with technology skills to work on-demand with students as they encountered technology problems. Students produced such materials as web-based, or paper-based, lessons on tuning a guitar, baking a cake, playing a board game, jumping a car battery, ironing a shirt, playing a Korean drum and so on. For about 15 years there were things we did *not* do – we did not get rid of lectures, of front-loading the course with principles and technical information, or of requiring defined deliverables so that every student proceeded through projects in the same sequence as every other. We did *not* emphasize the students' own experiences as a source of their decision-making in design. By this time it is fair to say that I had thoroughly unlearned studio.

The Studio Class

Over the next decade, however, I took multiple, parallel steps back in the direction of understanding design, not as science and not as art, but as a distinct form of knowing, thinking and acting. These steps included reading and studying design theory and philosophy outside the field together with my doctoral students, carrying out empirical studies on how scholars and designers think and work (also in collaboration with my students), and teaching an elective course in instructional graphics every summer. That course had been moving steadily toward a more and more traditional studio format. I was keeping field notes after every class period and conducting research together with my colleague Kennon Smith on various facets of the class, realizing that the more features of traditional studio we incorporated into the class, the closer we got to student performances we hoped to see.

I had been discussing with my peers in the department - badgering them about it possibly - my evolving viewpoint on design within the field and the summer course, which was my lens for putting that viewpoint into action. We were discussing some revisions to our master's program in that period when one colleague suggested, and the rest agreed, that we should offer a course in design thinking - an integrated approach toward design situations in which a designer determines responsively what to do using multiple modes of thought and action instead of a single, prescribed model of response.

Bob Appelman and I determined to re-envision the production course format so that it required the use of design thinking, rather than to create a new course in which design thinking was addressed "as a topic." This made sense to us because we had always explained the course as being one in which design and design principles were half the content, and mastering basic development technologies was the other half. I had recently been teaching an elective course in full studio format, and had been pondering the main difficulty with it – that my students had no rich mental store of design examples (precedent) to draw upon as they worked. The idea that our students should learn to focus on instructional designs in a detailed way as part of building such a mental store of examples was therefore already in mind. From there it seemed that the idea of asking students to document an instructional design, and to have them practice media and technical skills by producing an actual documentary, popped into my head on an exercise walk.

I outlined the idea of a single-assignment course to Bob, pushing the idea strenuously to tell the truth. Bob was positive about the idea and gracious in agreeing to run with it. We launched the course, him teaching one section and me another. In this new course, the one design brief (or assignment) was presented this way – *find an existing, functioning instructional or performance intervention and create a documentary that describes it as thoroughly as you can*. The documentary can be linear (usually video) or open navigation (usually web-based), must include some time-based media, and the audience experience of the documentary must last approximately 20 minutes or more. The process sequencing is open-ended for the students, as is their choice of the intervention they will document – they have to show progress three times during the semester, but not a specified *form* of progress. While they have to 1) decide on the object of the documentary and sketch a plan for addressing it, 2) show a prototype and 3) show the work at these three progress points respectively, what constitutes a sketch or a prototype can be distinctly different for any two students depending on how they conceive of their individual projects.

Teaching in the Studio

The beginning few weeks of this course are familiar from other non-studio, project-based, courses in which students choose a topic or project to use as the basis for a structured assignment. Here we ask the students to identify an intervention that they will describe, and we spend a good deal of time helping them figure out what that intervention will be. This gives a bit of a quest feeling to the course. We watch the students head out into their respective worlds seeking an object (a single course, a training program, a change intervention, a museum exhibit) to document. Some actively try to apply an ISD model to the object after the fact (perhaps because they have just come from a basic ID course); some try to find the ISD model in how a design got to be the way it is. More than a few want to find the individual designer of the object and they want that person to tell them how they designed it; most cannot and they are anxious when they can't. Some online students really want to document their own projects completed at work, which we don't allow – the kind of critical observation we want is too challenging to achieve for most of our students when describing their own work.

My experience is that I engage with their nascent thoughts, some tentative and some definite, trying not to squish any of them outright while also steering people toward those that would later allow the documentary to have some integrity as a designed communication; the scale of the object should not be too large and their access to it should be possible, even if it is difficult. This takes a good deal of time. In fact, I consider that expenditure of time to be a perennial tension in courses I have designed with this feature; so far this point of failure has not been resolvable for me. I am unwilling to give it up for two reasons. First, their understanding of the project does increase as they struggle with the choice of what to document. In addition, their commitment to the projects is also palpable when they have chosen their own subjects (as compared with courses in which I have supplied subjects). Even so, for some of them the decision process drags on and I know it eats up time they will probably need later.

For my part, I have a strong personal commitment not to push them toward the documentary that *I* would create, or even one that I imagine will work for them (even if they cannot see it). When I have pushed in this way, I see over the course of a semester that their command of what they are

Figure 7.1 Four stills from Nicole Hatch's documentary featuring the Newseum in Washington DC. This choice was challenging because of the scope of the project, the need to get permission for access, and the challenge of collecting photos and video footage within the museum guidelines. After a contact visit to the museum, the project looked more feasible.

doing slips further and further out of their grasp until, finally, I am coaching them one step at a time toward the end product that I have been able to imagine and they have not. *Not* pushing involves drawing out of them what they do imagine their product might be. Often I imagine out loud some tentative directions, looking for the spark of interest that signals to me they have caught hold of an idea they consider to be workable. This is usually not the idea I thought I was describing, but that doesn't matter. It is the excitement, or the motion *toward* something, that signals to me the end of that first groping process.

Once they get going, the course settles into a pattern that I recognize from my own studio experiences. This format feels so comfortable for me – a kind of relaxation into a familiar pattern of interactions. Students follow a pattern that goes, roughly, panic, ruminate, plan, stumble, recover, plan, do, do, revise, do, revise, do. They take action – sometimes tentative and sometimes bold - represent that action in some way, get a response (critique) from me or from someone else, and take additional action that has been reinforced or refocused by the response and by their own response *to* that response. While this feels familiar and comfortable to me, a little reflection will show that it is *not* how many other courses proceed. In other courses I have taught on a lecture-assignment-deliverable-feedback model, student actions are less frequent, less frequently represented (they may write a paper at the end of the term, for example, or participate in online discussions at weekly intervals), more likely to be evaluated than critiqued, and less frequently revised in response to input.

At set points during the course students are expected to show progress toward development of their documentaries, but we do not dictate what that progress should be. This means that the course does not proceed in the kind of orderly progression instructors and students may be used to. Students do not take the same path toward their goals and they do not all make progress at the same rate. So what is a regular class period like? One or two of the students may not be present; they will have let me know this in advance because they are in the field capturing media. The rest are expected to be in the classroom or a nearby digital lab, even if they are also working outside class hours on their projects – and all of them are. For me, class is a matter of circulating around the room making myself available for questions and asking questions myself. To start, this can either seem awkward ("What if no one needs me?") or intrusive ("I know you're busy, but stop and show me what you're doing"). Soon, though, I find that students are anticipating me and asking questions as I walk by – in fact, I need to watch the time so that the first one or two students don't keep my attention in preference to the rest. I find also that seeing their work evolve period by period (instead of seeing it only at designated review points) allows me to approach them in one class period with observations and inquiries that are relevant to what they are doing in this class period. As the term progresses, the sound of this classroom develops as a quiet hum. More and more students consult with each other, trading technical information and looking at each other's work or showing off their own.

While I recognize and generally relax into this format, the students are not generally as comfortable as I am – and they can make me uncomfortable too. They are used to being told exactly which actions they should be taking, and are often unused to producing anything but written representations of their ideas. They expect me to push them in the right direction when, in fact, I make sure they know that I cannot make any move to help them until they have made a move first – and if they do not act, then I do not make such moves. These are graduate students used to being successful in their studies and, for many of them, in professional work. Their reaction is often to question my competence as an instructor and as a designer of the course, and my reaction to that doubt, as often as not, is, I have to confess, to doubt myself. It's perpetually paradoxical. I am quite comfortable with the rhythm of the course and nature of the interactions, but perpetually doubting what I'm doing with each student. I think this is because their questions do not come at me directly; they do not come right out and ask, "Do you really know how to teach? Because you didn't break this task into part-whole segments and sequence them from simple to complex as I would have expected from a competent course designer ...." Instead they come at me sideways as, for example, with efforts to gain my informal approval for detailed, but hypothetical, project steps in advance of their being taken. In the middle of a conversation like that, I do ask myself whether I am being perverse not to give a student concrete direction when it would be so easy to do so - and when the student is clearly uncomfortable, clearly expecting that I do the helpful thing, which is to provide reassurance by approving just one little process step. I do hold off, though, so their decisions will be *their* decisions and most of them adjust rapidly to making such decisions.

Most students come into the course concerned, not with the questions of design and design thinking that we view as central, but with the nuts and bolts of media production. They have to *produce* the documentary, not just plan it and their concerns tend to center on this aspect. This is an aspect of the course that had continually challenged us, as much as the students, in the past - none of the students come in with all the technical skills they will need. Most are insecure regarding some, or all dimensions, of their skills. Also, we do not have the resources, or the time, to teach them directly everything they need to know how to do. In more traditional design programs (and perhaps in some instructional design programs), there may be special labs or courses focused on technical skills, and there may be personnel devoted to technical training; we do not have these and may or may not ever have them. Coincidentally, with this new course launch, the university invested in a license for a well-known and comprehensive system of online technology tutorials. We took advantage of this fortuitous circumstance, requiring the students as part of the course to log a certain amount of time with the tutorials. But we left it to them to decide which ones to complete and to explain their decisions, which actually allowed us to address a key aspect of their future practice – making media decisions that take resources into account along with the instructional or communicative affordances of those media. I have been pleasantly impressed at how easily these tutorials have filled our needs as instructors. On the part of the students I observe that the online tutorials do require more of their time than the short tutorials which were all we could provide in the past; they routinely spend more time with the tutorials than we require. But it is clear that they rely on the tutorials heavily. They describe setting up two computers side by side in order to follow along with the tutorials to learn efficiently from them, and they post reviews of the tutorials on discussion boards along with pointers to the critical parts of them in order to help each other get the most from them. From the standpoint of teaching, I find that fairly often I need to turn the students back online when they encounter technical problems, sometimes to blogs or public discussions – sometimes to each other. They have followed a tutorial beyond the point of my own knowledge, so my contribution is to encourage problem-solving rather than to contribute full solutions to specific problems. Once again, this form of teaching requires me to be comfortable with not knowing - and with suspecting that my students think less of me for not knowing.

I have to admit that teaching the previous media design course in our program used to offer me enjoyable opportunities to develop materials and conduct class sessions. It was fun to plan, and satisfying to deliver, visually-based lectures on design principles and engaging demonstrations of using technology. I felt confident when I recited a principle from one of my lectures during the evaluation of a tidy, but flawed, deliverable from a student. I struggled with helping students master technology skills in order to complete their projects, but managed the scope of those projects so that I did know how to solve most of their problems. Sure, I worried that perhaps the better projects in class were due to prior design experience on the part of the students more than to newly acquired design sensibilities. But I applauded the gains routinely achieved by our students: appreciation of how difficult media development can be, awareness that developing instruction requires multiple decisions that affect each other and the original strategies for a project, new technical skills. At the same time, I despaired of moving many students past a rudimentary stage in any of this learning. Bob and I saw that material from lectures and demonstrations did not "stick;" students who needed that information didn't remember it, couldn't apply it, or didn't believe it was relevant. Many came into the course dreading it and left vowing never to have anything more to do with media design. Some who left the course vowing to work in media design after graduation took an inflated impression of their prowess with them.

Teaching the course as it is designed now, I have already mentioned the persistent self-doubt characterizing the experience for me. It is difficult not to know what is going to happen with each student and each project, or what is going to be required of me on a given day. It can take weeks sometimes to see whether or not I have assessed the right move on my part correctly, and the period in between is stressful. I find myself wondering whether those studio instructors I had years ago, the ones who appeared so confident, were actually wondering whether they were going to be able to help enough – but not too much – each time they interacted with me. It's been a revelation to realize that what I saw as them not noticing or caring about my struggles was very likely to have been a form of self-discipline, much like the one that studio teaching demands from me now. I understand that the experience of having learned in a mode much like this one does allow me to trust in it and, in spite of my misgivings, in myself as an instructor. That baseline trust also allows me to enjoy the problem-solving aspect of the course. It is never routine and it foregrounds *my* design thinking as a model for my students. And all that material I used to pack into my lectures? It comes up in the context of the students' projects every time.

So what actually does happen during class? Without the ritual of setting up for lecture, walking into the classroom can be awkward at first for me and for the students. They soon learn to begin working on their projects, and I wait until they do before I come in so that I can circulate around to speak with most of them instead of being cornered by an early bird before the others arrive. As the term progresses, I am called on steadily to answer questions, comment on a judgment the student is weighing, or simply to admire work in progress. Early on, I look for openings to start discussions with each student myself, and during the term I remain on the lookout for anyone who is not asking questions or volunteering to show me what they have done. I stop at the desks of these students and ask what they are working on, what's new since last class period and – as I become familiar with their projects – specific questions regarding their work. This is hard for me; I do not like to impose and these are often the students who are reticent, insecure about their work, or covering for a lack of progress – in other words, not making it easy for me. Still, eager or reluctant, the student talks to me or shows me some work and we speak about it. They practice describing design thoughts and moves. I practice responding to what I am asked and leading to the conceptual or experiential knowledge that is relevant to their situation so they can see how it connects to their work. When a student has a problem, we combine our efforts to solve it. Also, when their work suggests to me that they need a revised production path, a new tool, a refined conceptual approach or simply more challenge, I start by describing to them exactly what I am seeing or what I am hearing them say.

They are usually quick to follow some aspect of this description and we engage in speculation, critique, expansion of their ideas, and problem solving from there. In the classroom space it is easy to eavesdrop, and the students do.

Figure 7.2 Documenting a weekend English language club, one student included text describing the informative bus driver who drove the members to meetings. Reviewing the documentary very close to the due date, she decided a photo was important to the story; she reworked a section of her documentary and returned to the field to collect the photo.

Sometimes they listen passively as they work. Other times they raise related questions, and this can lead to an impromptu "verbal essay" on my part covering a topic that I know is relevant to several of them. I find that I am conscious of the whole room, and that the details of the students' projects are present to me in a way they are not in other classes, even when those classes involve project work. Instead of seeing their work primarily at milestones (design plan, prototype), I have been part of their evolution continuously.

Studio Re-Learned

Lecture-based teaching can definitely be tiring, but studio teaching can be exhausting. When I am not responding to one student, I am working to draw out another one, maintaining sustained attention on all parts of the classroom as I do so. There is little distance between me and my students, so their actions and reactions to what happens in class affect me, in my perception, more than they would in my non-studio classes. In the studio, I inhabit a position of co-responsibility for problem solving together with my students, but I have to assess their progress and their products separately from my

Figure 7.3 The classroom available for studio is unprepossessing, but allows for tables to be placed so that students can talk while they work and listen in on consultations I am having with others nearby.

own input. This requires me to monitor myself all the time I am teaching, as well as when I am assessing my students' performance. Have I modeled and demonstrated design thinking to scaffold their development, or have I usurped their position in our partnership? The right balance is different for every student at every stage, so this equation has to be re-figured continuously. The students surprise me constantly. When I do not structure their actions in advance, they go further and faster than I was used to in pre-studio versions of this course. Unlike a course in which my interactions with students are tied to defined milestones achieved through prescribed actions, the in-class interactions previously described are never routine. I find studio teaching to be exhilarating as well, however. With practice, I have built confidence in my ability to respond to whatever comes up without having to respond with a solution. In fact, while it requires great effort, I do relax into the reactive nature of this form of teaching and experience the effort as a positive flow of action. In addition, I find myself unable to contemplate returning to a form of teaching in which I would not know as much about the development of my students' modes of thought, about their design actions, and about their actual abilities as I am able to do in the studio.

Efforts to establish a studio experience across more than one semester, providing more practice to instructors and to students with non-prescriptive design and with problems significant enough to provide the opportunity for real design thinking, have not progressed as far as I would like at this time of writing. My current colleagues in the program are on board with the view of instructional design that requires us to shift the culture of our teaching. Even so, the path to a pervasive change has not been smooth. Physical and organizational barriers challenge the most willing participants. Several members of faculty, none with experience in the studio, have taken a run at studio teaching with varying degrees of comfort, mostly not high. Team teaching is not possible for the moment owing to budget constraints, ruling out peer mentoring to build studio teaching skills. We have had to find and, while not *hide* exactly, at least remain quiet about a small space that we are using for our studio students. Our students expect that courses in a program like ours will be confined to one semester in terms of assignments, be structured around milestone deliverables and offer declarative knowledge to support and assess all their actions. These expectations may be revised over time, as those of the administrators who approve space and course structures may be. Right now we are examining adaptations we can make to our curriculum and to studio teaching in order to support the shift we are making to teach design consistently with our theoretical and philosophical views.

8 Constructing | Connecting | Conveying

A Beginning Studio Student and Instructor Journey of Meaning and Experience

Jill B. Pable

This design case describes IND3217 Studio I, the first fully "interior design"-oriented studio that undergraduate students in the interior design program take. As the instructor of this course, I have come to see it not only as a foundation skill-building course, but also an introduction to the idea of experience. With a design of any kind, including interior design, *human experience* is an unavoidable factor that pervades both the process and final outcome of a project. By this I mean several things: first, a designer cannot help but have a personal experience with a project as they gather its facts, wrestle with competing influences, and ultimately reach a solution for its intended users. Secondly, and perhaps as importantly, a designer must also be sensitive to the fact that the solution's intended users will *also* have an experience with the project's constructed outcome. Ideally, this client experience is one that is anticipated and accommodated by the designer.

These embedded issues of experience seem similar to the notion of constructivist learning, a long-known and widely (but not universally) accepted idea of how we consider and embrace ideas as we learn and think. Specifically, constructivist proponents suggest that we really can't separate our learning from our life experiences, and that it is these life experiences that in fact shape what we think and believe, and vice-versa. This consideration pervades the Studio 1 class in various ways, not only for the students but also for me as the instructor. I'm fascinated by how experience seems to have a hand in everything in this instance – how we learn, what we choose for design solutions, what others think of our design solutions, and even how I teach.

As straightforward as learning from, working with and designing for experiences may sound, it is the experiential outcomes of a design project that can be the trickiest to navigate successfully, especially for new designers taking the Studio 1 class. A designer's intentions are one thing, it seems, and the translation of an idea can sometimes come out in the end in a different, unintended way. For example, things like project concept development can either be a project's strength or its liability. This design case will reflect on the various ways that experience flavors the Studio 1 class, and conclude with concept development as perhaps the most confounding of these experiences to contend with.

Course Context and the Student's Prior Experiences

The Studio I course is required as part of the Florida State University (FSU) Bachelor of Science degree in Interior Design. This course is a part of the Program of Interior Design housed in the College of Fine Arts. The Studio I course has been in the curriculum for decades and is the beginning of a Studio I-Studio VI sequence that forms the heart of the program for undergraduates. Constructivist thinking underscores the course as a whole in that students are presented with design challenges in these studios, and apply knowledge in space planning, materials, lighting, building codes and similar content to these challenges. Students learn by doing and generate highly individual and diverse solutions to these projects, influenced more often than not by their own experiences.

Students are sometimes attracted to this major because they enjoy portrayals of interior designers as presented in the media. These depictions tend to over-emphasize the "fun" in the profession and the effects of surface finishes. By the time they get to Studio I much of the "HGTV" mindset of shallow decorative-only philosophies have been discarded.

The Student's Experience Prior to Studio 1

A student that is accepted to the undergraduate program takes three courses in the first semester: first, a required Design Foundations course that introduces her to the nature of a problem-oriented studio class (see Table 8.1). This class examines fundamental art and design content, such as the elements and principles of design, color manipulation, positive/negative space and similar information, in an intensive applied project format. She also takes Technical Design that introduces precision drawing (as found in construction document sets) and, lastly, a survey-style lecture course that introduces the fundamentals of interior design. It is in this last course that HGTV pre-assumptions are addressed, injecting a more realistic understanding of the profession.

Table 8.1 First summer and fall semesters of the four-year Interior Design undergraduate program of studies.

INTERIOR DESIGN Four-Year Curriculum	
Summer (Freshman year)	*Fall (Sophomore year)*
IND 2002 Survey of Interior Design	IND 2300 Graphic Techniques I
IND 1406 Technical Drawing	IND 4601 Social/Psychological Aspects of Design
IND 1203 Design Fundamentals I	IND 3217 Interior Design Studio I
IND 1204 Design Fundamentals II	Liberal studies class
Liberal studies class	Liberal studies class
Liberal studies class	
FIRST YEAR REVIEW	

It's interesting to note that some students opt to change majors at this point when the rigors and not-so-fun parts of the profession, such as building codes, life cycle cost estimates, and criteria matrices become evident.

The preliminary courses that precede Studio 1 are a collective high-stress event for a student because her performance in this course series determines her admittance or rejection from the program. In the past as many as 120 students have applied and only 40 are admitted per year due to space and staff restrictions. At the end of this first semester the student submits her work to a First Semester Review procedure, and faculty as a group assesses her likelihood of success. The parameters include course grades, creativity, evidence of high quality craft/construction and ability to grow from constructive criticism. The Design Foundations and Technical Design courses typically have a project due every week, keeping the pace of the content and endeavor very brisk. Thus, when the student gets to Studio I it is with a sense of relief that can be accompanied by relaxation (of either an appropriate or an excessive degree), as she knows she has made "the cut" and has officially entered the interior design program.

A Student's Experiences and Understanding That She Brings into Studio 1

The student enters Studio 1 with a beginning understanding of interior space. It is my observation that her application skills can fall along two basic lines that contrast significantly:

1. The previous design foundations classes have introduced her to artistic skills and information that require her to stay loose with her thinking, such as sketching, assessing greyscale values, and assembling quick projects in 2D and 3D forms.
2. Her technical design class primarily addresses design documentation, and she has created a beginning set of construction documents by hand. This exercise is a necessary one in helping her understand that what she designs must be communicated and feasibly built, and that precision is a necessary aspect of design follow-through. It prompts the student to communicate ideas in tight, precise ways.

Studio I content similarly challenges the student to continue this left-brain/ right brain juggling act. It is common to see her clinging more than she should to one side or the other during this stage of her development. For example, she might create unnecessarily perfect preliminary sketches with straight-edges. Or she might find comfort in creating fantasy-style design solutions that would be impossible to build.

Not surprisingly, she is exhausted by the end of the Studio 1 course, and it is probably her central focus of the semester. As her instructor I'm fine with this as I feel the studio experience should probably be the lynchpin course around which other courses revolve (but I don't come out and say this to other instructors). This is because Studio 1 is the playground (or at least I think so) where other simultaneous class content is applied, such as social/psychological information, graphics and also previously learned skills. The student in Studio I is sophomore level, though on paper she may be junior if she has already completed sufficient liberal arts credits. The students as a group are usually 80 percent or more female, which reflects an ongoing problem for interior design programs in general.

Evolution of the Course

I have been teaching this course for seven years - the majority of my ten years of employment at FSU. As there are usually two sections of Studio 1 consisting of 20 students each, I have taught one section of this course and a faculty colleague, an adjunct faculty member or a teaching assistant has taught the other one. After I had taught this course for the first year in its original form provided to me by previous faculty, I started to feel that the students weren't being pushed enough to inject their own ideas into the outcomes. It seemed to me that Studio I was the place to lay a firm foundation of critical skills, such as the pre-thinking "programming". This activity lets a student really understand a challenge, then translate what is necessary for a client's solution from text, abstract idea and concept, coupled with functional requirements, into a dynamic and self-made creation. I didn't sense a great deal of excitement from the students all the time, and I suspected it was because the projects were too rigid and pre-manufactured, with little room for driving a solution in a direction a student would feel was their own. In a way, it is understandable that previous instructors took this tack. In my experience, this level of student is excited and eager to get their interior design-specific learning underway. They sometimes feel they know more than they do and, if given a good deal of freedom to craft the boundaries or parameters of a project, they can go too far. This problem might be manifested by a solution that relies too heavily on artistry at the expense of function, does not understand or empathize well with the client's point of view, or tries to express a concept that is too obscure. (More on the intricacies and challenges of concept later in this chapter.)

After I had taught the course with others for two years, the senior adjunct faculty member left the program for another opportunity, which now meant that I was the longest-serving person interacting with this course. I felt more freedom at that point to evolve it into a stronger experience. Since that time, this course has been considered my playground to create, evolve and facilitate for both sections. That being said, there are significant amounts of content that must be present in this course in order for accreditation to be maintained.

Sensing it was time for a refresh and update, I began a fundamental series of changes to Studio I about five years ago. The heart of this course is the five projects that introduce students to a set of skills, including pre-design discovery, information analysis, space planning, and concept development. A driving factor for the five-project approach to this class was built around the attendant length of time available for each project. As the Design Foundations (DF) classes were quick-paced one-week exercises, and Studio II (which comes after Studio 1) favors two to three projects of 5–7 weeks in duration each, I opted to split the difference and involve the students in projects that were 3–5 weeks in length. This way they would be engaged, applying new information to a variety of environment types (residential, institutional, ecclesiastical), yet would not feel intimidated because the projects were not that long compared with their DF experience. I would have to admit that these conclusions about the courses were more normative than anything, resulting from what's worked well in the past and avoiding choices that led to past student struggles. See Table 8.2 for the Studio 1 courses and their sequence.

Accreditation Standards Played a Part in Course Evolution

Another primary driver of the course's content is the impact of accreditation standards from the Council for Interior Design Accreditation. This is the primary college accreditation body in this field, and FSU has been accredited by CIDA (then FIDER) since 1979. Accreditation is important as CIDA carefully crafts these standards to reflect the evolving applied practice of interior design in the field. Also, accreditation indicates that FSU adheres to a widely recognized quality standard, which is important as students are increasingly choosing their colleges on the basis of such seals of approval. Lastly, the state of Florida predicates its requirement for practitioners' interior design licensure on achievement of CIDA or CIDA-equivalent course content. Therefore, CIDA criteria dictate such details as discussion of anthropometrics and proxemics, introduction of universal design principles, and even the scope and scale of the projects' square footages (as overall the curriculum must show an ascending level of difficulty in the projects' cognitive requirements). CIDA also looks favorably on collaboration of students with others such as outside professionals that can assist them in generating original programming information for project solutions.

The course's existing projects were the primary place to enact change. Because accreditation-required content forms a significant portion of what must occur in this course, I opted to make a laundry list of necessary skills and knowledge that a student must know, then to organize these skills into a logical order of when they need to be learned to make sense (as some build in a linear fashion on others). I then crafted the projects around these skills so that they were clear and had a compelling end result to maintain student interest. This last point was important because this course introduces many

Table 8.2 Studio 1 course project names, order, length and brief description.

	Project 1	Project 2	Project 3	Project 4	Project 5
Name	Student Dormitory Project	Poetry Project: Programming	Design Charrette	Poetry Project: Design	Shrine Project
Length	2½ weeks	4 weeks	3 days	3 weeks	4½ weeks
Overview	Students design a dormitory room for an art student at a career camp. An art movement is used as a concept that guides the solution. The 15' square space challenges the student to design efficiently and in the third dimension.	Students conduct fact-finding to design a corridor within the Chicago O'Hare Airport that captures the essence of a poem using space, light and principles of environmental psychology.	Working in teams of 5 composed of sophomores, juniors and seniors, students generate and communicate a design solution to a given complex problem in 72 hours. An example is to design a zombie safe house that provides 40 occupants and 3 dogs safe entry, food, water, and ventilation for 30 days.	Following up on Project 2, students develop an interior design solution for the Chicago O'Hare airport corridor that captures the emotional essence of a chosen poem. Students must create a universal design solution that accommodates all persons, including those with strollers, in wheelchairs and other disabilities.	Responding to a religion drawn out of a hat, students generate a solution for believers of that faith. The religion cannot be the one the student herself adheres to. Examples include Zoroastrianism, Druidism, Wicca, Cao Dai, Zen Buddhism and others. Pre-design research challenges the student to empathize and design for ritual, plus express a spiritual journey through interior architecture.
Major deliverables	Sketches, floor plans, concept statements, 3D foamcore white model.	Text that deconstructs a chosen poem, 'dump sheets' that show visual brainstorming describing possible solutions, idea generator drawings that demonstrate moving abstract ideas to constructed expressions.	Sketches, floor plans, annotated diagrams, finish specifications, perspective renderings, concept statements.	Universally designed signage, accessible floor plans, concept statement, perspective renderings, furniture specifications.	Floor plans, perspective renderings, materials specifications, concept, problem and design statements.

All projects must be verbally and visually presented at their conclusion to the instructor, student peers and others.

new ideas, which can get overwhelming. As such, the potential for students to get discouraged is very real. I have found it is better to have highly interesting projects that keep students motivated and feeling they have a sense of engagement and commitment to the outcomes. The Poetry Project is the most recent addition to the course, and students seem to especially enjoy the safety of referencing a chosen poem coupled with the freedom to interpret and express it in built form convincingly (see Figure 8.1).

Improvements through Extended Collaboration

Another change in this course occurred about three years ago, which eased the burden of topics to cover and probably simplified the student's semester experience simultaneously. Our faculty member that teaches graphics is very easy to work with, and we managed to schedule the graphics class so that it occurs right after the studio class. What's more, many of the graphics class requirements (like perspective drawings and sketch diagrams) were modified in the graphics class so that they now directly support many of the Studio I objectives.

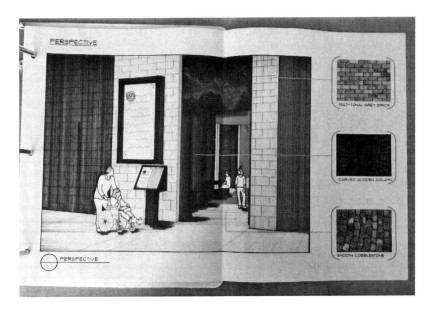

Figure 8.1 This Poetry Project solution by Katharine Galvin shows a perspective rendering of the airport corridor. The poem *Who Said that Love was Fire?* by Patience Worth is interpreted here as a human relationship that begins as a brightly burning soul-engulfing experience and that later settles first into long-enduring embers and then, ultimately, into ash – the thing that remains when love is spent. The floor plan's series of rooms carry visitors through a corresponding series of visual experiences.

This helps the students keep a singular focus while they burnish skills of various kinds in service to their work.

Also, physical classroom facilities in recent years have worked out so that the 20-seat studio classroom where the Studio/Graphics course sequence occurs are the only courses in that space - meaning that we can 'coopt' the room and use its display and desk spaces in a 'cold desk' fashion for only these two class sections. This permits the students to more truly move in, get comfortable, and leave their many drawing materials in the room for the entire semester. Most recently, the class activities have expanded to include the use of standard 'pin up' spaces for each student in both sections of the class. These in-class wall areas, about 3 feet wide and 8 feet tall, give students room to post their current development of a project for all to see. It also has the side benefit of making the classroom look very lively and colorful for visiting prospective students and also administrators.

The room for the class nicely accommodates breaking the students up into groups of three or four at clustered drafting tables. This tends to get students to work in cohort teams and share their designs with each other in a more 'safe' way (see Figure 8.2). It also tends to let students hear others' desk critiques better in a noisy classroom environment. This can be good from the instructor's point of view, as a student that is not prepared will know that their stammering and excuses will be heard by their peers. Guilt and unspoken peer pressure can be a terrific motivator. At the sophomore level I find that students are often at very different places with regard to self-organization and

Figure 8.2 The classroom layout of clustered individual drafting tables forms pods for a sense of community.

time management. These are the important, but largely unspoken, aspects of course success. Sharing techniques along these lines is helpful, and eavesdropping is the rule rather than the exception in student-instructor conversations.

Generally, the Studio I course has been under nearly continual evolution. Students are generally pleased with the results, and I have been quite happy that my student evaluations have been positive. I was really thrilled to have been awarded an FSU teaching award in 2010 largely as a result of this course. It was also gratifying to see Studio I cited for its quality and supportive content in the Department's 2009 and 2015 CIDA accreditation review reports written by the visiting teams.

In fall of 2013 my graphics colleague and I established a closer link with other faculty as well such as, for example, the instructor of Social/Psychological Issues which is the third required course students take during that semester. This new relationship enhanced the religious shrine project with its extended discussion of environmental psychological information within the "Soc/Psych" class (such as the implications of tall versus short ceilings, ascending versus descending hallways, and similar ideas). This helped free up more studio time for critiques than was previously possible. For example, this class had students visit, observe and document the needs of travelers at the local airport. This helped students plan for extended space in a floor plan that wheeling luggage makes necessary in the Studio 1 Poetry Project. These links with other classes the students are taking are somewhat time-consuming to develop and coordinate across multiple faculty, but they seem worth doing for the reinforcement and focus they bring to students' understanding.

Class Procedures and How We Interact

This course meets twice a week for 2.5 hours at a time, and the content of the course is entirely problem-solving in its orientation. Class activities are usually short 15-minute lecture-discussions that allow me to introduce complex ideas as necessary, then the teaching assistant and I conduct desk critiques for the balance of the time to provide students formative feedback on their solutions. Nearly every class period has something due for review or for final presentation. I feel the best class periods are ones where everyone can't imagine where the time went. This was not always the case with this class; I've learned that students are anxious to have project production time during the period and for me to offer them feedback early and often. This has led to the mini-lecture approach, which works well especially after students have read about these ideas beforehand. In this way, it's a quasi-flipped class that lets us devote more class time to process and outcomes, and less to new knowledge on how to conduct that process. There is still significant work time required for students outside of class, and I warn them that 10 hours or more a week for homework is the rule rather than the exception.

Materials are mostly from a new course text, which I've been delighted to find because it not only shows needed skills but does so in a loose sketch fashion - necessary for students to see as they often enter the course with 'tight' time-intensive drawing styles that slow them down and make them believe every line must be perfect. This course, instead, promotes "process process process" – it's not all about where you got to, but how and how well you got there. Therefore, final project drawings can be on tissue-like trash paper as long as they are rich in ideas and visually organized well to tell the tale of the design's details. This emphasis on process also has the added benefit of giving students time to reflect on their own experiences, injecting them into the project solutions, and also on the most successful graphic methods to use to convey the target experiences to others. For example, the Poetry Project rendering shown in Figure 8.1 is somewhat 'loose' in style, which freed up more time for this student to develop the telling of the poem's tale in the space.

This is primarily an analog class, meaning that computer-aided design is not yet in the picture. This was the consensus choice of our faculty so that students first gain hand skills like drawing and doodle sketch diagramming. This is because in practice they will need to sketch solutions on the job site. Also the CIDQ (Council for Interior Design Qualification) licensing exam that students take after graduation is essentially a hand drawing exercise. We also find that students that can sketch get quicker and better job offers. However, I'm starting to see the virtues of earlier introduction of computer elements such as word-processed text for concept statements and the like, and also of using SketchUp, a free easy-to-use 3D design tool. The graphics instructor and I agree that as long as these digital tools are a supplement to hand skills, that's fine. However, I'm pretty sure the question of timing for the introduction of digital graphics will continue to be a dialogue. Students oftentimes default to digital ideas in software products that produce beautiful, precise imagery, and thus miss out on the extended development of multiple early ideas that a pen or stylus make possible. It's easy for students to get caught up in the romance of a dramatic image and be less successful in the quality of the idea and targeted experience that this image portrays.

The student's primary interaction with me is by desk critique. These one-on-one sessions both build rapport and help a student have another pair of eyes on their work so that they can make course corrections as the project progresses. Some of these are informal and others are tied to announced 'milestones' in the project, which permit a measure of documented, formative assessment to occur. In these cases, a written account of the grade for the encounter is given to the student so they know where they stand. I didn't always structure grading this way, and early on learned that delaying assessment until a project's end created problems – one, it gives students little or no chance to improve their work; and two, it could present unpleasant surprises to students that, despite honest desk critiques, thought they were doing quite well. I have found the new scheme of lots of formative grading is especially necessary for this level of student, who is usually quite eager to be validated and incorporate feedback into her project decisions.

On occasion I will also use quick group exercises, pair-and-share exercises and similar activities to get the students to interact with each other. I also regularly require students to explain and justify their emerging solutions to each other, and encourage students to offer unbiased, low-stakes critiques so they can make adjustments. I'm learning the power of these peer encounters to improve a design that can leverage shared student experiences in an exponentially positive way. In my view, taking the time to have students interact with each other is time well spent – given that the class cohort will be sharing four more studios together after this one, their positive engagement with each other ideally leads to mutual support, which in turn can 'lift all boats' in terms of their collective learning. Sadly, I've occasionally seen the effects of a class group that rejects this collegiality and is protective of their work, suspicious of others, and offer cutting or unnecessarily harsh critique of each others' projects. In such cases, the group can divert so much of its mental energy to protecting individual boundaries and fending off intrusions that there is less chance for collective growth to occur.

Studio 1 Presentations and Grading: a Work-in-Progress for All

Each project culminates in a student project presentation that is text and visual elements coupled with a credible verbal presentation. At first, these verbal descriptions are not graded, but the students' early attempts give me the platform to critique this important presentation component. By the end, the verbal presentations are included in the final grade. Distractions such as swaying, twirling hair, saying 'like' too many times (this one's a problem for almost all), are pointed out to the students so they can work on these issues. Prior rehearsal of verbal presentations is a must. Other faculty are often invited to serve as external critics.

Grading is primarily based on performance on the course's five projects in terms of creativity, quality and depth of process, and graphic clarity. Lesser amounts of the final grade are determined by my perception of the student's attitude, attendance and support of their peers. I have come to see the value of grading a student's affective attributes like these, as an optimistic outlook and engaging positively with others are the invisible but critical parts of working with success in a design office. A great deal of production and decision-making in interior design is accomplished in teams - so much so that to ignore a student's attendance to the courtesy in professional relationships is to miss a necessary part of their growth. The grading of projects is achieved by the use of an assessment template that is essentially a list of required skills in any given project. I evaluate each of these line items for performance from excellent, good, fair, to needs improvement, then also write a comment if necessary. In recent years, I have shortened the space on the sheet for writing comments and rely more on formative, informal assessment with the student at their desks - frankly, grading was taking an incredibly long time in the former method, and giving feedback earlier provides the students more of a chance to make adjustments before the final summative review.

Studio 1 is a very formative class, with emphasis on the journey and less so on the outcome. It requires students to address and apply time management, creativity, listening and visual communication. It is not always an easy class at this point for students who are coming up to speed with design thinking and problem-solving, in part because it requires juggling many developing abilities simultaneously. However, that is the nature of design, and I have not found a better way to emulate the thinking of designers other than plowing forward in this multifaceted way. I have found it's best to be patient, probing, prodding, and be a good cheerleader. Students must feel that you are on their side, and that you want them to perform at their best. Most of the time, students react positively to this coaching.

I have also found it helpful to decide that *everyone* on the course comes to class with certain vulnerabilities and that, by its very nature, design is to lay yourself out there for others to critique and to accept the constructive pain this might imply. Students seem particularly receptive to the idea (and somewhat surprised) that teachers, too, are vulnerable – and that to teach is to continually try to understand students' current understanding, which means that not every risky teaching idea will be successful. In this way, teachers too are wrestling with constructing and re-constructing inner and outer experiences, just as students are. This 'we're all in the same vulnerable boat' approach tends to promote a positive outward-looking atmosphere in the class.

Time Management and Other Student Challenges

There are many unstated goals and issues in this class that are part of successful design practice, and a significant one is student time management. Handled poorly, this is where exhaustion, crabbiness and poor presentations come from. Most students tend to sleep for an unusual amount of time after presentations due to the all-nighter they just pulled (from what I hear from other instructors and the students themselves). As a result, we spend time in class discussing a healthy sense of perspective. Some students get so worked up about this course that they lose all sense of balance. A few obsess about perfection and some of them can literally make themselves ill by working excessively on projects. One student several years ago was found in her car not knowing where she was because she had become so dehydrated. I've had more than one counseling session that resembles a checklist Maslow's Hierarchy of Needs, asking them "Are you drinking? Eating?" I see a little bit of my own educational experience in these obsessed students, and know personally the journey one has to take to reconcile with the realistic notion that "this project will never be perfect and it is *good enough*." The quest for perfection does not go quietly into the night, it seems.

At times, students' outside life events can interfere, causing problems of attendance, time management and successfully meeting deadlines. When encountered, some students rise to the challenge and overcome these problems. Most students handle this stressful state of affairs well. A few students react by erecting barriers that manifest as defensiveness or simply checking out. These problems vary from sorority and fraternity responsibilities (for which I have little sympathy) to significant life hurdles such as cancer and car accidents. In a tragic incident several years ago, one of the Studio I students was accidentally and fatally shot by her sister's boyfriend who was showing off a new gun. This student's memorial service was one of the saddest days of my teaching career, especially when the class had an entirely unplanned and tearful group hug at the event's conclusion.

Over the years I have seen better outcomes by applying firm but achievable standards for all, but also by being a mentor-like shoulder to cry on when students hit walls in their performance or behavior. They seem so young to me at this stage in their college careers (perhaps heightened by the sense that I seem to keep getting older and they stay the same age!). The Kleenex box in my office is regularly and thoroughly used.

This course is stressful for most students as they must pass it with a grade of C- or better to continue in the curriculum on schedule. To stray from this schedule adds a year to their college degree, which implies a great deal of money. It likely requires the most time of any course they take that semester, and the multitasking element of the later projects (working from small details to large and simultaneously working big picture to small) can be daunting, but I cannot think of any other way to address the totality of a project than to do both simultaneously. Early in a project students are urged to identify a single concept for the project's solution. A solid concept, arrived at early, is the best way to manage the stress – it's like the recipe from which so many other decisions about the project flow. Concept is discussed further below because, in my view, it is tricky to bring students to a point of successful selection and application. Concept selection is also a direct expression of the project's desired experience for the client, and is therefore central to a solution's success.

The Challenges of Teaching and Learning Concept Development and Application

The choice and application of a cohesion-lending concept is an important and nearly universal requirement in student studio project deliverables. When well-selected, a concept guides the overall direction of an interior solution while lending meaning and/or function. The Studio I class requires students to generate a concept that enhances and guides their choices in a project, including color palette, materials, and it can even extend to space planning. The best concepts do two things – they relate well to the client, and they support the space's intended function or use. That is, the best concepts offer the designer guidance on how to apply the elements and principles of design (such as line, form, scale, and emphasis), while also having a meaning to the space's users and a logical connection to the type of project. What's also interesting about concept generation is its relationship, once again, to constructivist thinking, and its notion that learners construct knowledge out of their experiences. In the case of concept for interiors, designers are constructing an idea that will be made manifest in a physical environment, which is a way of seeing the world out of the designer's own experiences. That is to say, a concept arises out of connections that a designer sees in the world, and that designer is betting on the fact that a client and their spaces' users will perceive these connections as well. In fact, this "I get it" factor that is so important in a winning concept relies on the idea that everyone sees these connections, and has a pleasant moment of appreciating the creativity of them, and/or the architecturally tangible ways they are expressed. Therefore, the trick with a concept is to choose an idea that is understand-able, relevant to the mission of the project, and is creative. In terms of constructivist thinking, this challenges the student to not only derive an idea from their *own* experience, but empathetically put the idea through the filter of its likely resonance with others. This seems to me to be among the most complex thinking tasks - that of synthesizing ideas for group consumption.

A good example can illustrate how concept relies on connections perceived by both designers and their clients. A hospital's design might reference a sailboat as a concept – because the hospital is near the New England coastal waterway and sailboats are an icon of the area – and because hospital patients could benefit from a referential idea that puts their minds at ease in the face of illness. It could be expressed subtly through boardwalk-like corridors dotted with windows, plank flooring that evokes a dock, and a vertical vaguely sail-like feature on the building's exterior. The effect is sufficiently evocative of mood, but not heavy, overly obvious or cumbersome.

The best concepts result in a flexible, subtle, suitable, and delightful space that early grounding in this idea makes possible. To express a concept well is to acknowledge that human beings have an innate preference for meaning-making and, by extension, are shaped by previous experiential memories. The concept can not only address the users' state of mind, but also can be a work-able visual organizer for the space and offer guidance on materials palettes.

In particular, students struggle with identifying a relevant concept, then applying it in appropriate ways to a project. There are benefits to doing so, however – concepts lend unity to projects, make them memorable and make a connection to clients that honors their life experience and values. In my opinion, all interior environments have a concept - it's just that many of them are not intentional, appropriate or as meaningful as they could be. My experience has been that concept seems one of the most difficult ideas to get students to understand and then to apply in a capable way. The problem seems to lie in that a concept may be ill-suited to its use, ignore its client, or will be inappropriately expressed in the solution (usually the culprit in this latter issue is the concept that is too blatant or overwhelms the space). The problem is that the best concepts are applied lightly, but subtlety is not something easily learned, I believe. Therefore, I find it's important to provide students with many positive precedents of applied concept, offer a clear definition of what is concept and what is not, and then offer them an incremental way to derive concept. I have also found that it is imperative that students wrestle with content not just by listening to lectures or reading readings, but must themselves select, justify and apply concept in order to learn how to do this well.

A Current Approach to Teaching Concept

Through much trial and error, and not a little bit of failure in the past on my part, I have landed on the approach that Studio I students first learn about concept through a series of mini-lectures peppered with many examples from practice. Their first original response to this information is a concept board that includes photos, sketches, text and other elements arranged on a card-board backing for in-class presentation. I have seen that students learn most efficiently when they are asked in these concept boards to think about concept analytically by responding to four requirements, explained here with an accompanying example:

1. **Identify**: describe the concept idea or image with text or visual elements. The concept is a teapot – okay, but is it a Michael Graves post-modern teapot or an old English tea service porcelain style?
2. **Interpret and justify**: *how* does the teapot relate to the student users of this space? Does it subtly represent home and hearth in a residential project, for example?
3. **Deconstruct**: what qualities or elements of the teapot are extracted for use (spout, convex curve of the bowl, the liquid coming forth?)
4. **Reinterpret**: how would the deconstructed ideas be used in a new architectural way in the space? (perhaps the liquid is interpreted in a fountain, the curve of a wall shape, or perhaps simply a high-gloss surface finish?).

The concept board is also useful as a way to compel students to make explicit these often unspoken choices. Breaking down this elusive process into a series of steps (identify-justify-deconstruct-reconstruct) seems to help students see if the process is succeeding or not, both within themselves and also when they share it with their peers. Figure 8.3 depicts a student concept

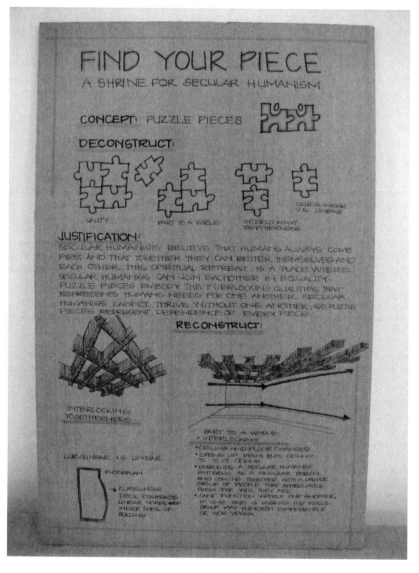

Figure 8.3 Example of a concept board for a shrine for secular humanism by Katie
Timmerman. Steps include deconstructing the concept idea of a puzzle
piece, then reconstructing it using architectural expressions.

board for the final Studio 1 project, a religious shrine devoted to secular
humanism. Figure 8.4 shows a portion of the resulting project that applied
this concept board's conclusions.

Teaching concept requires patience and a certain amount of repetition of
content in order for students to get it. I have found that at least a third of

Figure 8.4 In Timmerman's final model of the solution, the concept of puzzle pieces finds its outlet in an overhead trellis intended to reinforce the logical underpinnings of secular humanistic belief.

any given class will not deal with concept particularly well in the first exposure to the idea. It takes one-on-one brainstorming sometimes to fine-tune a concept so that it doesn't "beat somebody about the face and neck" with its final expression. To teach concept requires that the instructor him/herself is adept with concept. In fact, showing one's own prior work and application of concept is a great credibility builder and precedent example. This is where a teaching assistant can really shine by bringing in their own previous projects from their experience with the Studio 1 course – assuming, of course, that their project is worth showing as an exemplar.

As an instructor, I struggle with students that latch on to an example idea I throw out to them about concept like a life preserver in an ocean storm. Years ago, I would provide an idea like this, then forbid students from using it as they needed to go through the exercise themselves. In later years, I have seen that students sometimes need a fairly detailed "first push" on the first project, then they find their feet on the subject in successive exercises by themselves. As a result, I am less hung up on their use and development of an idea that I derived with them on the first project.

A concept board in the Studio 1 class is required, starting with the Student Dormitory project. This first project challenges a student to develop an art student's residential space at a fine arts college. The art student inhabits this dormitory room for three weeks as they attend workshops. Each dormitory space must have a concept of an art movement that guides its design, which the Studio I students select from a hat. The difficulty in the project is that the student must also simultaneously deal with design efficiently in a tight space - in this case 15' x 15' x 15' in size. This forces the student to design volumetrically in the height dimension and solve issues of stairs or ladders in addition to serving many functions in an overlapping fashion. The best projects figure out how to integrate the art movement concept seamlessly with this compressed, highly functional space. Past solutions have married an abstracted shipyard aesthetic with the work of metal sculptor Richard Serra, or paired the nonsensical nature of the dada movement with the notion of a discarded concept (with the art student living amongst abstracted paper partitions and a superscale figurative trashcan that sneaks up the walls). It's good, I think, to impart to students that concept is not stand-alone – it must contribute to the other required aspects of a solution such as the client's needs and function (see Figure 8.5).

Concept is repeatedly addressed in all of the Studio 1 class's five projects, as I believe it takes repeated wrestling with this idea to hone one's skills. I have found generally that students are able to act more quickly on ideas as the semester proceeds and later produce concepts that are more sophisticated. This is good, because the last project, a religious shrine, requires them to deeply understand a belief before selecting a concept, then expressing it not only in perhaps spatial arrangement or materiality, but also in lighting and shadow (see Figure 8.6).

Ongoing Questions and Struggles with Concept

Given that a concept's value resides in its meaning for a project's users (and is entirely subjective in its nature), this is a tricky topic to convey to students.

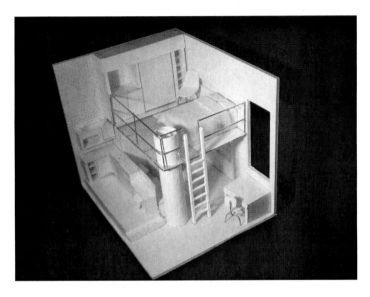

Figure 8.5 Example of the resulting model from the Student Dormitory project – a residential room for a single person by Victoria Davis. Given the artistic movement of graffiti, Victoria chose the concept of a billboard (an all-too-often palette for these artists), expressed here in metal railings, catwalk-like metal flooring in the second level and vertical orientation of the space's circulation.

I remain concerned with those students that never seem to get concept, and I tend to question myself and my own judgment at times with the proper selection and expression of a concept. My internal struggles with teaching concept rest along three lines: the validity of my current "crowdsourcing" approach, the times when my opinion differs from those of students, and questions regarding the best subject matter topics for concepts. These are discussed below.

The "Crowdsourcing" Approach to Critique

Essentially, concept is a matter that rests between the designer and the client and is a fully subjective topic. When faced with a student who has proposed an awkward, obscure or otherwise problematic topic, my current strategy is to harken back to "crowdsourcing" arguments that fall along the lines of "well, I would estimate that at least 50 percent of people would not get your connection between x and y, and on this basis it would never pass the 'I get it' test."

I had a recent experience with this when I substitute-taught in the Design Foundations class. The project at the time was to abstract the idea of having to use a wheelchair for mobility. The goal was to identify a person's

Figure 8.6 Example of the model from the course's final shrine project by Hae
Jeong Hwang. Lighting and its effects is a major part of the project along
with functional space planning and concept. This project expressed the
Wiccan religion as a paradigm of the natural world echoed here through
abstracted tree forms.

emotional reaction to this and to express these emotions in a three-dimensional art piece. I spoke with a student during class who wanted to evoke the concept of "freedom," in that she found a wheelchair to be an enabling device. This seemed like a viable idea to me. However, she further proposed a concept of an eagle as expressed in a military medal of honor, because she noted US soldiers were often confined to wheelchair mobility as a result of their war injuries and wheelchairs restored their dignity. This led her to a somewhat murky early draft of the project that combined an eagle's somewhat literal medallion-like outstretched wings combined with circles referencing the wheelchair's wheels. The ideas in combination lacked a necessary synergy, and I think the reason was that the idea was "lost in translation" and tried to address too many visual icons at once. This notion is somewhat akin to the parlor game "six degrees of Kevin Bacon," in which game players have to draw a connection in six steps or less between anyone in Hollywood and the actor Kevin Bacon. The underlying premise to this game is, if pressed, anyone could draw a connection between two ideas in a series of steps. The same process of drawing associations applies to developing a concept. However, with regard to concept, another requirement is present: is the "I get it" factor preserved? Happily, this student ended up abandoning the medallion eagle reference and generated a solution that captured the idea of freedom with fluid lines that integrated references to the wheels of the chair.

My Struggles with Rendering Worthy Critique on the Subjective Nature of Concepts

I am also continually struggling with the occasional student whose concept judgment differs from mine and, in fact, refuses to change the concept using my guidance. Who am I to say that their judgment won't be adored at some point in the future by their clients? Does concept savviness rely on having one's finger on the pulse of current culture? Am I so up on things that I can be the ultimate arbiter of taste in such matters? If I believe that the success of a concept relies on connecting in a dialogue with the user's prior experiences, I need to acknowledge that just because I don't understand a concept may simply mean I lack the necessary prior experiences for it to exert its charms on me. Ultimately, can I penalize a student based on the fact that their judgment and selection of concept is not a winning one in my opinion? At the formative point in their education that Studio 1 represents, I sense I must render an opinion for students, and therefore feel compelled to believe that my judgment would be held by sufficient percentages of other people to matter (including my fellow faculty). To not "call it as I see it" would seem an injustice to the student. My struggle is also underscored by the occasional student who starts out with a concept I sense is not a good direction, but they persist with the idea and it turns out just fine.

What is Appropriate Subject Matter for Concepts?

Currently I also struggle with how strict concept guidance should be. Right now I start teaching that concept must be an object (like a beach ball or a book), but not every literary source on developing architectural concepts feels this way. This last semester I began strictly adhering to this notion, but then loosened the requirements of concept in later projects, such that concept could evoke a mood, rather than strictly be something tangible (that is, "chaos theory" could be a concept). Generally, this went okay and gave some students more latitude to explore ideas without losing rigor or the "I get it" factor in their final project outcomes. However, results on this revised strategy are that not all students seem ready to relax the standards of concept that opens up doors to more flexibility. That is, some students end up with a solution that seems unfocused or embraces too many goals at once. It may be that reducing restrictions on concept needs to wait until a later time in the curriculum. If I had a crystal ball, I would really enjoy seeing the students' future work in their professional practice, and especially their use of concept. I think this would tell me what the students took away from these early Studio 1 concept explorations.

We're All Negotiating and Reckoning with Meaning

When I think about concept and the larger picture of the type of information and skills required in the Studio I class, I see that the students are in the process of constructing and reconstructing meaning that the spaces make possible, negotiating it in themselves and how they express it to the world. Not only do they have to convince themselves that a concept is valid, they also have to negotiate and place their bets on their clients' likelihood of "getting" the concept and buying in on the design solution ideas that support it. I like to think I am there to help them foresee what a client might say - and perhaps this is my highest utility as their instructor. Meanwhile, the course places me alongside the students in my own land of meaning-making – not only for myself, but in my hopes that the course is building for the students a constructed framework that they can parlay into their later careers. I get the sense that this course must continue to evolve, not only to help students as the profession changes, but also to serve as a platform for new ideas on learning and meaning-making that I uncover for myself.

9 The Lake Course
A Studio Apart

Jay Wilson

Introduction

This chapter examines my experiences in offering a class based on a design studio framework. As part of the Educational Technology and Design (ETAD) area in Curriculum Studies design studio is a part of all of the courses I teach. The course that is most true to the idea of studio design is Educational Technology and Design 879.6 Advanced Video Design. It is a full course that focuses on video design and production for graduate students. It incorporates face-to-face, virtual, and intensive design studio experiences.

To understand my approach to design studio learning it is important for me to share some insights into the context and learners with whom I work. It is also helpful to know about me. It is my belief that successful instruction is linked to the success of many components. Design, resources, context, content, and institutional climate all contribute to how deep and successful student learning can be. The key to making these elements work together is the commitment and actions of the instructor. In the spirit of the "instructor as a vital component," I share my approach to the 879 course as it is a different approach from others that I teach. It represents my most complete attempt at design studio learning. It moves beyond the previous frameworks I have utilized and includes many aspects that make it unique. I will share my journey as an instructor through/to the world of design studio learning as well as the practical elements that I feel contribute to the success of the course.

Who AM I as an Instructor?

I teach design in a number of areas: instructional design, visual design, video design, evaluation design, and multimedia design in a post-secondary teacher education context. Most of my teaching experience has centered on helping pre-service and in-service teachers develop skills and resources to make their instruction more effective and diverse. Teaching at both the undergraduate and graduate level has given me access to two distinct groups of learners. There is variety in each group but also commonalities in the understanding of design and the application of design principles. Most of those I work with have little or no formal exposure to design or designing of any kind. The undergraduates in particular are primarily consumers of content and design created by others. Those in the graduate courses have produced instruction, often for many years. They may understand the design process intuitively but do not know the specifics, processes, or language that is an important part of being a designer. They do not have a designer identity. They do not yet understand how instructional design is helpful in developing an understanding of the creation of resources or how to best share with others what they are creating.

Due to the tradition of providing student access to hardware and software more than anything else, my first 12 years of teaching were situated in on-campus labs. Following this time-honored tradition students at various points during a course could learn a skill and then produce an artifact that was then shared only with me. I would assess the work and share my thoughts directly with the learner. Although time-tested and effective at achieving student teaching objectives and learning outcomes, I believed there were opportunities to improve on this traditional practice. I began to slowly adapt what was happening in my face-to-face settings.

We learned and worked in close quarters in a computer lab setting most of the time. This particular environment allowed students to easily see what each other was doing and to interact with ease. I noticed students sharing among themselves when working in close contact. When I was unable to rush across the lab I encouraged them to exercise collegiality and help a neighbor or ask a neighbor for assistance. Small group sharing and helping created connections and community in the courses. I began to encourage students to share one-on-one with classmates and in wider class discussions. This tactic worked

Figure 9.1 As the instructor, I am able to connect deeply with the students.

periodically but was not promoted well by me in my early years of teaching. I also began to see that a work in progress was just as valuable and sometimes more valuable than a finished product. Seeing a partially completed work allowed learners to understand what was happening while it was happening.

How Teaching has Changed Me

What I saw happening on a small scale in my courses lead me to believe that to have deeper meaning and greater relevance, materials of any kind created by students have to be shared with people other than the instructor. As I reflected on the evolution of my own work as a student it became clear to me what I needed to change in my teaching. So often what I worked so hard at as a student was confined to the student-teacher relationship. It was only when, as a graduate student, my work was shared with a broader audience that I began to understand the value of openness and sharing. My Master's thesis was circulated and became required reading in a university department that was related to my research focus. My first attempt at writing an article was shared with an editor and reviewers. My dissertation became a conference presentation and a book chapter, which added even greater value to the learning experience that made up my program. I received positive feedback from all of these situations and it was only then that I felt my work had value. These milestones became foundational for me in gauging and valuing my success as a learner.

Early on in my university teaching career I focused on teaching with an emphasis on content chosen and delivered by me as the instructor. It was only after I had reached a comfort level with the process of instructing that I was able to make the courses more about learning from the students' perspective. Becoming more experienced in the classroom allowed me to make the environment more learner-centered. This change appeared to be successful but there was still something that prevented me from sharing total ownership with my students. A turning point was when I taught my first graduate course. It was after this experience that my teaching evolution evolved quickly. I discovered that graduate students do not need the same guidance around learning new material and concepts. They want to interpret the material their own way. They put more of who they are into their work. This helped me make a shift to a more student-centered focus and, by giving up even more control in the classroom, I was able to reflect on how my teaching could support and empower learners even more.

My first official attempt at radically changing my teaching model to incorporate more design studio elements began with an early version of my graduate video production course. I changed the final project wrap-up into a gala premiere at a movie theatre with all of the finished projects being shown on the big screen for my students and whoever was interested in attending. Instead of sharing only with me and maybe a few others on the course, the broader public was invited to be part of the audience. This extension of the final project gave greater significance to doing a good job on the work. It helped the students to spread their message and make the work in the course much more meaningful. I began to use this approach in both the undergraduate and graduate versions of the course.

The next step in the evolution of my course design was to do a better job of facilitating the sharing process between students. I did this by adding blogging as communication tool in the course. Students were required to research and choose a blog tool and make it their means of communicating to the world about what they were doing. Blogs worked well as they gave the students a chance to see what others were doing and to compare this work to their own. Blogs provided an interaction forum around everyone's work. As production courses are very visual in nature students used the blogs not just for text-based communication but also to share storyboards, images, video, audio and other multimedia-rich artifacts. Feedback and critique came from me in a very public but constructive and caring manner. I considered ways to effectively use discussion boards but I felt that blogs worked better in these courses.

What is ETAD 879... Really?

Using an approach called design studio is at the heart of all courses in our program. This format includes blogging, sharing, open assessment, flexible assessment, and student choice for topics and groups. The course that is the most intensive application of the design studio is the most recent version of Educational Technology and Design (ETAD) 879.6 Advanced Video Design. It is a full course that focuses on video design and production for graduate students. The course is offered every two years, it begins in May and it runs for approximately four months. ETAD 879 incorporates the elements listed above and adds even more innovation.

The course uses a blended approach that starts with an online component to create initial connections between students and to begin building community. The assessment in the course is based on the completion of a script (20 marks) and a final video (80 marks). The initial online component is followed by two mandatory face-to-face workshops. The face-to-face workshops place an emphasis on production and post-production. Each of the workshops is followed by a month of online interaction. This interaction takes place in what we call the virtual studio. It has many of the same characteristics of a face-to-face learning space in that it allows students to make, reflect, and share. It is a means to keep members of the course connected before and after their hands-on group experiences. Many of the artifacts of the regular design studio exist here such as counselling, yelling for help, teaching each other, and celebrating discovery. The first workshop looks at the concepts behind good visual design and moves into the practical skills of planning.

Based on sound instructional design principles students review a variety of existing video projects and projects previously completed in 879 to determine how they were planned and completed. These projects vary but are mostly focused on educational themes. Examples include a Division-wide resource on literacy assessment, a series of complex graphing videos for senior science and math, a way to engage students in the many aspects of Biology, and Northern Saskatchewan plant identification. Once they have a sense of what has been done previously, discussion takes place around students' experience and ideas related to video design. They can refer to the previously completed projects and, as they do so, they create shared understanding and new knowledge. Learners also unpack the concepts of treatments, script writing, and audience needs. Each student is shown how to create and use a blog. During the first session groups shoot footage and learn the practical skills related to audio, lighting, shot composition, and set dressing both in studio and on location. When the students are "sent away" they dive back into the virtual studio to complete and share their assignments with other students. All coursework is publicly accessible and, although not always discovered by those outside of the course, it is a resource that is always available.

The critiques, scripts and initial footage are shared in advance as a part of the blogs, but we discuss the material further in the face-to-face setting. In the second face-to-face session we use Apple computers to begin to learn how to use the software they know (like MS Word™ and PowerPoint™) in new ways and to learn software they don't know such as Final Cut™, Celtx™, Audacity™ and Photoshop™. The second workshop focuses on post-production with six or more hours spent using computers. Students have tutorial material made available to them in advance of this day but the hands-on work helps to solidify their understanding. They can turn to a colleague and watch what they are doing and ask questions of the entire group. The group footage from the previous workshop is edited into small videos. Students also bring in their completed scripts and share their vision for completing their final project.

It is at this point that the students fully become the managers of their own project. Scripts have been shared and approved. Ideas about planning are shared with me and among the other classmates. Students now have approximately one month to carry out their shooting. During this month they are asked to share regular updates on their blog. They share clips, scripts, stills, and stories in this virtual studio. They can ask others for advice and are expected to give advice and input to others. After the month the students are expected to begin post-production.

The next phase of the course is the truly unique part. The group is invited to a weeklong face-to-face design studio experience at a northern Canadian lake. They are transported to a location where community is further strengthened; some would say cemented. The Emma Lake Kenderdine

Figure 9.2 Students collaborating in the close quarters classroom environment.

Campus, founded in the 1930s as an art school, serves as the location. The location is a quiet lakeside retreat located in the northern forest. Cabins, workspace, and meals are all supplied. Students spend up to five days working here. They may continue to shoot and develop ideas, but most of the time is used to complete editing and post-production. Free of distractions and with the support of others they are able to accomplish a tremendous amount of work. There is constant sharing and 'grand rounds' of sorts as students reach milestones and conquer new heights. The instant responses to questions and shared excitement around successes bring the group together. Impromptu teaching led by the instructor or other students is a common occurrence. The videos are screened in the fall in a real movie theater with invited guests, faculty and the general public in the audience. Students are guided through the entire process but are expected to choose, develop and complete their projects. The hope is that the content is educational, useful, and has a positive message.

There are many aspects that make this place a great learning environment. The location is rustic and not a resort. It is isolated and, as a result, people spend most of their time together. They eat meals together, they share cabins, they use communal facilities, and they interact with other groups using the site. This shared experience is key to bringing people together. Although working independently they are in close quarters dealing with the same general creative issues. Only students enrolled on the course are allowed to attend so there are no distractions; very different from the schools and offices they have left behind.

As the site has been used for many years it has developed an almost mythical reputation. There is definitely a 'lore of the lake' that makes learners

Figure 9.3 Images of the lake site.

want to make the Emma pilgrimage. The feeling of connectedness to nature and the equality among the students help them to craft a new creative identity here. The lake is a very special place where learners take on a sense of the natural creative setting. The lake studio transforms them.

Table 9.1 A timeline of the course with major themes and milestones.

Building community.	Confidence and skills.	Sharing.	Creativity and risk taking.	Producing in a community.	Sharing.	Authentic learning and celebration.	Continued community building.
May	**June**		**July**			**August**	
First contact.	Face-to-face workshops.	Post-workshop virtual studio.	Script writing.	Week at the lake.	Post-lake virtual studio.	Premiere of final projects.	Official end of course.

The duration of the course breaks some of the University's rules as the course begins and ends outside of the official dates in the university calendar (Table 9.1). This flexibility allows students to begin and end when it works best for them. This flexibility can have its positive and negative outcomes. All students receive an 'In Progress' mark as official grades are due six weeks into their journey, hardly enough time to create what they need to for the course. They appreciate the freedom to work as it suits their schedules. Some complete early while others are scrambling just before the deadline. For me it is important to regularly check student progress through their blogs and with one-on-one production meetings to assist them maintain momentum regardless of when they plan to finish.

Design Studio Instructing

A key aspect to successfully applying a design studio model is to support the students on their journey. The course experience must allow them to learn, give them access to the content, knowledge and tools they need, and allow them to discover, make mistakes and experience success as they frame it. As a result of my own evolution this approach now feels natural to me. The sense of trust and support is strong and must be strong for students to achieve success. Students are not forced into anything. They are learning required content but discover on their own or through interaction with others what they need to be successful through their work. A true community is created through the virtual and face-to-face studio experiences. At the face-to-face events we form groups and teams. Someone who needs a hand finds help and learns during the entire process. Part of the instructor's job is to recognize and foster this collegiality. I model what is expected by giving honest, constructive feedback on student blogs. Social media is also used as part of this community building. The flow of tweets and posts is constant between the member of the course and others in the ETAD program.

How do I know the design studio is working? The first clue is that students tell me they love the course; I have them post-assess and they tell me they love the learning environment and the freedom to choose. Often the course allows them to complete a journey that has been on their mind for a long time. The technical issues at the lake around power outages and unreliable Internet connections are the only real problem in the minds of the students. If they have all of their material prepared and ready to use then not having reliable access to the Internet actually ends up helping them as they have fewer distractions. They forge professional and personal bonds that help them to be successful in other courses and while working in their "real worlds" as well. I see success in the quality of the work they produce. I see the countless extra hours they put into their projects as evidence. The high points are many along the way. Practicing camera work by following a family of ducks, late-night email flurries to assist a fellow classmate with a pressing problem, working on a script while a beautiful sunset unfolds, or taking still images of lichen and moss does not feel like work. It is the embodiment of creativity. There are many little discoveries and big victories, all of which are shared and celebrated with everyone on the course. The excitement and the unveiling that is the final project 'Premiere Night' provides the opportunity to show off their work on the big screen, with family and fellow students a part of the shared success.

The experience is different for me as the instructor. I have to be "on" the whole time. Making the course work takes a set of skills that most faculty do not possess at first. I know I didn't have these skills when I began. The preparation and planning alone will test your resolve but certainly in a good way. There are many new "jobs" that arise. Preparing for the intensive work-shop days. Fostering the early stages of the learning community. Providing regular and timely feedback on the virtual studio blog posts. Writing grant proposals to arrange funding. Setting up internal revenue accounts. Collecting and depositing student fees. Reserving travel and planning who sleeps in which cabins. Arranging for special diets. Equipment is begged and borrowed but not stolen. Materials and supplies are purchased and then materials and supplies are transported. A movie theatre is reserved. My tuxedo is cleaned and pressed. I fill the role of administrator, travel agent, controller, instructor, road manager, and social director. I have learned over time how the general process works but it is never the same from year to year.

I must be flexible yet make timely decisions. I have to establish strong communication links with students as they morph from consumers to designers and producers. I have to be critical but also sensitive to the developing skills and ideas of these learners. Being fair but honest is important as student work is put out for all to view. There are expectations realized very publicly. It can be tricky to critique someone's personal vision or dream for a project so I make sure I place a primary emphasis on technical skills so that feedback is objective and not just "I didn't understand it" or "I didn't like it". It is also important to protect the learners when it comes to selecting and crafting project ideas. I have to ensure that what they are doing will not cause them harm academically or as professionals. Most have positions of leadership in their organizations so it is important that what they do supports their status and does not erode it.

My level of commitment may seem over the top but it certainly does not feel that way from my perspective. I am no martyr. I am able to share an amazing experience with my students, fully connecting with them in a manner that I cannot in most teaching and learning situations. The work takes commitment and it takes energy but it is also self-sustaining. I am lucky that the students are able to connect with my vision for learning that is embodied in the course. They help me move the learning forward. They are not obstacles to the success of the course; they are integral. If I am not "all in" then it does not work. If the students are not "all in" they do not maximize their benefits. I have observed transformations happen every time I have offered the course at the lake. I see those who plan to come for a day stay for the whole week. I see people who are determined to give it everything at the beginning rise to even greater heights. I see the pained look on the faces of those who have to leave early knowing what they are missing out on. The intensity level is high for everyone. It begins with the first meeting, continues with the online interaction, and rises to new heights at the lake. Students are transformed in positive ways as a result of their involvement.

I encourage colleagues to try design studio on a small scale to see if it is actually for them. My approach has built up over time so to jump right in with a fully-fledged studio course would be overwhelming. You really must know your material and have experience managing and organizing in non-academic situations. So many things that are taken for granted in a regular university classroom or teaching lab do not exist in this course. If the students are at home working on material you do not really know their environment. If they are up at the lake there may not be power, or the Internet, or batteries. You have to plan for the worst and hope for the best. Be patient with people and learn to work without hard deadlines.

Theoretical Features

As I became more interested in developing the notion of sharing in my courses I needed to know how others had approached the idea. After completing a survey of published research I discovered the rich history of applying a studio design model in designing courses. Concepts such as academic design studio (Cennamo and Brandt 2012), communities of practice (Wenger 1998; 2007), and studio learning (Greenberg 2009; Clinton and Rieber 2005; 2010) gave increased clarity to my efforts and opened up a formal world of design studio literature. It was not until I read about design studio learning that I started to call it by that name and to think about it as a cohesive model. This evolving literature based around my own interest in authentic learning (Herrington and Oliver 2000) contributed to the evolution of my courses and supported these initial feelings. Once I had a formal concept it all just made sense to me. I also discovered that a majority of the application and research on design studios focused on art, architecture and computer design. Why not look for a fit in my own courses? The major features I was using were present in existing theory but I approached the design using my own instincts as well. I trusted what I already saw working in my courses and what felt right to me as an experienced teacher. As I mentioned earlier, I felt a bit undervalued as a student and I needed more motivation to be doing what I was doing. As a teacher I was informed, entertained, and intrigued by my students' work so I engaged with them about it. Why should this experience not be shared with everyone?

My initial forays using the design studio model created a great amount of direct and indirect feedback from students. They told me that they learned more than they had in their other courses. The comments I saw again and again were: "Best course ever" and "Can we do this in the next course?" When I have contact with these people now we discuss the transformational nature of the learning that took place. How it made them reflect on their own instructional practice. It was this feedback that has encouraged me to continue with what I am doing.

Things I Wonder About

As the formal concept of the design studio is still fresh in my mind I continue to look at what I have done and have still to do. Because students have freedom in the course they jettison the aspects that don't fit with their plan, customizing it to their needs. The fluid nature of the course based on enrollment, purpose, and student focus means that we try something new each time. It is what makes the course exciting for the students and for me. There are still aspects of the course I feel need to be addressed as part of the evolving nature of design. No course is perfect and 879 is no exception.

A major stress each year is related to securing operating funding. Annually I apply for a small grant that allows me to offer the course in the studio format. This helps to subsidize the student costs, rent or purchase equipment, and purchase consumables. There is never a guarantee that this money will be available year to year. It is possible but it would be very difficult to offer the course without this money. We could still offer the virtual studio and face-to-face workshops on campus but not the most transformative aspect of the course at the lake. Administrating the course is also stressful as I am solely responsible for the course and there are no stresses on my colleagues or my departmental or college administration. Booking university equipment has become a pain based on new accountability rules that ensure a grown up knows where I am with the gear. It is part of a larger program of risk management and accountability at my university.

I have resisted the desire to hold the entire course in a face-to-face setting without a virtual studio. I firmly believe the learner needs time to process, digest and create. The intensity of all three face-to-face sessions helps to create a wonderful transformation but students cannot maintain such a level of energy and commitment. It has been said that pressure makes diamonds, but not quickly and not all the time. I like that the students have flexible time to work on the assignments but sometimes I feel I give them too much time. Many of the pressures of real world production deadlines do not exist, only the final deadline of the premiere night, which is many months away. Deep learning and well-crafted documents take time so maybe I should not worry about time as much.

An area of growth I have identified is ensuring student projects have an element of social value. It may be too much to ask that they have to benefit a non-profit organization but it also is possible to provide resources for schools and other educational entities.

One difficulty for the students is knowing what to do when they are responsible for their own schedules (Figure 9.4). Those used to a more structured learning environment struggle at first. Those who are already self-directed learners find the transition to this course easy. They lead others in the creation of community in the course, which becomes so important. In time everyone on the course learns how to trust and interact in good faith with other students. Much like the rest of the course, the lake site has many

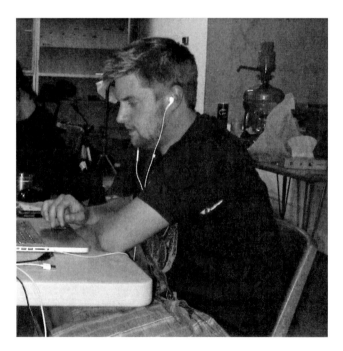

Figure 9.4 Students work in an environment they create and control.

uncertainties that must be addressed just like a real production situation. Students need to learn how to deal with these uncertainties. There is anxiety for me as well when I do not know exactly what the students are doing. I know this is part of any course where there is prolonged independent student work time. In the same way that the students must trust me so I need to develop trust in them. There is the stress of providing honest and constructive feedback. There is the stress of not knowing if my virtual interactions are understood or helpful. There is the stress of learners not investing in supporting other students by not sharing.

I would like to do a better job of documenting the process properly. Writing this chapter has been a great help but the perspective is primarily mine, making it very narrow in scope. It is hard for me to teach effectively and gather data at the same time. As I do not think I could give up the teaching component, it might help to have a research assistant document what is happening from a different perspective. I recently observed another lake-based course and it was very helpful to be a fly on the wall to see what happens when the instructor is not present. To observe the relationships and connections being made would inform my understanding even more deeply.

Another change I intend to make is to have people submit final projects earlier so that I can do a more thorough analysis and critique and allow them time to implement changes. The project still has to meet the needs of the student but part of the learning is having an expert review. Currently I encourage students to do this but it is not a requirement. It is not a criticism of their creativity but a review of the technical delivery of their message. I often have a chance to preview but I am not in contact as much as I would like towards the end of the process. The process of screening to look for major issues works well in my undergrad face-to-face video production course. The students learn from the critique but it ruins the surprise at the end for me.

The commitment to the lake is stressful for the students. Attending the lake studio is a big commitment for those with families, especially at the end of the K-12 school year. For a small portion of the students it is hard to give up all aspects of their outside life to commit to five days away. I encourage them to attend as many days as they can but some have to back out of the lake session close to when the event is scheduled. These last-minute changes are frustrating for the students, for me, and for the administration at the lake site. If I am able to foster a deeper awareness of the lake experience early on in the virtual and face-to-face sessions then they may understand the opportunity the studio time presents. Once they hear about it from colleagues who have attended previously they are convinced.

It is my hope that a design studio can work in other courses. There have been no significant program design changes as a result of my studio course but others in my college are using a modified version. We are talking more and more about the possibilities for broader course and program change and increasing involvement from other faculty and administration will help further the influence of design studio modeling. There is a fear that the lake site is not valued by central administration, causing concern about the future of the site as an option for the course. It may be necessary to relocate to another site, which presents its own challenges and opportunities. I believe it would be possible to recreate the intensity and closeness of the lake but losing the inspiration of the natural beauty would be hard to replace. I am unsure what removing the magic of the lake would do to the learning and the learners.

As I reflect on the course for this paper I can proudly say that it is a model that works for my students. It is a combination of the instructional courage of others, the trust of the students, and my willingness to do things differently. Although effective as it is there are opportunities to define the course. I believe that, through the course, my notion of design studio will continue to evolve and improve. We will try new approaches and modify existing ones. We will work to make the experience more about what the students need for their learning. Hopefully the reader has found value in learning about this particular course and has found ways to improve their own courses.

References

Cennamo, K. and Brandt, C. (2012) 'The "right kind of telling": Knowledge building in the academic design studio'. *Educational Technology Research and Development*, 60, pp. 839–858

Clinton, G. and Rieber, L. P. (2005) 'Creativity, flow, and the training of graduate students in design and development skills'. *Instructional Technology Monographs*, 2(2). Available at: http://itm.coe.uga.edu/archives/fall2005/gclinton.htm

Clinton, G. and Rieber, L. (2010) 'The studio experience at the University of Georgia: An example of constructivist learning for adults'. *Educational Technology Research and Development*, 58, pp. 755–780

Greenberg, S. (2009) 'Embedding a design studio course in a conventional computer science program' in P. Kotzé, W. Wong and J. Jorge (Eds) *International Federation for Information Processing, Creativity and HCI, Vol. 289, From Experience to Design in Education* (pp. 23–41). Boston, MA: Springer

Herrington, J. and Oliver, R. (2000) 'An instructional design framework for authentic learning environments'. *Educational Technology, Research and Development*, 48(3), pp. 23–48

Wenger, E. (1998) *Communities of Practice: Learning, Meaning, and Identity*. New York, NY: Cambridge University Press

Wenger, E. (2007) *Communities of Practice. A Brief Introduction*. Available at: http://www.ewenger.com/theory

10 Evolving into Studio

Andrew S. Gibbons

This study uses the changing landscape of instructional design from about 1970 to show why training that includes studio experience is becoming a new imperative. I describe four historical stages in the evolution of the designer's working environment to illustrate how design has acquired more of a social aspect than ever before. Today's emerging views of design are more likely to take into account how expert designers think and how teams work together collaboratively. In a changed professional world, studio training has become a new standard: one that supplies many of the intangible skills that can no longer be taken for granted.

The Evolution of Instructional Design

Knowing where design and design training should go depends on where it has been. My personal view of the past is framed, of course, by my own experience. For me, the evolution of instructional design as a field of practice can be summarized in four general phases:

- A revolutionary phase in which the idea of designed instruction was fresh and new and began to form into a body of practice;
- A tooling phase in which computers and authoring tools became the "new, new thing;"
- An expansion phase in which the emphasis turned to serious new instructional forms that used more of the computer's power and escalated the demands on the designer;
- A new design phase in which design thinking and design logic are replacing the process, the tool, and the device as the most important problem.

The Revolutionary Phase

Following WWII and the Korean War, training system designers with years of experience in man-machine system design with the military and government joined university faculties. One of these, Robert Gagné captured the expertise gained from this experience (1965a, 1965b) and translated it into terms to which educators could relate (see also Gagné 1970, 1977, 1985). A close colleague, Leslie Briggs, wrestled with the problem of integrating programmed instruction with teacher-led instruction in the classroom. He first focused on this as a media selection problem (Briggs 1967) and then recast it in larger terms of systematic processes for the design of instruction (1970). Others saw that this filled a knowledge void and wrote several additional descriptions of systematic development processes (see Andrews and Goodson 1980). Among these was a handbook for all military services called the "Interservice Procedures for Instructional Systems Development (IPISD)" (Branson *et al.* 1975), from which the acronym ISD was derived.

Over time, these ideas, along with taxonomies of educational goals introduced by Bloom (1956) and Gagné (1965b), came to dominate thinking on educational product development for the field that came to describe itself as Educational Technology (Ely 1963; Association for Educational Communications and Technology 1972; Seels and Richey 1994; Januszewski 2001; Januszewski and Molenda 2007). The trend of these ideas was an emerging focus on the development process, formulas, and simplification so that a wider audience of developers could be empowered. Another leading figure of this time, Robert Glaser, focused instead on research into the learning processes and became the co-founder of the Learning Research and Development Center at the University of Pittsburgh (Steele 2006). This provided the seed for the Learning Sciences movement.

In their time, the ideas of Gagné, Briggs and the others were revolutionary. The military market for these ideas had already been established, but now they were poised to engulf commercial and corporate development as well. Initially these ideas had to be digested and tested under titles such as SET (systems engineering of training) and SAT (systems approach to training) through government-funded projects. These projects demonstrated that process models were a useful management tool for keeping projects manageable and predictable in terms of budget and timeline, as well as producing instruction of acceptable quality. My own experience with some of these projects gave sufficient evidence of the usefulness of the ideas to make me a disciple, and I spent the first five years of my career teaching systematic process models to military-civilian ISD teams and then applying the process with these teams to create large bodies of instruction.

Turning development into a process made it possible for large teams of subject-matter experts to produce instructional materials according to templates designed by a trained designer – me – who was supplied by a contractor - my employer. This gave maximum leverage to the customer at a minimum cost. The government was also trying the alternative, a large contractor-owned development workforce using the same systematic approaches, but that was proving more costly.

I was prepared to be captured by the systematic approach by my work as a graduate student on the TICCIT project (Gibbons and O'Neal 2014), which also used a template approach for large-volume production of computer-based instruction for junior college use. TICCIT was an NSF-funded project aimed at proving the minicomputer as an instructional device. At the same time, NSF and other government agencies were funding an alternative mainframe computer system, PLATO, which assumed neither systematic development nor template instructional formats (Alderman *et al.* 1978).

Systematic design ideas were revolutionary at the time. They provided an alternative to hand-made, instructor-produced, one-of-a-kind instructional products. They described an approach to instructional design and development that for decades afterward became the gold standard in the military, industry, government, and commercial development firms. Unfortunately, because they reduced the need for critical, insight-producing thinking, they diverted attention away from the deeper issues of design. For a more lengthy account of the spread of these ideas and their impact, see Gibbons, Boling and Smith (2013), and Smith and Boling (2009).

The Rise of Tools

A key turning point for me and for the systematic approach came with the marketing of the first IBM personal microcomputer in 1981. After this, anyone could create whatever the programming tools would allow. The rapid proliferation of newer and more powerful PCs and PC-compatible software packages made every user an experimenter, and an experiment that occurred to almost everyone was the possibility of instructional use. A large audience was already familiar with the PLATO system (TICCIT had much less effective public relations, and PLATO had several years' worth of a well-funded head start), and the authoring pattern for PLATO was that every university instructor could also design and build instruction.

Everyone could be a designer, but everyone couldn't be a programmer, so almost immediately application development tools began to emerge that took the pain out of programming. This extended the reach of the user, but unfortunately it also limited the options available to the developer. Moreover, the instruction created tended to mimic classroom and textbook delivery styles. The attention of designers was taken up with learning to operate the tool, so there was little time to devote to the deeper issues of design. Even formalized design processes tended to suffer. The new tool-using designer was interested in "keyboard development" – just getting going, making something with the tool - and was not versed in systematic development procedures. Fairweather and Gibbons (2000) referred to this as an instance of the "one step forward and two steps back" phenomenon that has since marked each major advance in computerized instruction.

Some computerized development tools like TUTOR (Sherwood 1977) and TenCORE (2015) preserved the character of program code but, in order to simplify programming further, many software producers incorporated simple program constructs into their development tools. The most common architectural structure was the "frame," which consisted of a display component and a logical behavior component. Together, these two parts of the frame could display information in some audio-visual form and then respond to different kinds of user input. Again, I had become well acquainted with this structure through the TICCIT project. Moreover, I worked after 1980 for a company that built computer-based instruction systems, including authoring software. It was inevitable that I should become a devotee of the frame-based authoring system, learning to use it at the connoisseur level, because I had to demonstrate its power to potential clients weekly. As I made this new commitment, however, I did not forget the systematic procedures of the revolutionary period. I still practiced them, but I had to do it in private, out of the customer's view, because my employer's product was different now.

The Rise of New Artifacts

In the early 1980s the customers for whom I demonstrated my tool authoring tricks had, in most cases, never seen nor imagined the computer as an instructional tool, so there was a need to demonstrate a wide variety of ways in which the computer could be used. This pushed me and trained instructional designers working for competitors to begin pushing upward expectations of the computer-based instructional product that had already set at a low level. We began to imagine new kinds of application that could be built using the tools we had, which were also on an upward escalation path as customers, now awakened, became bored with yesterday's idea.

We were under pressure to find ways to build old artifact types using the tools we had, and new artifact types had to be invented. This forced us to keep inventing. We pushed against tool barriers, but we also had to be able to make the case for the effectiveness (or the efficiency) of our artifacts, so we became aware of what our formulas and systematic procedures could *not* do.

This was a defining time in which I, and many of my colleagues, had to face questions for which we had no answer. Was our product idea in fact more effective? How did we know this? Was computer-based instruction more effective? How did we know this? Did systematic design procedures produce more effective instruction? If instruction was more effective, was it the result of the computer, the authoring tool, the instructional approach, or the design approach?

For me, the answer to these questions began to revolve around a particular type of instructional artifact that I had found effective, efficient, appealing to customers, and innovative in its demands on the design process. It was the intelligent simulation, which I still believe today to pose one of the most demanding design challenges in all of these categories.

Designing simulations presented me with a forced choice. I discovered that systematic design procedures had little to offer to a simulation designer. They tended to funnel my choices toward direct instruction tutorials and made it hard for me to know just how to approach design. The familiar thread of the didactic narrative – the "presentation" – was not an element in simulation design. What was missing in process models? (See Gibbons 2003 and Gibbons 2014 for my current answers.) Moreover, I was confronted with the question still being asked today by the Learning Sciences: What is it that makes the essential difference during instruction (see van Lehn *et al.* 2003; Clark 2009)? In a major change of career, I took an academic position, seeking grounding for the answers to my questions.

Where was I at this point? I had discovered that the revolutionary systematic procedures of the 1960s, though useful in many ways, were not applicable in all situations. I had discovered that formulas and taxonomies delivered efficiency but did not even come close to covering the full range of learning needs, types, situations, and design problems. Robert Gagné also realized this, as he continued his search for a more universal set of learning outcome types (see Gagné *et al.* 1971, Chapter 5).

Instead, I had come to the conviction that the critical issues of instruction were centered on principles for making the kinds of performance and practice environments made possible by instructional simulations. At this point I became model-centered in my thinking (Gibbons 2001; 2003). I began to believe that the core of a design consisted of some kind of interactive model. At this point I was having my students read *Ender's Game* (Card 1994).

I had also discovered that interdisciplinary teams working together were imperative because of the growing complexity of virtually all of the technologies involved in design. I had lost a lot of my designer arrogance.

The Rise of Design

The study of design has become, for me and for many of my academic colleagues, an important research pursuit, but the "design" term as it was used during the days of revolution did not mean what it means now because, as we are discovering, deliberate design of interesting artifacts is a much more complex activity. I believe:

- we have to describe anew what we design;
- we have to describe anew how we design;
- we have to describe anew what is/can be created by designing.

What we design is defined in terms of what we know *can be* designed (individually, not collectively). Boling and Smith's concept of *precedent* is important (Boling and Smith 2011). Designers draw on the sometimes nameless terms of design languages (Waters and Gibbons 2004; Gibbons and Brewer

2005; Gibbons 2014) that represent their store of mental concepts. These define the boundaries of their design range. Teaching these subtle concepts – helping the design novice to realize that they even exist – is a greater challenge than a textbook and a classroom lecture can handle. This is a strong argument for studio instruction that will be examined in the next section.

How we design is becoming an increasingly frequent topic of discussion. One source of new perspective for instructional design is the design practices of neighboring design fields, including architecture, business, medicine, computer science, engineering, the arts, and technology - design fields that Simon (1999) says have been neglected by the academy. The growing field of design studies accepts as a basic premise that there exists some degree of underlying commonality among design fields that can be studied in an interdisciplinary manner. What then differs between design fields is discussed by Schön (1987, See Table 1, pg. 59), who shows how some design terms are shared *between* fields but that others are *unique* to a field. The implication is that there may be theories of design in general (Schön 1987; Simon, 1999), but there may also be theories that are domain-specific (Gibbons 2014).

The question of *what is created* as we design - the nature of designs - has been given scant discussion. Examples include a discussion of computer designs by Blaauw and Brooks (1997), Dorst's discussion of design frames (2015), Alexander's discussion of design patterns (Alexander 1964; 1977), Schön's examination of the evolution of a design (Schön 1987), and work I have done on design layers (Gibbons 2014). Boling and Smith's work on design precedents is also in this vein (Boling and Smith 2011). The lack of discourse on this topic creates problems for designers. Without a sense of the form of a design, its expression, its nature as an artifact itself, and its documentation, designers who wish to escape the landscape of sameness and traditional forms are hindered; they have no image of how to express designs, how to move design knowledge forward and what to move toward.

In the sections that follow, the questions of how we design and what is created are given particular attention. There is no easy answer to these questions. Instead, the answers evolve in and are limited by the mind of the individual instructor. As the design insight of the instructor matures, the instructor slowly, by stages, moves toward a studio to accomplish the task of training designers.

A Note on Varieties of Studio Instruction

A studio can be described both as a place and as a form of instruction. In the sections that follow studio, the place, is of less importance than studio, the technique. It is my conviction that adopting the studio technique will over time lead the instructor to request a venue suitable for exercising it, but the form of that will depend on the specific characteristics of the technique. If an instructor is evolving new insights into design and the teaching of design, the form and furnishing of the studio will evolve correspondingly.

Evolution of an Instructor Toward a Studio Technique

My experience training ISD teams and managing their projects in industry only partly prepared me for instructing in the university. One of the big differences I found was that when you tell university students what to do and how to do it, they ask "Why?" and expect there will be a good answer. In 2003 I took an academic position at Utah State University. There I was assigned immediately to teach basic instructional design courses to Masters and PhD level graduate students. I also taught courses in Implementation (of instructional products) and Instructional Simulation.

My industry experience proved useful, but it didn't fully prepare me to answer the "Why?" question. One of my first realizations was that I had never really asked myself the question enough, and it was then that I began to seek better explanations for why things were the way they were. What I discovered over a period of many years was that the ISD process does not explain *how* you make a design. It describes data-generating processes that may contribute to a design, it makes development processes manageable, and it defines development processes that lead away from the design processes, but it does not deal with questions about *what* is being designed or *how* to actually create a design. In virtually all ISD models there exists a box labeled "create the design" or something similar. This box is of greatest importance to the professional designer, but it is the least helpful as it is described in the ISD literature. The result is either design from prior examples, resulting in a lack of innovation, or invention of idiosyncratic design processes and invention of a new, suitable design model.

I have described how the nature of designed artifacts has changed over time as client expectations escalated, and how it has become increasingly apparent that the traditional ISD process needs to be joined by other views. Simulations showed me the need for the design and development of dynamic content models that ISD did not anticipate. Moreover, with simulations there is no longer the familiar narrative presentation structure that so often supplies the designer with a familiar architecture (that leads to the *telling* of the subject matter).

A Different Design Approach

By the end of my Utah State experience I was gaining new insights into what might lie within the "now-create-the-design" box in ISD models. I had begun to see the need for emphasis on the architecture or functional nature of the thing being designed, and on the architecture of the design itself.

Between 1993 and 1998 Peter Fairweather and I co-authored a book on the design of computer-based instruction (Gibbons and Fairweather 1998). It had a split personality that straddled the divide between traditional development processes and formulas, and the demands of simulation design. The first half of the book (up through Chapter 14) is very traditional; the second half (from Chapter 15 on) was about using the functional elements of the artifact as an approach the design. Three parts of the book define what have become "layers" in a book I published later in 2014 (Gibbons 2014) – strategy, message, and display, or representation.

I began to use these new concepts in my teaching, especially in my simulation courses, and I found they provided a key for explaining not only the design of simulations but also of traditional didactic forms as well, which I consider to be "frozen" simulations. I began to see that the concept of layered design was already being used in a number of other design fields. Since my time at USU, the number of examples of this I have encountered has continued to grow (see, for example, Baldwin and Clark 2000).

Layer thinking does not eliminate the need for a systematic process for managing design projects and processes. What it adds is much-needed detail about design that is not supplied by systematic design models during the key creative moments that actually populate the design with theoretically- and pragmatically-motivated substance.

The Impact of Layering on My Teaching of Basic Design

The impact of the functional-layer approach led to important changes in my teaching methods and eventually resulted in my increasing commitment to studio methods.

At USU I had been using lectures and a term-long individual development project, which students chose for themselves. Assignments for each of the ISD processes were due at points scheduled throughout the term, and they were checked during the term at key progress points according to quality criteria I provided in a course manual. Each assignment submitted by each student was checked, given feedback, and recycled (in some cases multiple times) as required until I judged that a basic criterion had been satisfied. This system worked because of the explicit ID model it was based on.

The downside of this approach was that the products the students were designing were mechanical and unimaginative. Only rarely did a student design anything other than a didactic tutorial that relied heavily on the presentation of information. Moreover, students that I challenged to try to design something different and innovative were unable to see how applying the systematic process facilitated the creation of the design. When I faced the same students in the instructional simulation course, they were at a loss as to how to proceed until mid-term.

I realized that the problem was that I was not teaching students how to design by thinking like a designer; I was teaching them to perform the stages of a process mechanically and efficiently. When they practiced their skills in the real world, their creative range as a designer would therefore be restricted to traditional instructional forms, and if they designed more non-traditional forms, such as museum displays, simulations, or learning environments, they would find themselves uncertain how to proceed, just like the simulation class students.

Classes using the ID model system at Utah State were held in a well-equipped multi-media classroom with students seated at tables facing the front of the room. Instruction included lectures, demonstrations, and dissection of examples. Examples of student work were used (by agreement) during these (friendly) critiques.

I used this pattern of instruction until I moved to BYU, each semester spending more and more time explaining to students the layered approach that was becoming increasingly clear in my own mind. At this time the concept of model-centered instruction (Gibbons 2001) was also gaining traction in my thinking and with students as a conceptual description of the core simulation mechanism.

Over the Watershed: Commitment to the New Approach

Shortly after I arrived at BYU I was predictably assigned to teach the basic instructional design course and, soon after, the advanced design course. I became committed to using the functional-layer approach, which was becoming defined in sufficient detail to be practically useful. The dilemma this raised was that I now had two approaches to design that were not mutually exclusive and that I wanted to crowd into the space of a single semester. I couldn't send students into the working world without an understanding of ISD terminology and processes, but I also wanted to give them a conceptual design edge for the problems they would meet that didn't fit the traditional mold.

The classroom at BYU was a standard multi-media classroom with 35 of the most rigid, uncomfortable and hard half-desk student chairs ever manufactured - arranged in straight rows. This was a step backward. Sticky feet on the bottom of the chairs made them hard to rearrange, and the classroom space was so full of chairs that any rearrangement required piling chairs on other chairs. This was not a friendly place for teaching the kind of ideas that would, in the future, require a much more open, flexibly configured space. Moreover, the room configuration did not lend itself to team design, which I decided would have to be an important element of the advanced design course curriculum. It was at this point that new subject matter, a new teaching technique, and a terrible teaching space collided to send me to the Dean's office with a campaign for the creation of a design studio. This idea was also championed By Peter Rich and Rick West, new colleagues who had joined the BYU faculty and added their weight to the project.

Even before the studio was approved (which took a matter of years), I decided to split the semester evenly, reduce the number of ISD processes taught, and introduce experiences with layer design into the last half of the semester. The order was ISD first, layers last.

This turned out to be the wrong order. What I discovered was that teaching ISD gave the students a concrete way to intellectualize designs. When the more abstract idea of layers was taught in second position, it confused students who had already adopted a process frame of mind. It stifled creative approaches before they could develop in the students.

Accordingly, in the next basic design course, I introduced the layer approach first, using multiple, rapid design challenges one to two weeks long at most, followed by a studio critique of the products, deriving principles opportunistically. What students discovered was that they already knew a good deal about design intuitively. The rapid-fire projects and the lack of process structure showed them this. It also made it possible during the second half of the course – the systematic process portion – to refer back to the creative issues of design they had experienced at the beginning.

At the beginning of the course, even before any terminology had been introduced, critiques were focused on close observation of the examples, noticing details, and intuitively judging what worked and what didn't. Only during analytic discussions of examples did we try to give things names. Deficiencies in student work (judged by the class) usually hinged on missing design decisions within different layers. This led to discussions of the layers and the decisions characteristic of each layer. This led naturally to a discussion of the multitude of design decisions everyday designers make without realizing it. This led them inside the mystery box.

In my own thinking the question surfaced: "What makes it a studio?" Accounts of studio innovation were appearing more frequently, including the account of Georgia's curriculum reform experiment (Clinton and Rieber 2010). What did make a studio? The place? The method? The role of the learner? Clearly, my own shift in thinking was not due to a change in physical space but to a change in the subject matter, teaching style, and a new conceptual approach to design.

Following the layer portion of the basic design course in the first half of the semester, many students found the ISD portion of the course a welcome change because it was more concrete and made them feel more secure. But by the time they encountered the process model they were used to thinking creatively. As expected, the designs they created in the ISD portion of the course became more creative and divergent than they had been in the ISD-only course or in the ISD-then-layer course. Students were more confident in attacking the ISD problems. This order of teaching became my preferred pattern.

The Advanced Design Course: A Studio Becomes Real

When I began to teach the advanced design it became apparent that some essential areas were not being addressed in the basic design course:

- acquiring more mature design judgment;
- engaging in innovative design thinking within a team structure;
- appreciating design as a process of discovery;
- learning to sequence decision making strategically;
- learning how to approach the design of non-traditional instructional forms.

The uncomfortable chairs were by now banished from the classroom and replaced by reconfigurable tables and (somewhat) more flexible and comfortable chairs. Whiteboards appeared on all of the classroom walls. This was when new colleagues Rick West and Peter Rich, who both had experience in the University of Georgia studio system, introduced to our faculty, and to the Dean again, the idea of a separate, protected design studio space reserved just for our department and just for design courses. Rick and Peter designed a configurable workspace, private storage areas, and a variety of media appliances for sharing design representations. Over the next four years this goal was realized thanks to their efforts. One of the things that became clear at this point was that a public, viewable representation of an evolving design was paramount. The new studio design addressed this problem by becoming a flexible representation space.

It was clear that, in order to address the course curriculum goals I had set, the advanced course had to be team-centered and that the design problem had to be high-stakes, real-world, visible, and challenging. I felt there had to be a chance that the class-team could succeed (or fail) in a visible way, but if they succeeded (and I made sure they would) there would be plenty of medals to hand out and considerable new confidence generated.

From the beginning, we had a string of fascinating projects that required the student teams to move outside their traditional stereotypes of "instruction." This brought us face-to-face with the issue, "What is designed?"

- A magazine wanted us to recommend new article formats that would encourage parents and children to engage in activities together.
- A cultural history museum wanted portable cultural experiences for public school classrooms.
- A second history museum wanted a way to connect children of the current era with the experiences of children of other historical periods.
- A client wanted a large space designed to house and give a coherent theme to a number of interactive "science of light" displays (Ashton *et al.* 2011).

- A client wanted to create a culture among its high-level employees that would unite successful but disparate elements of its organization.
- A client wanted a design for the "e-book of the future", including a sustainable business plan for its marketing.
- A client with a multi-venue family park wanted one of its venues redesigned using out-of-the-box ideas, but with a particular type of family learning experience in mind (Nyland *et al.* 2015).

These projects underscored the idea that the traditional definition of "instruction" was changing and that instructional designers are experience designers of both formal and informal learning environments.

The instructional challenge for an advanced course using a real project is that it can't be staged like a basic course. The sequence of design conversations that a real design problem presents can't be scheduled beforehand. They often occur in response to momentary needs and prior decisions.

The instructional approach I chose for the advanced design course was to keep both the layer and ISD design approaches in the background and let expediency reveal moments when one or the other could help if it were pulled into the foreground. The most pressing expediencies in a real-world situation are the nature of the problem, deadlines, client relations, team organization, resources, team skills, and the design environment. The most critical aspects of the design environment directly related to progress on the design itself are team communication, team leadership, and the public representations of evolving design decisions. Project management tools are important but secondary, because new problems bubble to the surface in an unpredictable order. If the schedule becomes too much the center of attention, the design process begins to drive the project, and creativity takes a back seat.

The Future

The studio as a method and as a place will continue to grow within our department. Our department's main studio proponents (Rich and West) have continued to pioneer studio instruction and have reached out across campus, forming relationships with design instructors in several design-oriented schools and colleges. Recent developments from their sustained efforts include: (1) the design and teaching of multi-department, multi-disciplinary design courses, (2) the launching of projects by interdisciplinary design teams, and (3) a project underway to create a dedicated design space in the BYU library as a high-tech interdisciplinary campus design studio.

Conclusion

The purpose of this chapter has been to give an account of the evolution of a classroom instructor into a studio instructor, and an account of how, as a result, a suitable place for studio instruction became necessary. What was important was not the creation of the place but the instructional need for such a place.

In order for this need to occur, it would not be necessary for an instructor to undergo the kind of fundamental change in thinking that I experienced. A studio can be used to teach any form of narrative about design and how it occurs. Hopefully, our store of narratives will increase in the future, and hopefully the number of studios will increase. One might speculate whether the teaching of design to classroom K-12 teachers in a studio setting might be long overdue.

I would hope that this account of the maturation of a designer - one who felt secure in one particular approach to design - might be encouraging to other designers to see themselves and their design knowledge in dynamic rather than static terms. Our knowledge of design is expanding in a time period that is fast becoming a new Design Age. Perhaps others will find an evolution in their own thinking taking them down a different path – one that will not only illuminate design for others, but one that will carry them toward the studio as a place for instruction in designing.

References

Alderman, D. L., Appel, L. R. and Murray, R. T. (1978) 'PLATO and TICCIT'. *Educational Technology*, 18(4), pp. 40–45

Alexander, C. (1964) *Notes on the Synthesis of Form*. Cambridge, MA: Harvard University Press

Alexander, C. (1977) *A Pattern Language*. New York: Oxford University Press

Andrews, D. H. and Goodson, L. A. (1980) 'A comparative analysis of models of instructional design'. *Journal of Instructional Development*, 3(4), pp. 2–16

Ashton, S., Foisy, A. M., Marwedel, R., Popham, J. A., Proctor, K. R., Randall, D. L., Tateishi, I., Thompson, C. A. and Gibbons, A. S. (2011) 'From takeoff to landing: Looking at the design process for the development of NASA Blast at Thanksgiving Point'. *International Journal of Designs for Learning*, 2(1), pp. 56–73

Association for Educational Communications and Technology (1972) 'The field of educational technology: A statement of definition'. *Audiovisual Instruction*, 17, pp. 36–43

Baldwin, C. and Clark, K. (2000) *Design Rules: The Power of Modularity* (Vol. 1). Cambridge, MA: MIT Press

Blaauw, G. and Brooks, F. (1997) *Computer Architecture: Concepts and Evolution*. Reading, MA: Addison-Wesley

Bloom, B. (1956) *Taxonomy of Educational Objectives, Handbook I: Cognitive Domain*. New York, NY: David McKay Co.

Boling, E. and Smith, K. M. (2011) 'The changing nature of design' in R. Reiser and J. Dempsey (Eds) *Trends and Issues in Instructional Design and Technology* (3rd Ed.). New York, NY: Prentice Hall

Branson, R. K., Rayner, G. T., Cox, J. L., Furman, J. P., King, F. J. and Hannum, W. J. (1975) *Interservice Procedures for Instructional Systems Development* (5 vols)

(TRADOC Pam 350-30). Ft. Monroe, Va.: US Army Training and Doctrine Command, August 1975. (NTIS Nos. AD-A019 4860-AD-A019 490)

Briggs, L. J. (1967) *Instructional Media: A Procedure for the Design of Multi-media Instruction, a Critical Review of Research, and Suggestions for Future Research.* Washington, DC: American Institutes for Research

Briggs, L. J. (1970) *Handbook of Procedures for the Design of Instruction.* Washington, DC: American Institutes for Research

Card, O. S. (1994) *Ender's Game.* New York, NY: TOR Science Fiction

Clark, R. E. (2009) 'Translating research into new instructional technologies for higher education: The active ingredient process'. *Journal of Computing in Higher Education*, 21(1), pp. 4–18

Clinton, G. and Rieber, L. (2010) 'The studio experience at the University of Georgia: An example of constructivist learning for adults'. *Educational Technology Research and Development*, 58, pp. 755–780

Dorst, K. (2015) *Frame Innovation: Create New Thinking by Design.* Cambridge, MA: MIT Press

Ely, D. (1963) *The Changing Role of the Audiovisual Process in Education: A Definition and a Glossary of Terms.* ERIC Document Service, ED016409

Fairweather, P. G. and Gibbons, A. S. (2000) 'Distributed learning: Two steps forward, one back?' *IEEE Concurrency*, 8(2), pp. 8–9, 79

Gagné, R. M. (Ed.) (1965a) *Psychological Principles in System Development.* New York, NY: Holt, Rinehart and Winston

Gagné, R. (1965b) *The Conditions of Learning.* New York, NY: Holt, Rinehart and Winston

Gagné, R. M. (1970) *The Conditions of Learning (2nd Ed.).* New York, NY: Holt, Rinehart and Winston

Gagné, R. M. (1977) *The Conditions of Learning (3rd Ed.).* New York, NY: Holt, Rinehart and Winston

Gagné, R. M. (1985) *The Conditions of Learning (4th Ed.).* New York, NY: Holt, Rinehart and Winston

Gagné, R. M., Twitchell, D. and Merrill, M. D. (Eds) (1971) *Robert M. Gagné and M. David Merrill in Conversation.* Englewoood Cliffs, NJ: Educational Technology Publications

Gibbons, A. S. (2003) 'What and how do designers design? A theory of design structure'. *Tech Trends*, 47(5), pp. 22–27

Gibbons, A. S. (2001) 'Model-centered instruction'. *Journal of Structural Learning and Intelligent Systems*, 14(4), pp. 511–540

Gibbons, A. S. (2014) *An Architectural Approach to Instructional Design.* New York, NY: Routledge

Gibbons, A. S., Boling, E. and Smith, K. M. (2013) 'Instructional design models' in M. Spector, M. D. Merrill, J. Elen and M. J. Bishop (Eds) *Handbook of Research on Educational Communications and Technology* (4th Ed.). Berlin: Springer

Gibbons, A. S. and Brewer, E. K. (2005) 'Elementary principles of design languages and design notation systems for instructional design' in J. M. Spector, C. Ohrazda, A. Van Schaack, and D. Wiley (Eds) *Innovations to Instructional Technology: Essays in Honor of M. David Merrill.* Mahwah, NJ: Lawrence Erlbaum Associates

Gibbons, A. S. and Fairweather, P. G. (1998) *Computer-based Instruction: Design and Development.* Englewood Cliffs, NJ: Educational Technology Publications

Gibbons, A. S. and O'Neal, A. F. (2014) 'TICCIT: Building theory for practical purposes'. *International Journal of Designs for Learning*, 5(2), pp. 1–19

Januszewski, A. (2001) *Educational Technology: The Development of a Concept*. Englewood, CO: Libraries Unlimited

Januszewski, A. and Molenda, M. (2007) *Educational Technology: A Definition with Commentary*. New York, NY: Routledge

Nyland, R., Langton, M. and Gibbons, A. S. (2015) 'A new farm country: Designing transformative family learning'. Design and Development Showcase demonstration, AECT Annual Convention, November 2015

Schön, D. A. (1987) *Educating the Reflective Practitioner: Toward a New Design for Teaching and Learning in the Professions*. San Francisco, CA: Jossey-Bass Publishers

Seels, B. and Richey, R. (1994) *Instructional Technology: The Definitions and Domains of the Field*. Washington, DC: Association for Educational Communications and Technology

Sherwood, B. A. (1977) *The TUTOR Language*. Control Data Education Company. Downloaded 27 July 2015 from: http://www.group-s.net/tutorlanguage

Simon, H. (1999) *The Sciences of the Artificial* (3rd Ed.). Cambridge MA: MIT Press

Smith, K. and Boling, E. (2009) 'What do we make of design? Design as a concept in educational technology'. *Educational Technology*, 49(4), pp. 3–17

Steele, B. (2006, May 30) 'An academic giant in our midst'. *Pitt Chronicle*. Downloaded 27 July 2015 from: http://chronicle2.pitt.edu/media/pcc060530/GLASER_tribute_2006MAY30.html

TenCORE Authoring (2015) Downloaded 27 July 2015 from: http://www.tencore.com/index.html

Van Lehn, K., Siler, S. and Murray, C. (2003) 'Why do some events cause learning during human tutoring?' *Cognition and Instruction*, 21(3), pp. 209–249

Waters, S. H. and Gibbons, A. S. (2004) 'Design languages, notation systems, and instructional technology: A case study'. *Educational Technology Research and Development*, 52(2), pp. 57–68

11 Orchestrating Learning

Katherine S. Cennamo

or•ches•trate (ôr′kĭ-strāt′)
tr.v. or•ches•trat•ed, or•ches•trat•ing, or•ches•trates
1. to compose or arrange (music) for orchestra.
2. to arrange, coordinate, or manipulate the elements of, as to achieve a goal or effect.

Random House Kernerman Webster's College Dictionary, © 2010
K Dictionaries Ltd. Copyright 2005, 1997, 1991
by Random House, Inc. All rights reserved.

This case describes how I teach a graduate course in "Applied Theories of Instructional Design" using studio pedagogy. Although there is no dedicated studio space where students toil for long hours, I have adopted elements of the studio pedagogy to teach graduate students to design instruction that is grounded in a variety of learning theories.

You might wonder how a theories course can be taught as a studio but I believe that any design-based course can be taught in this way. Whether learning to design functional products, buildings, instruction, etc. – anytime the solution to the problem involves a multitude of possibilities, there is no one right way to solve the problem, and details of the problem reveal themselves through the process of problem solving, then the studio method is an appropriate way to learn the necessary skills and dispositions. In my investigation of academic design studios across various disciplines (for example, Brandt *et al.* 2011; Cennamo and Brandt 2012), my colleagues and I have described how the pedagogy, epistemology, and surface structures such as dedicated desk-space, long blocks of time, and other observable features of the studio come together to create a unique learning community. As I reflected on my work with studios in other design disciplines, I realized that it's the epistemology that really matters – beliefs about what it means to learn, and consequentially teach, in a discipline. This is what instructors need to know about, examine in light of their own beliefs, and choose to embrace if they want to teach using the studio method.

In the following sections I briefly describe the context and content of the course, but the particular course activities and setting matter little. Beliefs about the role of the student and the teacher, and how they share the responsibility for learning, are absolutely critical to orchestrating learning in this class and, I believe, in any successful studio.

In the Beginning

I negotiated access to this course close to 20 years ago. As a new professor, I had been teaching large lecture sections of "Computer Applications for Educators" for several years. I found lecturing to 75 people quite boring. Although I incorporated group activities when I could, I found myself making grocery lists in my head as I went through my PowerPoint™ presentations, telling the same jokes at the same time in the presentation. Ugh... I hated it.

My colleague was thinking about writing a book for that audience so I saw an opportunity for him, and for me. I offered to let him teach my course in exchange for me teaching his course on "Applied Theories" for instructional design and technology (IDT) students. Quite honestly, my primary goal as I embarked on teaching the Applied Theories course was to never, ever lecture again!

At the same time, I was working with a science educator to develop video cases of science instruction for use in pre-service education classes. This was in the early 1990s when the field was just beginning to grapple with constructivism and exploring the use of constructivist methods such as case studies.

Researchers in IDT were also beginning to question the epistemological foundation of our field and how the preparation of designers aligned with the way design was practiced. In fact, as a practicing designer, I had observed a student with a newly minted master's degree coming into our well-established and well-functioning design shop and telling us we were doing it "wrong" because we were not overtly following the design model through which he had been trained. I was committed to developing designers who were more sophisticated than that - who were able to recognize, and enact, good instructional design practices in all their various disguises.

So three things came together to shape the class: my interest in preparing instructional designers for the realities and variances of professional practice; my immersion in the literature on case studies and other constructivist methodologies; and my desire to never lecture again.

In the beginning, I only had a vague idea of how I would teach the class. The course was intended as an advanced learning theories course. I decided that it was not going to focus on learning *about* the theories but, instead, it would focus on *applying* the theories. That first semester whether a particular approach worked or not was pure luck (or perhaps it was design intuition?). I selected a book, created an open-ended syllabus, and figured out what we would do in class week by week. From that first year, I've retained the basic organizing structure of the course and simply refined it throughout the years. I still use an open-ended syllabus and figure out what to do week by week but, after all this time, a predictable pattern has emerged.

Guiding Beliefs and Course Goals

The overall goal of this course is for students to learn to use theories to inform instructional design decisions. In an introductory instructional design (ID) course, students are often exposed to a limited set of instructional strategies such as Gagné's Events of Instruction. The purpose of this course is to expand their design toolkit. But, rather than give them a course in instructional strategies, I have decided to develop in our students a way of thinking about learning theories that enables them to derive instructional strategies, as well as other design decisions, from learning theories. Along the way, they also learn more about the theories they examine, instructional strategies that align with particular views of learning and knowledge acquisition, and instructional design, but the emphasis is on the analysis and synthesis process. I want my students to be able to design based on any learning theory that they may come across, not just the ones "in the book".

Personally, I am as passionate about theories as I am about design. Every design discipline has theories that guide their work. Architects have theories that they draw upon to make a building structurally sound on a given site. Graphic designers have theories of design aesthetics. We have learning theories that can guide us in building "structurally sound" instruction for a given set of learners and context.

But I don't think we should look to theories as a prescription - in fact, I find prescriptive theories (instructional theories) very limiting. Instead, theories can and should be used to broaden our perspectives, provide a variety of alternative approaches to a design problem, remind us of things we might want to consider. As a designer, I go into a design situation and often act on intuition - but then I can go back to theory and, 1) based on my knowledge of theories, I think about which one might be most appropriate given the goals and context and learners, and then 2) I look at how my intuitive design aligns with the theory, to make me aware of things that should be *considered* in order for the product to more closely align with a particular theory of how people learn. Theories don't dictate what to do; they just give me another perspective and prompt me as to what I might consider adding in order to maximize opportunities for learning from a particular theoretical orientation. In this way, theories can help refine intuitive designs. Intuition, of course, comes from experiences and beliefs and values that include knowledge of theories. Theories also give us a language to use to justify our intuition and design decisions. As a designer I find them quite useful.

Recall, for example, how this course came to be. I never wanted to lecture again. I coupled that very intuitive design decision with my emerging knowledge of constructivist methods and research on instructional design practice to shape the design decisions I made as I developed the class activities and flow for my syllabus. These design decisions were refined as I went along, week by week, based on intuition, yet informed by research and theory.

So, given my beliefs about the value of learning theories for instructional design, my goals for the course are that, for any given theory, students will be able to 1) know it when they see it, 2) design based on it, and 3) describe their design decisions using the language of the theory (or "talk the talk").

The Context

In this class, I expect students to develop the ability to create a technology-based learning experience that aligns with a particular, any particular, learning theory, and to justify their design decisions from the perspective of that theory. Early on, I draw parallels between architectural design and instructional design. I point out that an architect may prefer a particular kind of architectural style, but that most architects need to be able to design houses that are consistent with a variety of other styles, based on the preferences of their clients. Instructional design is the same. We may prefer a particular theoretical orientation, but if the content, context, goal, or whatever lends itself to a different theoretical orientation, then we should be able to design in that way too.

I've learned throughout the years that this course is most meaningful to students after they have a little experience in the program. At the very least, they are expected to have a basic knowledge of instructional design and learning theories. Some technical proficiency in a few software tools is also helpful. This course is where their instructional design skills, knowledge of learning theories, and hard skills in development tools come together.

The course is offered as a three-hour graduate credit class that meets on campus once a week for three hours. We typically examine five or six different theories of learning and, for each learning theory we examine, the course progresses through a predictable sequence, although the point at which we start, and the relative emphasis on each activity, varies depending on the skills the particular class members bring. Students are provided with readings that establish a common vocabulary with which to discuss the theory (i.e. to "talk the talk") then, when they come to class, they are put in groups and asked to either a) examine learning materials from the perspective of that theory (i.e. know it when they see it), or b) design a learning experience based on that theory (i.e. design according to it). Class time is typically divided into hands-on group work for the first half of the class, followed by public critiques after a brief break.

I'm a big believer in group responsibility and individual accountability, so the next step is for students to do an independent activity for homework that builds on what we did in class. Typically, they are asked to select a topic for their independent work, and then to design an instructional product to teach that topic from the perspective of the theory with which we are working.

As a cumulative project, students develop a working prototype for a technology-based learning experience based on the theory of their choice. Students present these projects in the last few weeks of class and, again, we critique them, discussing as a class how they match the theories in which they are grounded and offering ideas on how to make them match more closely. This activity serves as a good synthesis for the students because we compare the projects to the theories after some time has passed since the initial discussions on each theory. Students then have a few weeks to modify their projects based on the class input before submitting them to me for final grading.

Through these activities, students are provided with opportunities to develop and apply the three skills that I want to develop in relation to a particular theory: the ability to talk the talk, to know it when they see it, and to design according to it.

Public Critiques and Iterative Practice

What we do though is less important than *how* we do it. Public critiques and iterative practice are key to how I develop student competency in this class. Throughout the years I have learned that the optimum class size is around 12. I'll accept up to 15 students but, with more students than that, I am unable to provide adequate time in class for all students to demonstrate their knowledge, participate in class discussions, and to receive one-on-one coaching through detailed feedback on their projects.

Group Work

With 12-15 students, students are placed into three to four groups of three to four students each. The classroom has moveable tables where students can cluster to work on their group task. While students are working, I circulate around the room and listen to their conversations. If they are on track, I do not intervene. If they are off base, I ask probing questions to try to get them back on track. If that doesn't work, I start to co-design with them, thinking out loud as I puzzle through design decisions. Using the language of the theory, we work on developing a joint understanding of how the key ideas of a theory impact design decisions.

One primary way in which we come to a joint understanding of the terminology of each theory is through examining instructional products through the lens of a particular theory. Students are provided with access to the instructional materials and are expected to work in groups to review the materials, identify examples of strategies that are consistent with the theory, and discuss how learning occurs in the lesson, according to the theory. My goal in having students examine commercial products and other students' projects is to provide a collection of design precedents, so that students can begin to see how this theory can be exhibited in practice.

Students are then asked to design a learning product that is grounded in the theory under discussion. Usually, they work in groups prior to doing this independently, using a topic that has been assigned to the entire class. For example, students may be asked to develop a web-based lesson that teaches the concept of plagiarism to international graduate students from the perspective of behaviorism, schema theory, Vygotsky, and so forth, depending on the week. Given a particular theoretical orientation, students are asked to outline the goals of the learning experience, describe an appropriate assessment, and outline the activities of the lesson in sequence. The goal of the project, to teach "X," is the same for each group and each theory so that the students can begin to see different interpretations of the same theory, as well as the subtle differences and similarities among theories. I want for them to develop a sense of the parameters of a theory and the variances that are acceptable within the parameters of that theory. They also need to be able to defend their design decisions based on the language of the theory.

Class Critiques

I then have the groups present their conclusions or designs to the class. The students usually outline their responses on flipchart paper that they post to the classroom walls. Sometimes they post before the class break, and the students circulate around and look at the other groups' work over break; at other times they simply display the flipchart pages as they present to the rest of the class. The advantage of flipchart pages over computer-generated presentations is that we can display all of them simultaneously and write or draw on them as needed.

As students walk us through their design, we look for ways that the project matches the theory. As a class, we identify instances of instructional strategies that are consistent with the theory, and use the students' work to discuss how learning occurs – in this lesson – according to the theory. The students, however, don't always get it right. Frequently, there are misunderstandings and misconceptions reflected in their work. The other students are then invited into the design space to help their peers redesign their products. As the instructor, I might model my thought processes as I think aloud about how I would solve the design problem.

I use these critiques to diagnose the students' misconceptions and to supplement their knowledge. Critiques are the site of mini-lectures, grounded in the examples provided in the students' work. Throughout the presentations, I use the students' work to summarize the main points of the theory, pointing out particular good examples (or several alternative examples) from the students' work. If something is done well, I point it out and discuss why, from a theoretical perspective, this is a good example; if something falls short, we work together as a group to redesign it. I use the examples provided by the students' work to demonstrate how the theory looks in practice.

Conducting class in this way results in students who are much more invested in the discussion than they would be in a typical lecture – and, for that matter, more invested than they typically are during class presentations by their peers. After all, in class, they are all working on the same design challenge using the same theory - and they realize that they will ultimately be responsible for designing instructional materials based on this theory on their own.

Critiques are a safe place to make mistakes. Students are informed upfront that their work will be critiqued publically, and that this is a normal and expected part of how learning occurs in this class. Because students work in groups for these initial exercises, any misperceptions are those of the entire group. Insecure students often find that they are correct while more vocal students may have been wrong. When someone makes a mistake, I often thank him or her for bringing it up. It's typically a common misperception, and I point this out. I emphasize again that this is how learning occurs in this class.

Really, I've found that it is a matter of developing the perception that critiques are about skill development in a safe environment instead of being about evaluation. It's an attitude on the part of the teacher and cultivating an attitude on the part of the students. Students must feel we are on *their* side and want them to perform at their best. Once students realize that the critiques occur in the spirit of making them better designers, they embrace this way of learning.

Iterative Practice

The opportunity to redo work is another crucial element in creating an environment in which students feel safe to make mistakes. As I grade their independent work, I look for certain key concepts. Do they identify activities consistent with the theory? Are they sequenced appropriately? Do they justify them using the language of the theory? Typically, students either get it or they don't. If an assignment is way off base, I don't assign a grade; instead, I just give them an "R" for rethink and redo. They have two additional opportunities to redo.

I tell them on the first day of class that my goal is for them all to be able to do this, that redos are common, and how almost everyone will have to redo something sooner or later. I use as an example a student, who is now a professor at a well-respected university, who chose to sit through the course a second time because she did not do as well as she would have liked the first time. Because students are allowed to redo projects, the primary danger to successful completion is that they fall behind. Students who have not demonstrated an understanding of enough of the theories to achieve the grade he or she desires are offered the opportunity to take an incomplete and sit through the entire class again to learn the content in adequate depth. In any given semester, it is not unusual to have one or more students repeating the class from the previous semester.

I often use the coach analogy with my students. I remind them that even professional athletes have skills that they work to refine on a continuous basis and so, for the duration of this course, I am their coach. My job is to look for areas where their skills need refinement and then to provide activities ("workouts") that help them develop their skills in those areas in which there is room for improvement. My job is to get them ready for the game.

Teaching as Iterative Practice

Course prep, and teaching the course itself, is an exercise in iterative practice. Honestly, this course is never taught the same way twice. As in any course that incorporates studio methods, I use the students' work and the associated critiques to diagnose what they understand and what they do not. If a lot of students fail to understand a key concept, I'll add specific activities in class to help them understand better. For example, we often examine additional examples of instruction based on the theory and talk through how various concepts from the theory were operationalized in the instruction. As in a coaching situation, class planning involves reflection on the strengths and skill deficiencies I observed in the prior week and then designing activities to either strengthen deficiencies or to move on to another skill set.

I keep the syllabus and schedule deliberately flexible so that the course activities can be modified based on my assessment of the needs of the students during class time (see Table 11.1). I do have in my mind a checklist of things that I want students to be able to do – my course goals – and I judge what happens in class against those. Because I assign homework assignments that enhance or complement what the students have achieved during class time, I wait until after class to finalize the homework assignment. If, for example, we are working on schema theories in class, students know that they will have an individual assignment on schema theories but I do not provide the actual task until after we meet as a class. Thus, for example, they may have analyzed instructional materials from the perspective of schema theory in class. If they did well on this assignment, their homework may be to apply what they learned to design a technology-based learning experience based on schema theory. If, however, they were confused about terms and strategies, I may ask them to do additional readings about the theory, to try to locate an example of instruction that illustrates schema theory, or to simply come up with a unique example for key terms or strategies of the theory.

Table 11.1 Excerpt from the syllabus.

Course requirements:

---

1. Class participation: For this course to be effective, everyone must come to class prepared to discuss the readings that have been assigned. Class discussions will extend the ideas gained through your readings to applications in practice. This means that you must have read the assigned materials and reflected on the meaning of what was read. If a full understanding requires you to look up and read additional sources, please do so. Bring the additional readings and references for those readings to class.

   Make-up/or missed classes: Since most of the real "work" in applying the theories occurs during class time, it is impossible to benefit from the course by simply reading the chapter. Please see me for details.

2. Written Tests and Assignments: Throughout this course, you will be expected to respond to regular written assignments. The purpose of these assignments will be to compare, contrast, and synthesis your knowledge of the various theories we examine. Questions will focus on applying and integrating the knowledge gained from course readings and discussions.

3. Application project: The application project provides a chance to apply the theories we discuss to the design of instruction. Each class member will design and develop an asynchronous lesson grounded in one of the theories we examine. The lesson can be self-instructional or designed for distance learning. Your lesson must be designed to teach one or two "objectives" and the goals, assessments and instructional strategies must be all consistent with your chosen theory. You are expected to:

   a. Present a prototype of your materials to the class. You will present your materials in class for input by the class. Plan to present your topic, your goals or objectives, and how you plan to assess learning as well as demonstrate how you plan to present the content and sequence your instruction. Your classmates will offer you suggestions for the lesson. Think of them as your colleagues, whose purpose is to provide you with new ideas for your project.

   b. Revise and submit materials. After receiving input from your peers, complete your 1) learning materials and 2) accompanying paper. More details will be provided in class.

Grading scale:

Tests and Written Analyses	425
Application project	350
Class participation 15 classes @ 15 pts per class	225
Maximum possible points	1000

I've built the course with the expectation that students will have a basic knowledge of instructional design principles, an understanding of the major learning theories, and some technical development skills, but some semesters the students have more or less prior knowledge, often depending on the way various courses are taught in the program. So, in many ways, the course is a moving target. When an adjunct is hired to teach a prerequisite or the instructor of another course changes, I often have to modify my course.

That's okay with me though. I just try to respond to the needs of a specific group of students and push that group as hard and far as I can. The primary goals, assessments, and activities don't change but, in some semesters, I can move fairly quickly, cover the theories in depth, and push the students to do complex work, and in other semesters I need to be satisfied with a limited number of concepts. Sometimes, I am lucky if students can develop a goal, assessment, and sequence of activities consistent with one or two particular theories. I do have in my mind a checklist of things that I want students to be able to do – my course goals – but I consistently modify the quantity of content addressed and the amount of support that students receive based on their evolving skill set. I begin with a minimum of structure, but most activities can be more or less structured, depending on whether the students, as a group, appear to need scaffolding or not.

I've tried various things throughout the years. I usually bring in example materials that demonstrate the theory in action, although sometimes students are assigned to locate examples to share with the class. Typically, they do these analyses in groups to provide practice in using the language of the theory to justify their perceptions, but we may do it as a whole-group activity if time is tight. Sometimes our classwork only focuses on analysis of existing products, and all design work occurs independently. Usually, they are asked to select a topic for their independent work and then to design a lesson for that topic consistent with the theory with which we are working but, sometimes, I assign the topic for the independent work. I've randomly assigned theories for the final application project instead of letting them chose their own. I've asked students to present their application projects throughout the course, as we discuss the various theories, instead of at the end. Each of these approaches work almost as well as the other; each approach has advantages and limitations. The important thing though is to think on my feet and remain flexible. If students don't develop an adequate understanding the first time, I modify the course activities and try something different.

It's not an easy class to teach. It's quite time consuming to provide students with the feedback that I do, grading and regrading projects. The challenge is in deciding whether a project is correct or not. For me, as the instructor, I am constantly pushed to think about the limits of the theory. I know how I would design a lesson according to a particular theory, but I am always challenged in deciding if some projects are within an acceptable variance/parameter or not. Another thing I try to remember is that I could be wrong. As long as a student is able to offer me a reasonable justification based on a correct interpretation of the language of a theory, I am open to modifying my judgment of the work.

From my perspective, my colleagues have entrusted me to help the students understand these things – to teach these students to apply these theories and I have this one chance to make sure they get it. Students view it as an important skill – as reflected in their willingness to repeat the course on occasion to explore the content in more depth. All in all, I get positive feedback from the students and other faculty.

I frequently consider turning the course over to another faculty member; because I've taught it for so very many years, it's rather predictable. But then I teach the course again and I see the light bulbs going off for the students. I see their enthusiasm mounting as they begin to see, often for the first time, how theories are applicable to the design of instructional products.

Also, I realize that experience counts for something. The years that I have spent teaching the class provide *me* with the precedents I need to arrange the learning events of the class in a way that ensures students develop a sense of how the three pillars of ID – design sensibilities, learning theories, and technical affordances – come together to result in a cohesive instructional product.

Learning to Teach, Teaching to Learn

In addition to flexibility and the ability to think on your feet (and often to think on your feet aloud), the main skill needed to teach a class like this is confidence. You need to be confident in what you know, and okay with what you don't know; confident that you know how to do what you are asking them to do; confident in revealing your thinking to the students; confident in the skills you bring to the table, and okay with the ones you don't. You need to be confident in order to give up the structure of a traditional class.

When using studio methodologies, you have no idea where the class will go. You have much more control with a prepared set of slides. Yet, you're not really giving up control; you still have control of the class activities. You try something and if it doesn't get the results you want, you try something else. But instead of controlling the class activities by presenting what *you* know to students, you orchestrate – "arrange, coordinate, or manipulate the elements of, as to achieve a goal or effect."

From my perspective, studio teaching isn't about showing students what you know; instead, it is about orchestrating activities that reveal, and then strengthen, the students' knowledge and skills. It's not something that you can learn to do other than by just doing it – and reacting to the situations that emerge. It all comes down to your beliefs about what it means to teach and learn design - the epistemology of the studio. Over time, you learn to anticipate how students will respond to particular activities, and yet there is no one right way. Every group is different. Instead, you think on your feet, respond in the moment.

But then, when you think about it, isn't that life? Isn't that what we do when we travel and work and interact with our family and friends? We don't learn to do it; we just do it. If it isn't right, we do it again. It seems to me that this is an important disposition to model for our students.

References

Brandt, C. B., Cennamo, K., Douglas, S., Vernon, M. and McGrath, M. (October 2011) 'A theoretical framework for the studio as a learning environment'. *International Journal of Technology and Design Education*, 23(2), pp. 329–348. doi:10.1007/s10798-011-9181-5

Cennamo, K. and Brandt, C. (2012) 'The right kind of telling: Knowledge-building in the academic design studio'. *Educational Technology Research and Development*, 60(5), pp. 839–858

12 Reflective Practice
Educational Changes Based On Professional Expertise

Fred M. Duer

I received my MFA in 1982 at Ohio University. My undergraduate degree was a Bachelor of General Studies that combined two years of studio art and two years of theatrical design into an original self-written, committee approved degree. Between graduate training and undergraduate school I worked professionally for two years. The last quarter of my grad program was an internship at The Old Globe Theater in San Diego. I was subsequently hired as a resident assistant designer for five years. My freelance career was based out of San Diego, as I worked around the country, until I moved to Los Angeles and began working in television. I worked in both television and theater for the next 15 years until making the transition to academia.

I teach theatrical scenic design to both undergraduates and to my own nationally recruited MFA candidates. I will be concentrating on the first graduate scenic design course taken during their first semester in a three-year MFA program. I will also relate how the course changed and my teaching and mentoring was adjusted after nine years at a major Midwestern R1 institution, Indiana University, to a smaller east coast, urban school, Temple University. The context in which I teach this particular course is the goal to bring my small group up to the same base level so that groundwork is set for subsequent courses. An incoming class at Indiana could be three in one given year with a total of five MFA students at a time. At Temple University I only recruit one each year for a total of three in the scenic design program at a time. The "Fundamentals of Scenic Design" or "Scenic Design Two" courses also have grad students from other disciplines; lighting design, costume design and theatre technology. I have on occasion permitted advanced undergraduates into the course. At Indiana University the students I recruited had usually been out working professionally for a year or two before entering the program. At Temple University the grad students tend to be even older having worked in the field for eight-ten years and, in one case, a middle-aged student transitioning to theater design from a 20-year HR career. The large east coast city of Philadelphia, with its thriving commercial theater center, is more appealing to a grad student who may need to consider work opportunities for a partner or spouse. I prefer an older student with some work experience as I have found they understand exactly why they want the MFA, where they are headed, and specifically in what areas they need to improve.

When I first started, I assumed the younger undergraduate student would be easier for me because they might not be able to see that I was new and inexperienced in teaching. This feeling was really just my initial insecurities coming out. In reality, the professional experiences I was able to draw upon worked to my benefit at either level. What I have found interesting is that the older students are actually harder to teach but, in the end, much more rewarding. The desire, perhaps demand, from a graduate student that we professors are superior teachers and mentors is what drives me forward. For these students, a simple explanation doesn't suffice in terms of explaining why a concept is being taught and, additionally, why it has become an industry standard in the first place. They want "it", the advanced degree, that badly and want to be pushed. The older student has put their working life and sometimes their family's life on hold to attend a three-year program, and they are often at a distance or in an unfamiliar setting without comfortable support and/or income. Adding to this, the student is extremely busy with classes, shop work, assistantship duties and homework for 16-18 hours a day. In addition, the older graduate student is secure enough to respond well to critique. Discussions of experiences to illustrate a concept can be a deeper conversation as the older grad student can bring their life knowledge to the table. In some classes I teach a mix of grad and undergrads and am always amazed at how the older MFA candidates can help the younger students with concepts, especially current pop culture references (that I may not be familiar with) as they relate to some of the traditional techniques I teach.

The challenge then is to read a new student and see what they need from you as a mentor. What kind of critique will be effective and what tools need to be strengthened for success in the working world? Along with this I had to remember that, as an instructor/mentor, I don't have to be their friend or their therapist, although that often happens. A colleague entering this level of graduate mentoring may have difficulty being able to give 100 percent to this type of teaching. I was late to academia after working professionally for 30 years. It was a conscious decision to "give" rather than "take." Before entering academia, I was working in Los Angeles in theater, television and film, but predominately in prime-time situation comedy. That particular environment is an overindulgent atmosphere where money is wasted and salaries are extravagant. When 9/11 occurred the industry shut down as we all began to question so many aspects of our lives. For me this was true as well. I had seen many of my cohort go into teaching after graduate school but I felt I needed to have something more to give with professional experiences to draw upon. At this point the timing was perfect for me; the right place and the right time. I have no fear of giving a student every single thing I was taught or every little thing I learned in the working world. I also know what I didn't get and what the student will need. A younger colleague may not be ready to "give" so courageously.

A first scenic design class is the leveling of the playing field. Often scenic designers start out in performance and then realize that back stage, specifically design areas, are much more rewarding with lower levels of competition. I teach about 50 percent of students wanting to go into teaching and 50 percent wanting to go into the professional freelance world. At the beginning of their programs, my teaching and mentoring is relatively the same. Later I am able to individualize the mentoring to a specific student's desired career path. This is a benefit of small classes and small programs. It can't be stressed enough that, when you have the opportunity to gather this kind of personal information, it can only help your teaching and your project creation; and in some ways your grading. Adjusting grading criteria shouldn't be the norm but an example of when it might be valid is when a grad student from another discipline, costume or lighting design for example, takes one of my scenic design courses, I can appreciate their willingness to step outside their comfort zone and to look to what they are getting in the process and not in the end result. In addition, I try to relate concepts being taught back to their own discipline.

As I began writing the syllabi for my entire graduate curriculum, I looked toward the concept of sequencing first-, second-, and third-year scenic design courses. Within that framework of six semesters, I also created a list of major scenic design constructs and inserted them into each course. Another element of this sequencing was dividing up genres of theatrical history and types of theatrical presentation with entertainment disciplines. The goal of helping the student to create a diverse portfolio at the time of graduation was also a component of how I divided up the courses and projects. At Indiana University I created three sequenced "design" courses and initially one was to be taught in sequence each fall semester.

Combining all the elements needed for a well-rounded scenic design sequence was an entirely new experience for me. I wrote each concept, historical genre, theatrical style, entertainment genre and script I wanted to teach on an index card. I was then able to arrange the cards on a large surface until three courses' worth of projects were cataloged. The analog method of moving around index cards also helped me visualize the larger sequence that I felt was necessary for an effective MFA program. As I began to stack cards alongside each other I found that some things were interchangeable and that it was possible to combine, for example, sculptural space, theatre in the round, colored pencil on black paper, and Greek Drama. Another example of this would be; multiple location design, proscenium presentation, musical theatre, and finished presentation model. The combinations were limitless but certain concepts began to fit together nicely. I found I could also build on previous components across a semester and from year to year. In this way student challenges, as mentioned above, were worked out sequentially.

There was some overlap of course, but the projects were ever changing in a way that made me believe the students would still be encouraged to explore, and not to rely on "tricks" that they knew had worked on a previous project. "He liked it the last time, he's sure to like it this time." In fact, it isn't about "what I like"; it is about effective design and the communication of that design. It helped the course stay interesting to me as well because my mentoring was always fresh and I couldn't rely on my own personal mentoring "tricks." Granted, from year to year patterns started to evolve in what I saw from particular types of students from particular types of educational backgrounds, as I mentioned before. None of the patterns in my unscientific data collection was true research, just small indicators that I was doing something right because similar student struggles were illuminated to me.

At Temple University however, there were six semesters of scenic design for the graduate students, with a constantly shifting enrollment of other design disciplines from both the graduate and undergraduate population. I had control of who was let into the graduate classes but I was encouraged to keep enrollment numbers up. The idea of sequencing projects, as mentioned above, was next to impossible. For the Temple courses, I combined all the projects from all the sequenced scenic design courses I had previously written into a list of 14 projects with over 50 script choices. The list was carried through the syllabi of six semesters. In this way I could guide a particular student to the project that best fit them at a particular time in their studies. Each project has unique objectives and specific concepts to address and, for the MFA candidates, I reserved certain projects to first, second and third year so there was a semblance of sequencing for them. This was an interesting challenge for me because it was a whole new way of looking at the sequence that I had been teaching for nine years. It is always helpful to rethink one's personal pedagogy. Similar patterns of mentoring began to emerge even when working with diverse students on differing projects. Due dates were the same even though the script choice differed. With a bit of guidance, I am able to suggest particular projects that work well together at the same time, across the room. An example might be that a student working on a large "golden age" book musical would be tackling the same design constructs as a student working on a multi-location Jacobean period piece such as *The Duchess of Malfi*. It may sound a bit absurd but both could be dealing with the seamless movement of changing scenery.

The course consists of discussion, demos, and presentation of design projects. I space out the due dates of larger projects with in-class work made to be completed in 75 minutes. Most presentations are made informally, with emphasis on a safe environment "around the table" for feedback and brainstorming of a student's ideas. I teach a structured sequence of steps through a design process from script analysis, scenic breakdown, and visual research to thumbnails, sketches, and finished presentation of colored renderings. Some projects will culminate in a rough or finished portfolio quality scale model and/or drafting. Each major project group has an overriding concept such as, actor's movement in space, solving the specific scenic requirements, designing for multiple locations, or designing for a specific actor/audience relationship, as in the theater's architecture. In each case, the student being able to present ideas in a logical and effective manner drives my mentoring. Theater design, as with most visual art forms, is not an exacting science; and thank goodness for that. Outside the classroom, the creative process can be threatened by budget, time, manpower and resources; as well as the challenge of collaboration. By the time a theater artisan gets to graduate school the concept of collaboration is the exact reason they chose theatre design in the first place. With so many challenges to artistic creation, teaching a sequenced process will make it easy for creative thinking and readjustment later. I teach the communication skills linearly even though that is hardly ever the reality in the working world. To help drive this home I also will act as "the producer" during a presentation to get the student to think on their feet. Examples might be, "Your budget just got cut in half, how will you redesign?" or "The artistic director doesn't like what you and the team have come up with, you have an hour to rethink it and present it again." A challenge of the design classroom in a collaborative art is that the student must also be their own director. In theater a director usually creates the initial concept or path to the storytelling. On "paper projects" there is a bit of designing in a void. So if I can jump in and act as another voice, it will give them experience in dealing with this type of collaboration. In the working world, these types of revisions are actually the norm and not the exception.

I am reminded about the student who wants to be "perfect" right out of the gate. This sometimes manifests itself in "what do you, the professor, want?" In other words, what do I have to do to get an "A?" There is also the competition that occurs with students trying to impress me. Another similar situation is an undergrad trying to impress the graduate students to justify their admittance into the course. In all these cases I try to keep the assignment's objective at the forefront and to create a safe environment for experimentation or even failure. In general, there isn't a right or wrong in design.

It was interesting and eye opening to me initially that a huge part of design teaching turns into therapy. Obviously there are personal boundaries that a professor needs to respect. But simple questions as to time management, creative blocks and personal habits relating to school work are where advice can be offered. I shouldn't have been surprised about this because many artists fight these challenges, particularly perfectionism. When I realized this, it was an easy leap to helping a student merely based on how I worked through this to carve out my own successful freelance career. I know there are things I help students with that I never would have discussed with my mentors. Surprisingly enough, the more I taught, the more my freelance career, or summer work, was freed up. As I used my outside work as classroom examples, I found I needed to mirror good collaborative and creative strategies. In other words, how I get it "out of my head" and onto the paper.

Another component of effective teaching that I began to develop was the idea that "skills" and "design" had to be separated, particularly at the beginning. Too many times I heard: "I can't learn this painting technique or this computer skill fast enough to present my ideas." I also heard: "I have great ideas; I just can't draw them the way I see them in my head." I realized quickly that my artistic brain had melded skills and design together merely by working professionally and having to deal with deadlines on a daily basis. A paycheck means time management and you figure it out quickly or you don't succeed. When I turned to teaching, I had to get information out of my head that I had rarely had to stop and explain before. I just did it; I didn't have to talk about it. I wasn't even sure how I know what to do, as in "what to design" "or "how to draw it." I began to dig back to find out when and how I learned those skills. What had my mentor taught me and what had the working world taught me? In searching for these answers, I started to remember that my mentor didn't offer up solutions, he just gave the feedback that helped *me* find the solutions, and there were plenty of times I didn't find the best solution. Also, interestingly enough, I remember like it was yesterday the critiques where I didn't succeed and felt I had let him down. Those memories reinforced in me the idea that I didn't want to create that feeling in my students. After reflection on this, I distinctly remember that it all fell together and the connections (what my mentor was trying to pull from me and why) were made after a few years of working professionally. Also, as I said previously, the deadlines and a paycheck are a great motivator. The notion of leading the student to solutions was an effective one that I could mirror. There were others, however, that I did not want to adopt.

Part of my initial pedagogy was predicated on what I didn't get from my mentor and on making sure I was more effective than my own examples. My mentor hadn't had an extensive professional career before entering academia and I wanted to make sure I helped my students make the connection a bit earlier than I had. The market is tougher now and I believe it is my duty to give my students all the tools I can. In thinking it through one step farther, it wasn't that the working world would be at odds with a linear design process, it is just that the successful designer needs to constantly revise and adjust to changing situations or a production team's changing direction. Would I be able to get that into my pedagogy? The modern student needs more than me lecturing them at the front of the classroom with "Wait till you get out there…" or "Look around you, only 10 percent of you will survive in this business…." Teaching by intimidation is a thing of the past, as is "Listen to me, I'll tell you what it's really like." I needed to find my own version of what I perceived as scare tactics.

What came to me as I was writing my first syllabus was the sheer amount of concepts/skills needed for scenic design. Script analysis, research and its

interpretation, sketching, drafting, model building, and accurate communication are all major components of scenic design. I remember as a student
that it was all thrown at me at once. If I could separate the "skills" from the
"designing," I believed students would have more success. If I could tell
them the specific goals and desired outcomes early, then I could help them
stay on track. To be perfectly honest, I never had goals and outcomes listed
in a syllabus when I was in school in the 1970s. This seems so basic to
academia now.

Thinking through the idea of separating design skills from design content
also helps the student who suffers from "the first sentence disclaimer
syndrome." As they set their project on the table, they are not allowed to
start with: "I can't draw but" or (the worst) "It's not perfect but." I spend
a lot of time correcting misconceptions and encouraging critical thinking
related to the student's art and design.

Undergraduate programs in theater vary greatly across the country in
scale, depth of pedagogy, and in professional level of faculty. With diverse
educational and life experiences, I have also found their understanding of the
past is lacking. In theater, the golden age of American musicals from the
mid-1940s to mid-60s, and forward to the explosion of the rock operas of
the late 60s and 70s, and the multimillion-dollar British imports of the 80s
and 90s, are all references they need to know. Another area I find missing is
the concept of connecting American history to the arts. The modern student
may have had art history and American history but is unable to make the
connections between them through the 1900s and the timeline continuum
that it represents. I find myself thinking back and wondering if I had that
awareness in graduate school and, truthfully, I think I had a good amount of
it. To alleviate some of this, I started what I call "Need to Know" or "N2K."
I created a list of 150 individuals from fashion, pop culture, theatre, film, art,
including choreographers, directors, producers, illustrators, sculptors,
photographers, and fine artists. I try to stay away from mainstream artists
covered in art history survey courses or theatre artisans covered in theatre
history. The area of illustration is rarely covered and it is of particular interest
to me in scenic design because illustrators tell a very important story in a
single, effective/efficient image. However, illustrators were sometimes
shunned by mainstream artists or institutions; particularly children's book
illustrators and popular poster and graphic designers. At least once per week
throughout the semester, each student presents three of the people from the
list, in a predetermined order, so disciplines are similar across that particular
day's list. They only have to identify and give a few key pieces of information
(with a visual) on the individual and spend no more than three minutes on
each one. When they can make a connection with somebody else from the
list, we pretend to ring a call bell. Of course, I have ordered the artisans in a
particular sequence, but we ended up calling it a "ding." As in "is there a
ding for this person with somebody else on the list or from a previous day's

presentation?" I use the list throughout the three-year MFA program and, depending on how many students are in a particular semester, determine when we get through the list, to simply start over. It has been so popular that I had to create a second list of art and architecture, furniture and decor, and American popular history, culture, and music. Even if the presentation is short, the name recognition will help the student recall something that identifies an area of research needed to complete the identification. I have found that, after doing this for several semesters, I can begin to throw in the "ding" while we are talking about other things in other areas of the course or throughout the day. I imagine this sort of thing could fit just about any discipline. Because I try to catch them outside of the classroom it keeps it from becoming pure memorization and regurgitation of internet research. In the theater design disciplines, concepts, individuals and nomenclature are used not only in the classroom but in the practical education of production.

The course is two days per week for 75 minutes per day. This schedule of two meetings per week (usually Monday and Wednesday) gives a larger amount of homework time for a project later in the week or weekend, after having class only two days apart. I plan on large components of projects to be due after a weekend. On the meeting days that are 48 hours apart, I try to assign smaller elements of a project. I found this out the hard way when no additional or progressive work had been done on assignments on Wednesdays. My syllabi are very complete in their structure and all assignments and due dates are known at the beginning of the semester. Along with this (and other) class work, a grad student also has shop work for their assistantship for four hours every weekday afternoon and a practical design assignment on a production. These are assigned a year in advance. Not all students in each class have the same production assignment so I also try to take into account the production schedule when creating my syllabus. A production can have 18-hour days during the technical and dress rehearsals when a production is being finalized before opening night. It may seem like a lot to weigh all these factors in creating a syllabus, but I'll get much better work from a student if they are not rushing through an assignment late at night. All I have to say is "give yourself the screw-up time." In other words, give yourself the time to try again because it can only get better.

This also goes back to separating the skills from the design. I know where they are in their skills training, thus what can be assigned in the design class to sequence the use of those skills. The successful student learns very quickly the necessity of time management in an academic setting and, with reminders from me, how necessary time management is to making a living as a freelance artist. I believe the training and the constant reminder of time management are the same for either career path – academia or working professionally. I find myself saying, "if you think this is hard to balance, wait till a pay check is attached to the creative process and there are life commitments like family and a house, to name a few." To those who think teaching is the easier choice, I have to say: if you can't see yourself standing in front of the classroom and enjoying every minute of it, you may want to reconsider. For theatrical design in general, you need to not be able to live without it - you need to want it that badly.

Between large assignments, I include in-class work sessions or in-class work assignments to space out the due dates. The time between components, of which six or seven comprise a major project, allows for incubation time. Nothing is gained by rushing an artistic process. There needs to be time to let the ideas develop naturally and unrestrained by deadlines; to "simmer," "stew" or "brew." There are a host of cooking references similar to this: "putting it on the back burner" and "letting it marinate." Deadlines are real, so my advice to students is to learn how and what they did to get ideas out of their head and onto the paper. Remembering this when they have plenty of time allows them to draw upon it effectively when life gets in the way and time is precious. The creation time in grad school is a luxury and the perfect time to learn about oneself as an artist.

The physical facility for this course at Indiana University was a large computer studio (smart classroom) made up of drafting tables that included a PC computer station, scanners and large and small format printers. Along with being able to present from a master computer, the students' stations could also be projected to the front of the room. This made for easy presentation of my materials and theirs, but the large drafting tables and computer monitors created an obstacle for free discussion. Sometimes the students buried themselves in the computers. It was a circuitous walk around the room behind them to check on what they were actually working on. I rearrange the room to make space for a large table that the students could gather around. This was for discussions, demos and, with the close proximity to the master computer monitor, it was also used for more intimate presentations. There weren't drafting stools with wheels for the first few years I was teaching in that classroom, but these were acquired after suffering with stool legs being scraped across the floor. At Temple University, the design classroom had smaller drafting tables that did not block student and teacher views, and a wall-mounted large monitor. But there are no computer-equipped design studios in the theater department so students used their own laptops. Without a hard-wired system to the presentation monitor there is a lag time to get a student's laptop hooked up and communicating properly.

Indiana University is an extremely digital campus (with free student software) whereas Temple is not. Digital artwork and drafting were just beginning to be taught when I joined Temple's faculty. In my pedagogy both hand and digital techniques are used. As in most art forms, the groundwork must be laid with hand techniques as a basis for digital work. I believe an effective designer must be able to combine older analog art skills with digital techniques. I'll also add the word "efficient" to design because the digital environment has certainly helped that aspect of theatrical designing. Because theatrical production, and the design aspect of it, is fluid until the audience is included; changes, revisions, and adaptations will be made up until opening night. Working efficiently and communicating these alterations to a shop or a production team is paramount to success and longevity. In my early career, I assisted older established designers for several years. One of my primary jobs was to make the changes and communicate those revisions to the appropriate parties. This was before the use of computers. Although it wasn't easy for me to change, after hand drafting for 25 years, I needed to take the time to learn and keep up to date with digital technologies. My graduate students have been recruited by me personally and they know when they come to study that they will be learning to combine all manner of skills and procedures. The age of a prospective scenic design professor will determine what is being taught in a particular program. The same is true in the working world. A busy older designer may not have the time and the inclination to learn digital drafting and rendering, but their hand art work will undoubtedly be exquisite. Hence a younger designer looking for assistant work is able to bring digital skills to an established professional studio. Because I still teach many traditional hand techniques, students come to my program to learn what other programs with younger professors do not teach.

A course project consists of sequenced steps through the design process. There are some recognizable steps published in theatrical design textbooks that are great starting points for beginning students. I have adapted those steps and refined them based on my personal experiences. After a student learns to follow a process, they are then able to adjust to their personal style or a particular production's timeframe. This feeds right back into the concept of connections being made later, as mentioned above.

The first step is to analyze the script. It all starts with the written word. Unlike other art forms, a theatrical designer gets to start with a great document that is loaded with information. They are breaking down the script into informational bites; from time, place, and action to the realities of exactly what is needed on stage. Along with this is the design team's concept. In other words, how the story is being told. Research is the next step. It can be anything from an inspirational piece of artwork and evocative imagery, or photographs of an actual location, to historical visuals from the period of the script. In theater, the period can include when the script was written, when the piece is set and/or where or when the director's concept sets the production. The next few steps can vary in order. I prefer to start with thumbnails leading to sketches, proceeding to value sketches, with my medium of choice being grey markers. At this point, as other members of the design team may not have been added yet, a sketch is not precious and can easily be tossed aside when changes occur. I prefer a white model as the next logical step. A white model is usually made from card stock with a varying degree of detail, but it is to scale, defines the three-dimensional space, and can be created quickly. Color is eliminated until the designer and the team has progressed forward. Color is added through a colored rendering and/or a colored model. The term "rendering" is used because it illustrates a moment in the production, complete with lighting, as it will be seen onstage. Hence, "rendering" the light or "rendering" the moment. The color of the costumes and color of the lighting is added at this point. Other methods for communicating color are a color presentation model or a paint elevation. A paint elevation is an exact two-dimensional schematic (to scale) of how the color and finishes will be painted on the scenic pieces. Both of these components are viewed under white light, to be duplicated on the actual scenic pieces. They will subsequently be analyzed by the lighting designer using colored light on a model or color swatch to determine its effectiveness.

An important component of the process in scenic design is the drafting. Whether digital or analog, it is a step that can never be skipped in an actual production because it is how the design is communicated to the shop when being built. In a paper project, however, it is not always necessary to do a full drafting package as it tends to be the mechanical aspect of a project instead of the artistic component. Again, this is where the skills can be separated from design. This is an interesting correlation to what I mentioned above about assisting an established designer as a way of breaking into the business, because drafting is one of the skills that are most often needed when working as an assistant. In separating drafting from design, I don't want a student to only design what they can draft or fail to design a particular element because they don't know how it will be built. Designers, both professionally and in academia, will always be able to get assistance in how something can be built.

I have projects that encompass the entire design, to a finished presentation quality portfolio piece, as well as projects geared toward specific skills and steps. I don't have the same component due on each project group and a project could be all about the process and not just about the end product. The students know ahead of time what is expected on each assignment and project group. If a particular design begins to head in a direction that lends itself to a differing final component we can adapt because my classes are small. An example of this might be that communicating a scenic design may lend itself to a grey-marker storyboard of scenes with color indicated with a collage of research and swatches. This may be more effective/efficient than a full color model, which is time consuming and difficult to photograph or transport. Because the students are also sharing and presenting their journey throughout a project, the discussion of communicating ideas is what dictates the method or skill that is used.

The critical factor to teaching this way is to listen to the students in their first few weeks, perhaps through their first large project. This course is the first design class of their three-year MFA. I like to find out how they are used to working, how much I should "jump into" their process and if there are any hurdles that might be blocking their creativity. An example of the latter would be a student who loves the research phase. They load up their work space with piles of books with pages marked. Or perhaps they have folders full of digital inspiration, but they can't get to the next step because they are overloaded with imagery. Because they haven't defined how they will use the research, they don't even know where to begin in their selection process. In an unspoken manner, I am also setting the tone of how I mentor. A very independent student or perhaps an older student, who may be set in their ways, may find it difficult to have someone in the middle of their process making suggestions. Another example might be a student from a smaller liberal arts undergraduate program where there weren't a lot of structured courses in design. They just happened to be the one interested in design or were thrown into designing by their professor without complete training. If a student welcomes the feedback, then I also need to be careful to not do the opposite, i.e. handing them too much and blocking them from thinking on their own. My challenge and what I like the most about this type of mentoring is the individuality of figuring out what will work the best for each individual. Additionally, what works for one student may not work for his/ her classmate across the room. I have no problem in being perfectly open about this to help them understand why they are getting particular unique feedback.

The question of grading is challenging for me. My education began in a liberal arts university in studio art. Those two years consisted of two levels of all the areas of studio arts; drawing, painting, sculpture and 2D and 3D design. I remember feeling that a lot of my studio classes were evaluated on "good art/bad art." Perhaps I was young, not fully comprehending, or perhaps education was different in the early 1970s; but I promised myself I wouldn't grade in that judgmental manner. I also felt I had a lot of professors who taught by intimidation. What I mean here is exactly what I stated previously which was the process may be more important on some projects than the end result. Because I am teaching communication and collaboration in one of the most collaborative art forms, the idea of "gallery worthy" finished artwork is very subjective. The artwork being done in scene design is a communication tool, nothing more. Because my mentoring is very one-on-one, I owe it to my students to include explanation alongside a grade. I have found the discussion of a project or the progression through it has become much more important than the grade itself or, at the very least, they exist hand-in-hand.

I need to make sure they understand where I stand on grades. The grades and "points" will come into play if the students aren't bringing in work or presenting substantially on each due date. I have found that a student from a BFA program is all about "talking." Sometimes that includes talking to hear themselves talk, and in some cases to cover the lack of work on the table. Conversely, a student from a small program, or perhaps an undergrad program without a professional faculty mentor, may find it hard to talk about their work at all. I ask them about what they were feeling while they were drawing. Not to over analyze but to help them figure out how they got to a particular point so they could go there again. I try not to make this too much of a therapy session, but more to find what impulses are being blocked and perhaps what issues I have to adjust in them that were implanted by another teacher. I have found there is a lot of damage done at the high school level when Student A didn't win all the high school art awards, and then he/she was told they were not an "artist." I try to open up their minds and make sure they are ready for three years of effective thinking and exploring options. Theatrical collaboration is about freeing yourself to be open to all the ideas set forth by a team and successfully combining that with your own inspirations without letting your ego get in the way. An example might be an independent student whose reply to a question about process might be "I always do it this way," or "this is how I was taught." Their career will include critique, in academia and in the working world. Some students react better than others. I have heard students say "What exactly do you want me to bring to the next class?" and/or "Why don't we have more freedom on these projects?" You can't please all of them, all of the time. But, if an extra sentence from me helps the situation, I will always make sure the assignment objectives are clear; and clear could be as simple as "Try my method on this one and you can see if that works for you." Experience has taught me that my method will work for them and guide them to much more success down the road. The difficulty comes when a younger student has come straight from undergraduate school where many decisions are set in stone for them or handed to them by a professor who got it from their professor. That could be merely a survival tactic of a professor surviving in a smaller program where they are forced to wear many hats. A mentor, who hasn't worked professionally with several different types of producing organization, will not have the options that are created by diverse experiences. It is personally interesting for me to determine when a student's professor was trained based on how and what they teach their students. There are many design concepts and techniques that have been carried through from the original mid-century training programs that can now be rethought as technologies and aesthetics change.

I'd like my students to think critically while, at the same time, realistically. The latter would be my comment to the student who wants to impress me quickly upon arriving and tries to do more on a project because now they have the freedom. With that type of student I simply say, "thanks, but there really is no need." "You are in the program already, stop trying to impress." In most cases, I'd rather see a great thorough process that perhaps didn't culminate successfully in the end than more "stuff" hitting the table that cannot be backed up with substantial thinking. This is not the concept of suffering for your art, it is more the idea that I want to see them working through challenges. What is gained, even without acquiring a portfolio piece, will be put to use in the very next project. It might seem, from the previous paragraphs, that I might seek out the challenging student and that I may have contradicted myself when I had earlier stated my preference for older students who knew what they wanted and why they came to grad school. To be fair, the challenges are easier to write about. As a teacher, and personally, I tend to be a "fixer;" I enjoy the challenges. The reward comes with the hard work. The well rounded and grounded student pushes themselves and soars the minute they arrive at graduate school. The pleasure and return for me, and for them, is seeing how far they can go. An example is brought to mind of a student who did indeed come straight from an undergraduate program but was just waiting for the attention from an individualized mentor. He came in with a great work ethic and began to hold back work from the round table discussion because he didn't want to show up the rest of his cohort. He'd wait after class and show me additional work that was farther ahead of the assignments. Besides being a joy to see and a surprise, I asked him to include that in his presentations and to not hold back. I told him he could be and (indeed he was) a great impulse for pushing the rest of the class forward.

I have had, in some years, students who would like more time to work on a particular project, as cited in the phrase: "I can't learn it fast enough to create the perfect project." If I am able to present the assignment parameters with the concepts clearly stated then they have limits that can help creativity instead of hinder it. When I have graduate students from other theatrical disciplines in my courses that haven't had me as an instructor on a regular basis, I see the uncomfortable panic in the first few weeks. They begin to appreciate the projects are not "product" oriented but "process." Later, in all of their lives and careers, everything heads toward "product-"oriented success. This is the time to be able to create the working patterns of time management, and for finding out how their creative brain actually works. In reaching out to former students with a question about the effectiveness of this technique they mentioned that concentrating on the process helped the design "reveal itself" because time was given. In the working world, time is a precious commodity. Learning a process also helped them to participate with a design team and practice effective collaboration skills later in their working careers. Again, this is because proper time was spent and the steps along the process were presented in a similar fashion to showing a director or team a design as it is being created. Product-based pedagogy puts a lot of focus on the end product and then I feel it heads toward "good art/bad art" type mentoring. That tends to be subjective. I have found that, given the chance, students know if it's "good" or "bad," if we have to use those terms at all. It is really whatever their definition of good and bad is for themselves. Keeping progress presentations an open dialogue through the process actually helps them get to the end more effectively because they have had feedback along the way. Bringing a project in at the end without understanding or appreciation of its development tends to put too much weight on one component. Perhaps things just didn't come together on a particular final rendering or model. I can still appreciate what went into it and I know where it was headed. Plus, it gives me a hint as to where a student needs help on the next project. At the end of the semester I include in my syllabus a "Revisit/Redo" project, which lets them do exactly that with a previous project. Invariably it comes back much better, because the end product due date wasn't looming over them. Also, there is a bit of reflection on what might have gone wrong.

Once they get used to how each concept, technique, or element builds on the previous one, and that the parameters are set out in the syllabus, they realize success is attainable. I even go so far as to say "If something happens and you don't have your completed work on a presentation day, attend class anyway." The discussion within the room will be just as important for them to hear. I have found that this freedom to have a small misstep keeps them on track and focused. A grad student's workload can be overwhelming but, because they come to the program so highly motivated, very few due dates are missed and I am rarely taken advantage of. They are also told that, later, a missed due date could mean the loss of a job, so learning to multi-task is stressed from day one.

In general, I find I try to fit too much into a semester. I thought that, even if each project doesn't culminate in a finished portfolio piece, I could concentrate on one component of the process and squeeze more of those components and concepts into a semester. Most students love that the course keeps moving and they are never on one project for a long time. Many courses taught by my colleagues in other theatre training programs (at comparable universities) spend an entire semester on one large project. That seems too easy to me. I need to be inspired to mentor and I owe it to the students to work hard at giving real and constant feedback instead of looking at the same project and saying the same thing each week. When the student moves to another project within the same semester, they will invariably use what they most recently learned. This was a conscious decision because working on one large semester project means they will inevitably put off the work until later in the semester and/or boredom sets in. In talking with students from other grad programs that I work with during my summer freelance projects, they relate experiences of trying to come up with just enough or something different to get the professor to think they are still working hard on their project. I don't want my classroom environment to feel that way.

The concept of filling the syllabus up too tightly is an issue I address each August when I revisit and revise each course. I have now taught this course many times at two different universities and each time I reevaluate this issue. I record in the previous semester where things stumbled or what happened that caused revisions within the semester to make sure I address it in the coming year. I am not afraid to revise due dates, lecture demos, and in-class projects within a semester. I hate racing to catch up if things get off in the syllabus. I will be honest with myself and address it at an effective point in the semester to keep things moving forward smoothly. Early in my teaching I'd hold on to the syllabus as if made from stone. I have grown to be able to let go when needed, even though it can be hard to rearrange within a tight schedule. An example might be to put a "catch-up" day in the syllabus, later in the semester, for that exact purpose. I will also take an assessment of where students are when it is getting close to a big due date. If great work is progressing, but the semester is particularly busy with production or other course deadlines, I will move a due date. But, in order to do this, I need to see that they are all working toward the completion of their projects and just not procrastinating. In the long run, I'd rather not see a rushed project that won't give the student anything in their learning or for their portfolio. I'd rather see additional time used to get the projects to the next level successfully. Understandably this is the luxury of a small class roster. Each semester, each roster is unique and must be treated as such. If I have a few undergrads mixed into my grad roster, I'll take a bit more time on certain concepts. When I present something that is a hands-on type class demo, like the use of colored pencils, introduction of a computer modeling program, or white model construction techniques, I call it a "workshop." I put several days in the syllabus with the generic label "Workshop." I use these days to space out due dates but also to find out what is needed. In the first few weeks of the semester I can poll the class and see what concept or techniques need to be introduced or reiterated. If a student has had that workshop already and feels comfortable with it, then they don't have to come to class on that day. I can then present at a speed that works with the particular cohort attending that workshop session. What I have found interesting is that an advanced student may come to class that day anyway saying they could use the practice. Another adjustment might be to add a particular project into the listing if I have a designer from another discipline or another major. If I have an architectural student for example, I'll try to find a particular script that speaks to that aesthetic. Or, if I have a lighting designer with an interest in new media, I'll find a script that calls for projections. Conversely, I may guide them to something outside of their comfort zone on a different project just to push them a bit farther. All this rearranging and adjusting could seem hard on a professor, but it is what I owe my students and the reward will come back to me in seeing their success. I believe it has helped me gain the respect of my students in a way that makes learning inevitable. This probably doesn't work as well at the undergraduate level but it certainly does when mature discussions of the realities of life, as well as of multi-tasking and time management, in grad school take place. I have found very little abuse of this give and take.

When everything is working effectively in my classroom, the rewards are plentiful. A recent event happened in which I interviewed a current student of a past student who is now teaching at the university level. The past student had struggled but worked extremely hard to improve himself. Seeing the skills passed along to a second generation, and seeing my techniques and my methods being taught, gave me a feeling of joy and accomplishment and an unexpected smile of pride.

13 The Creativity Habit

Brad Hokanson and Marit McCluske

Introduction

Imagine you are taking a new class and at the first session, as one of 80 students, you are given a banana or an orange. Before you start to eat, you are asked to peel your fruit in a way that is different from how you ordinarily do, and in an unusual manner, and to sketch your efforts as you proceed. While you're familiar with the fruit, you've never given much thought as to how to be creative in this ordinary part of your life. This is the start of a different form of thinking in the class, one that will continue with a series of challenges and exercises to increase your personal creativity. The first assignment will build on this; it is to eat something different, and it is the first of a series of challenges called "differents" that encourage divergence through your entire life.

How this course, Creative Problem Solving, is taught, and how it has developed, is the focus of this chapter.

I knew this course on creativity was unusual... let's say different... the first time it was offered. Sometimes a course will have a life and power all its own, much like a novel or poem has its own momentum, and this certainly has been the case with Creative Problem Solving. In the middle of teaching the class for the first time, I was walking through the college administrative area and the assistant dean asked me if I was teaching a cult. Puzzled, I asked what prompted her question. It turned out that, independent of my knowledge, my students had all decided to wear aluminum foil in a class to which I was a visiting lecturer. Some had foil skull caps, others aluminum ribbons in their hair, and some wore foil jewelry. They were expressing their individual creativity while declaring their solidarity with me and with each other - and their difference from everyone else in the class. My understanding, both of the course and of aluminum foil, was changed substantially. Students were and continue to be enthused about how the course changes their creativity and thinking processes.

Having taught for years in the design fields – in architecture, in graphic design, and in instructional design – I've come to understand that creativity does not develop spontaneously, even in design or studio courses, but must be specifically addressed as a topic. At the same time, many aspects of the studio environment are critical, such as the action-oriented and direct

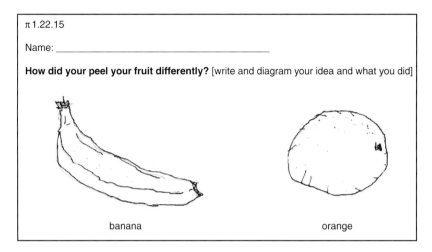

π 1.22.15

Name: _____

How did your peel your fruit differently? [write and diagram your idea and what you did]

banana   orange

Figure 13.1 Idea capture form, from first day of class. Brad Hokanson.

personal involvement of learners. It was in my college and graduate studio courses where I had the opportunity to be inventive and divergent, which helped me develop my creative capabilities. This time in studio has inspired my teaching methods.

The studio format was the constant, a structure for learning and working. Studio was always a presence, a way of life, and then there were other classes. That was true in art, in architecture, in urban design, and in instructional design. I'm not sure if I was *taught* design, but rather I was in an environment where I *learned* design. No one ever said, "Here's what an idea is. You should have one." It was something you discovered. The challenge of design centered around a guiding concept, which was central to a lot of my learning.

The necessity for creativity, for human ingenuity, is without doubt. Creativity is a skill that can be employed for a small task or for a large project and in everyday life. Creativity is important in any field, from business to mathematics, from engineering to the arts. Businesses around the world recognize this skill as essential and seek out the most creative workers for their enterprises. It's also recognized through the achievements of a lifetime; research has shown that creativity is three times as strong an indicator of future lifetime achievement than intelligence (Plucker 1999). The goal of this course and this proposal is to increase the creativity of each student.

This course is looked on as a continuum; as a set of projects that act together, like a longer-term treatment. The real goal of the class, to develop creativity, can be seen in the various aspects of the projects and exercises; to develop the ability and habit of generating more ideas (ideational fluency); to develop the capability of finding, refining, and stretching problems, leading to different types of solutions (ideational flexibility); and to build a capability to keep (retain, save, select) and develop ideas that are unusual and unexpected (originality). Developing a *habit to vary* will continue the impact of the course; recent research has shown increases in measured creativity are retained after two years (Im *et al.* 2015).

Understanding the nature of how any course is developed, presented, and improved has great value to education and the design of instruction. From our writing, we hope to better that understanding and to build our own classes and knowledge. The authors are the lead instructor of the course and a former graduate teaching assistant for the course. Most of the narrative is by the lead instructor, Brad Hokanson, with additional discussions in the text boxes by Marit McCluske.

> I was a teaching assistant for four semesters in the course, teaching six different sections of the course. At the time, I was a graduate student completing my MFA in graphic design, and I'm currently a faculty member in graphic design and I teach an interdisciplinary design thinking and creativity course developed from parallel research to this class.

The Idea

From the beginning, the central concept of the course was not to *teach* students *about* creativity, but rather to *train* them to *be* more creative. This changes the nature of the course from presenting information about creativity to trying to consciously change the character of the learners and, over time, to build their creative skills. This is our calling, since creativity among US schoolchildren, as measured by the Torrance Test of Creative Thinking, has declined significantly since 1991 (Kim 2011). The opportunities to become creative as a child have decreased just when the value of creativity is being most recognized.

So I *teach* a class that is different from most, different in many ways, not least in the process of how it is done and how much of what I work on can be considered "training." My goal is to build a series of self-directed habits for creativity, a habit to vary. This would be a different conceptualization for any course. It is a course that is experiential, not abstract or mediated. Learners do the "differents" themselves, in person, reporting back to the class about their experiences and process.

Most design faculty believe that creativity develops within their design studio, not recognizing creativity as a separate skill with a need to be explicitly taught. Based on my research, creativity does increase in studio courses somewhat, but not to the extent that it does with dedicated instruction. Teaching specific design skills often drives out the general creativity skills.

All parts of the course are used to develop creativity; from warm ups, to demonstrations, to exercises, to taking attendance. Assignments are integrated into students' everyday lives, changing how they eat, how they talk with others, and what they wear. In every session we do exercises and activities in class, and learners are pushed to generate more ideas. Every week they do something... Different. Repetition, development of positive habits, and conditioning all play a part in the course curriculum.

> Effective communication of the relationship between the learner and the idea being presented becomes paramount to the success of each project. Almost every discussion session would involve some type of exercise designed to facilitate effective communication of creative ideas. Group exercises helped develop greater understanding of empathy and the personal realm of creative possibility of another: What is deemed creative for some is routine for others.

More than the development of declarative knowledge, this course seeks to improve the skills of learners, showing them methods of generating new ideas. It builds the habits of learners to produce long-term systems that encourage creativity, and it works to change the beliefs of learners about their own creativity and their own limits.

Figure 13.2 Wearing Something Different. Marit McCluske.

Being more creative comes from a set of characteristics, including knowledge, beliefs, skills, and habits. In this course knowledge, the traditional lead component of most university courses, is the least important aspect.

Belief

Belief comes from our experiences and exposure to ideas as well as our positive opportunities to be creative. The most important component of being creative is a belief in our own creative capability, and that creativity is present in us all. Importantly, our level of creativity can be increased if we choose to do so. However, our belief in creativity must be followed by acting in ways that help us to develop that creativity by challenging our assumptions and personal limits. All of us are often constrained in what we can do by what we believe and by our social context.

Therefore, much of the effort in building one's own creativity is to develop the courage and persistence to be divergent; the ability to withstand the judgment of others. As most new ideas are unpopular, there is a natural tendency to continue with the existing status quo. To bring forward ideas, one needs to have the capacity to experiment and try new things, often at the risk of not succeeding or being embarrassed.

Vygotsky (1978) held that learners can only learn material for which they are intellectually ready, only accepting new information "adjacent" to their own understanding. Similarly, learners in this class are often constrained by societal and personal pressure to conform to existing standards of behavior and response. Excursions outside of expectations are self-edited or repressed. Most times, students cannot be *that* different from the norm. A conscious effort to extend student responses into the developmental zone will enable later responses, effectively building a callus, not a scar, for the learner. We seek, in the class, to stretch the personal envelope of each student.

There are generally two groups of students that make up a class. One group consists of those that have a conscious need or desire to develop their creative thinking skills, often approaching their weekly Do Something Different (DSD) with a defined problem to solve. The second group of students are often much more hesitant and timid at the beginning of the semester due to the divergent nature of the course. A distinct sense of fear is apparent upon asking them to do something out of their comfort zone. What quickly evolves from this mix is the empathy needed to approach problems from multiple points of view. The nature of the course allows for a culture of empathy to exist in an environment typically lacking in personal engagement.

Skills

The specific *skills* of creativity need development, whether in the process of making something habitual or in the conscious use of a creative methodology. Practice in using creativity techniques will make skills more habitual, even for the simplest task of generating more ideas. At first, there are personal limits to how many concepts or ideas an individual student can develop, but the ability to create more will come through practice. Methods for creativity must be internalized and be part of the student's everyday experience.

Generating a lot of answers involves both inspiration and the ability to withhold judgment. Each class has an exercise or a drill to generate a lot of ideas. This is both a practice within the classroom and a presentation of the various methods of idea generation for the student to use long after the course has concluded. Exercises gleaned from a range of creativity techniques are used and include brain writing (rapidly generating multiple answers), random-word stimulation (answers triggered by a random word), mind mapping (graphically representing idea connections), and random-image stimulation. An online and mobile phone app has been developed to continue this practice away from the classroom.

One successful method for generating multiple ideas is the Attribute Listing method. It begins with an existing object or process, from which a listing of every possible attribute is generated. This includes functional,

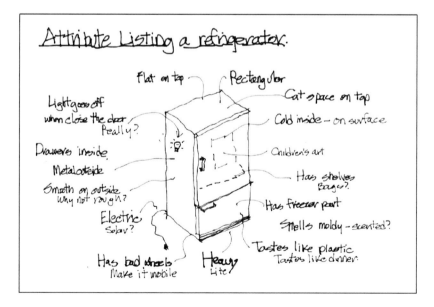

Figure 13.3 A sketch depicting an Attribute Listing exercise. In the exercise, attributes of an object or process are listed, then changed to generate new ideas. Brad Hokanson.

visual, acoustic, taste, and smell. Each attribute is then changed in some manner to create a new product idea. For example, the refrigerator door that has children's art display space can be transformed to hold and display new digital art... or recipes. Also the smell of what's been in the refrigerator can be sniffed by the appliance itself: "Maybe it's time to change the baking soda!" the refrigerator of the future could tell you.

> Students practice idea generation tactics for fluency, frequency, and originality, and students are able to see how they compare and just how much improvement may be needed. Much of the course is re-learning the creative thinking skills they may have once had, and within a school setting. Therefore, I would draw on a lot of research from games and play to help mediate group work. Sometimes too much focus is placed on the "challenge" aspect and students forget to realize that a part of creativity is curiosity, playfulness, and fun.

I would often have students engage in short design prototyping experiments in which one sense (sight, hearing) is substituted for another. Students would generate alternative uses of an object or a space, and then redesign an experience for a partner in which the primary sense engaged is swapped for another. Alarm clocks, way-finding signage, and cell phones were reinterpreted, designed to emulate how children experience the world through multi-sensory engagement, or how visually impaired users can navigate a space through sound. The goal was to generate a large range of ideas that explore how a routine habit could be creatively altered by altering the primary sense engaged.

Habits

While often viewed as restricting creative action, regular *habits* can work to develop, demonstrate, and increase creativity. These types of habits include consistent development of multiple divergent ideas, regularly providing more responses than are required, involving oneself in challenging and different activities, and consistently seeking to be more creative. Assumptions and personal limits on action can be addressed and overcome at the same time.

Perhaps the most important habit for learners to develop is the *habit to vary*; habitually doing divergent things, taking on new challenges as a matter of course, and extending one's limits. We can vary many things in our lives, from the routes we travel, to our music choices, to what to have for dinner, with positive effects on our creativity.

The large assignments, the "differents," of the course are designed to change student habits; to encourage them to move past their current habits of what to eat, how to sleep, and what to wear, and to develop in them a larger habit of adventure and exploration. This takes time and repeated practice and, of course, it requires doing something different.

Differents

While the course has changed a lot over the years, the overall direction was set from the beginning as a course that trained the students to be more creative through a series of challenges to "do something different." These differents can be seen as starting points for becoming original and creative.

Many ideas for the course were inspired by teaching I did with Gerry Allan at the Minneapolis College of Art and Design in the early 1980s. Early instances of differents were used in general studio classes for art and design students. Each Different or DSD is organized along a specific theme, such as eating, talking, or giving. We begin the differents with changing everyday activities, such as what to wear or how you travel to your home, and increase the complexity to be more reflective and engage with others.

The differents begin with basic challenges that can be minor changes to one's regular habits or more substantial redefining of a problem. Subsequent challenges are more complex and reflective, pushing the learners to directly think and examine their own lives. They include doing something your "other" does that you never do; remembering something you did as a child; finding somewhere to sit without electronic stimuli and then listen for an extended period of time; and selecting one of the previous DSDs to re-do. Perhaps the most personally challenging externally related DSD is to "give" something different.

The first challenge is often to eat something different. Entering college provides a number of opportunities for students to change dietary habits and to explore new foods. For this project, many students immediately seek out different ethnic foods. Some manipulate their current eating pattern by wearing their food, eating it upside down or under water, or reshaping or blending their normal diet. The more adventuresome expand eating to go beyond traditional foods and consume flowers, twigs, ants (as a garnish to chocolate-covered strawberries) or grass. The most exploratory answers involve redefining the challenge, as students end up eating their words, or eating breakfast in the back of a police car, or eating pineapple upside-down cake ... upside down.

One of the more memorable examples of an "eat" something different was a student who made pancake batter - from dry ingredients, oil, and egg - in his mouth. After mixing thoroughly, he spat it out on the grill for cooking and later consumed the finished pancake. With syrup. And relish.

In an online version of the course, one student from Cambodia noted she often ate tarantulas, which, where she lives, are common, tasty, and often served as a snack. What made them different was to have tarantulas on a sandwich. She had never eaten a sandwich before.

Figure 13.4 Wearing something different: clothes to read the newspaper at the bus
    stop. Jude Michael.

A more complex example of a Do Something Different is the challenge to
do something your significant other always does that you never do. This
requires reflection and observation of one's roommate, parent, boyfriend, or
pet, and selecting those traits, such as peeing standing up (boyfriend), obses-
sive compulsive behavior (parent), chewing tobacco (roommate), or riding
in a car with your head out the window (dog), that are interesting and repli-
cable. Implementing the task on a day-long basis can be both embarrassing
and surprising: One single dad copied his nine-month-old son and wore (and
used) an adult diaper through the course of a day.

Perhaps the most normal and yet divergent different of this type was a guy
who went to Victoria's Secret and convinced them to fit him for a bra. He
measured a 36AA, and the salesperson deftly noted that Victoria's Secret
didn't carry that size but provided him with a training bra. In the changing
room, and with his girlfriend serving as the camera operator, they recorded

Figure 13.5 Eating something different – bagel with cream cheese, via one's feet. Lindsay N. Smith.

his experience in trying it on. While he did need some instruction from his girlfriend, he was clearly in "different" territory.

Each challenge becomes more complex and begins to be judged in the context of the class and not in society as a whole. After weeks of personal exercises, interacting with others becomes important to developing one's creative skills. About ten weeks into the semester, students are challenged to generate a DSD for someone outside of the course to complete. Most often this person is the roommate or friend who has been photographing the previous DSDs. In some cases, however, others are recruited to participate. As evangelists for creativity, the students strengthen their own personal creativity and develop an understanding of the nature of creative challenges. Rather than specifically directing an activity, each student needs to *give* a challenge instead. Brothers have been dramatically made up, fathers have received pedicures, and mothers have snuck out at night to cover a neighbor's tree with toilet paper. Changing gender appearances has led to unusual outfits and adjustments in restrooms.

I did wonder who that guy was; sometimes, near the beginning of class, you don't remember all the student faces, and the guy in the back with the mustache and stocking cap looked sort of familiar. He listened intently as we sat through the other students' work and then, when Annika took off her

Figure 13.6 Something your "other" does. Annika Q. Yan.

disguise and describe how she had used the men's room without incident all day, it became clear....

Evaluation of these projects through the critiques and discussions of each assignment becomes part of the learning process of the class. While there are parts of the assignment that are very objective – such as requirements for pre-planning, multiple initial ideas, photographic documentation, and a written description – the essential aspect, originality, is a subjective evaluation.

While most of the course focuses on fluency, the ability to rapidly develop multiple new ideas, the DSDs are evaluated subjectively on *originality*, the novelty and uniqueness of creative efforts and whether the idea was creative or merely different from their ordinary activities. As creativity is often evaluated in comparison with society, the instructors of the course base their decisions on their own experiences as guiding heuristics. If they have done something similar, it's merely different, and not yet original. If they could imagine completing something similar, it's moderately creative. If they laugh or gasp at the idea, indicating cognitive dissonance, it's very original and gets the full score.

As the term progresses, learners are also asked to work with others as partners, as part of a team, and eventually to convince a willing civilian to attempt their own DSD. The series concludes with the construction of a Rube Goldberg Machine, a contraption that completes a task in an inventive, yet overly complex manner.

One difficulty with the defining feature of the class is the nature of creative ability itself. Explaining the complexities of creativity as it relates to weekly projects becomes tough when the concept is challenging enough to define as it is. I found that sometimes students want or need extra guidance and feedback regarding the quality of ideas and "if they're doing it right." There's always some disorientation that's associated with the novelty factor of the class, and it tends to emphasize some of this need.

As the value of success is rooted in the idea, students are encouraged to report on the results of their work regardless of success or failure in execution and planning. The point is it had a result and they can learn from it. Additionally, oftentimes students become too engrossed in the thought of just getting out of their comfort zone.

During the projects that required a reflection on habits and beliefs, students frequently quickly evolved from overt "differentness" – generating the most unique idea possible - to executing a more subtly creative idea that offered up commentary on their daily experiences as college students. Many student projects explored the ingrained biases against what's different from their own experiences. Students have used these projects as a gateway to explore homelessness, either through interviews or through the act of giving to strangers, with the intent to provoke others to think more critically about biases.

The differents evolve through the semester as students gain more experience. The differents change relationships with peers and social groups as well as the student's understanding of and ability for creativity. Students become more capable of doing something that, just weeks earlier, would have been unthinkable.

Evolution

The course began as a freshman seminar in 2000. It continued in seminar form for six years, and over that time the course material developing iteratively.

The course subsequently developed into a large lecture course when it was required by one of our departmental majors. This necessitated a number of changes in course structure, including the use of a course management system for collecting course assignments and grading and the use of teaching assistants to lead discussion sections.

About half of the students in the course are from our Retail Merchandising major, with the rest of the students coming from across the University.

Students are generally not design students, and come from areas such as journalism, mechanical engineering, and business.

The course has recently shifted to a full online version for one of two annual offerings. In alternate semesters, the course will continue to be offered in an in-person format. It is unlike many other courses that move to the online environment that focus on the delivery of information, development of learning through discussion, and evaluation through digital quizzes. It also functions like an online studio course, with substantial work away from the computer, located in the daily life of the learner.

Project collection in both versions is done through an online course management system, with each assignment requiring written documentation and visual recording of the activity, ranging from single images to polished videos. In the discussion sections, the DSDs are presented and critiqued by the instructor and teaching assistants. The best-in-section examples are collected to be presented to the full class where a best-in-class is selected.

As with many other studio courses, there is constant pressure to be more productive and to reach more students, and this will shape the future of this course. The first format changes, from a small seminar to a larger lecture course, are understandable in any university environment. The move to an online environment is a similar shift.

Projects often become a lens through which the spectrum of personal meaning is discussed, even very early on in the semester. The associations between creativity and personal significance or expression are made through assignments that ask the student to "do something different." For example, in the case of wearing something different, students need to consider what is different for their own personal comfort zone, but also what is considered different for their culture.

This can add another level of complexity in critiquing the assignments. It's very similar to being in a studio class and critiquing a design or a work of art in which the creator has expressed a lot of personal value. There is a challenge in being able to provide feedback on the quality and creative skill of the assignment as a whole while separating it from the personal significance to the student, and not critiquing their personal experiences or values.

This is something I find to be a unique way to observe and understand the dynamic of meaningful communication through creative experiments as a whole, which is arguably the most fundamental component of design.

Table 13.1 Percentile increases calculated from raw scores.

	Average Standardized Scores [mean = 100, SD = 20]						
	F2009	F2010	S2011	F2011	S2012	F2013	S2015
pre-	101.76	115.56	107.17	110.69	111.65	110.18	112.03
percentile	53.51%	78.17%	64.00%	70.35%	71.99%	65.62%	68.46%
post-	129.35	129.67	129.25	128.01	130.05	132.03	132.8
percentile	92.89%	93.10%	92.82%	91.93%	93.35%	91.01%	91.78%
Number [N]	50	33	36	80	41	89	46

Assessment

Providing an outside benchmark for learning, everyone in the class is tested using the Torrance Tests of Creative Thinking. The Torrance Tests were developed in the late 1950s and are the most used standard test for evaluating creativity. The TTCT focus substantially on the aspect of divergent thinking. Learners are tested at the beginning of the term and at the 12th week, with results provided to students to help them understand and internalize concepts of the measurement of creativity.

Measurements of student creativity indicate a class development from a beginning average 67th percentile to a final average at the 93rd percentile in measured creativity. Personally, the course remains interesting and one that is consistently changing and different from previous experience. The theoretical background continues to develop and the research opportunities remain strong.

The Torrance Test provides an important personal connection to a research-based understanding of creativity, as well as a vocabulary to discuss concepts of creativity such as fluency (the ability to generate a number of ideas) or originality (the development of rare or unique ideas).

Instruction

This course does afford me the opportunity to work with a limited number of graduate teaching assistants in a teaching and learning environment. Their development and collaboration has been an important part of the growth of the course.

In a similar way to the students, teaching assistants evolve through teaching the course, from a more didactic approach to one of leading students to become more creative. In the end, the operation of the course must be a performance in and of itself; fluid, dynamic, and improvised, not choreographed.

Teaching assistants are also challenged by the skills nature of the course, comparing the course, consciously or unconsciously, with their own learning experiences. For this course, most have been selected for their ability to interact with younger students as opposed to a specific skill in a discipline. They must deal with a topic that is more abstract and ephemeral, and less visible than, for example, graphic design or drawing. Studio courses in general are about providing questions and challenges, and not answers. Within this course, we go beyond the traditional discipline-based course and focus on a different skill.

Finish

One of the concepts of the course is to have learners build their learning experience in the "real world" and within their own personal experience. It is about changing their processes, their thinking, and most of all their habits, and encouraging highly skilled and motivated students to engage in this open-ended, complex learning method. In many educational experiences, most skilled students quickly seek and find the one correct answer to a problem, getting to "done" as soon as possible. However, this class specifically seeks more and different answers. One central tenet is that the only wrong answer is *one* answer, a model that is strange and cognitively challenging for many, but essential to creativity.

Students are often surprised by this as a course and challenged by the nature of the learning. Their previous experience in education is often one of information delivery and retention and not of skills development. They do not expect a vision that includes the experiential or problem-based procedures of the course. Most of these students have already been highly successful in didactic, lecture-based, information-delivery teaching situations, and seek to continue that success through doing the same things, not by being encouraged to do something different.

References

Plucker, J. A. (1999) 'Is the proof in the pudding? Re-analyses of Torrance's (1958 to present) longitudinal data'. *Creativity Research Journal*, 12(2), pp. 103–114

Im, H., Hokanson, B. and Johnson, K. K. (2015) 'Teaching creative thinking skills: A longitudinal study'. *Clothing and Textiles Research Journal*, 33(2), pp. 129–142

Kim, K. H. (2011) 'The creativity crisis: The decrease in creative thinking scores on the Torrance tests of creative thinking'. *Creativity Research Journal*, 23(4), pp. 285–295

Vygotsky, L. S. (1978) *Mind and Society: The Development of Higher Psychological Processes*. Cambridge, MA: Harvard University Press

14 How I Gave Up ADDIE for Design Thinking, and So Did My Students

Monica W. Tracey

It was August 2007 in the desert – 120 degrees with dust swirling under the beating sun as the world's largest mall sat unfinished – when I realized that this was not my typical design project. I had been hired to lead a small team tasked with designing instruction on how to clean the soon-to-be-open Dubai Mall for over 400 non-English-speaking laborers. All the information generated from our initial meetings, our initial needs assessment, and even the client's initial request had suddenly become irrelevant. The project had veered onto a new course as the mall was behind in construction, the laborers were not yet in-country for training due to visa issues, and the instruction that we had already designed was no longer wanted. I was in a foreign country, with most of my design team in the US, when I realized that everything I learned in my ID (Instructional Design) courses could not have possibly prepared me for this. The only way I was going to be successful in this design project was by pulling from my 20-plus years of experience, my ability to live daily in the uncertainty of this project, and my willingness to rapidly design numerous solutions knowing that none of them might work and that I would likely have to go back and start again. This project forced me to realize that the students I was teaching would not be able to do this work if I continued to teach design the way I was taught and the way it was currently being taught in the classroom. Although I always knew that the step-by-step approach to teaching design did not apply outside of the safe confines of the classroom, I had not up to this point realized I was actually doing a disservice to my students. After seven years of teaching design, my methods of instruction were permanently altered by this epiphany.

From Business to Academe

In 2001 I made the transition from full-time instructional designer to full-time academic when I accepted a tenure-track position at an urban university in the Midwest. I stayed at that institution for five years when I was offered a position at a neighboring university. It so happened that I earned my PhD from this same university, so I was returning to a familiar place. My new (and old) home was an Instructional Technology program that is over 60 years old and offers masters and doctoral programs. The program was solid and steady but changes were imminent as retirements were occurring and new faculty with new ideas joined the program. I was given primary teaching responsibility for our introductory Instructional Design (ID) course. I took this same course 13 years before and it was almost identical. As I was preparing to teach this course, in the back of my mind I was remembering when I took it, and how I was already working in the field. What I was learning in the classroom at night often did not align with what I was practicing the day after class in my workplace.

ID Is More Than What We Think It Is

This course is a first-semester requirement for all graduate students in our program; hence their range of experience, knowledge, and motivation is quite broad. The course, as it stood, marched students through the ADDIE process in a linear, step-by-step fashion. This was perhaps typical for similar introductory courses in ID but I knew from the start that the layout of the course was *not* how real designers practiced, at least not based on my experience in the field. Design is based on constraints, and designers make decisions not by following a model but from their experiences and the constraints of the project they are constantly faced with. Design is not systematic, but rather a space where designers work with others to innovate solutions to constantly changing complex problems. On top of this, the course had to be offered online, as it was a first-semester requirement for our online master's program. I was resistant to losing regular, face-to-face contact with my students during this critical period in their graduate training. They would be exploring and developing the foundational concepts that would indelibly shape their educational and professional experiences, and I felt it was imperative to have personal, face-to-face interaction with them individually and as a group during this time. Design is a messy business filled with uncertainty, and having my students not immersed in that messiness and uncertainty is a disservice to them when they go into practice. Thus, these two issues (real-world relevance and the online context) emerged as the most significant and pressing constraints as I planned my approach to the class.

Change is Difficult

As a new faculty member, I wasn't sure how far I could go in terms of revamping the course, so my initial changes were measured and preliminary as I gained my footing. Rather than using the previously assigned text and the traditional assignments (conduct a needs assessment, create a design document, create an evaluation plan, etc.), I started with a new book, *Real World Instructional Design* (Cennamo and Kalk 2005), and introduced cases, problems, and group projects to the syllabus. During that first semester,

I pushed students to move beyond ADDIE and other simplistic models in favor of a *designerly way* to solve these complex design problems. I knew they had to be exposed to instructional design models, but did not believe that was the first thing they should be exposed to when learning about design. In a 15-week course there was still too much time spent teaching the waterfall approach to design that I was struggling to move away from. As the semester progressed, it was clear that these initial changes were not enough; my students were not grasping basic design thinking. They continued to look for a simple formula to design complex problems. It is difficult to explain that, when working in design outside of the classroom, they were not going to be able to spend four weeks conducting a needs assessment, then four weeks creating a design document, and so on. Rather, they would be working on all of these tasks simultaneously and would need to be working in a constant design/reflect space. This is not an easy concept to model and teach.

The other professors in the department were supportive but did not have similar backgrounds in design and did not understand the issues that underlined our failure to prepare our students for practice. In addition, some of the students did not have an interest in design at all; since the class was required for all graduate students, they were just taking it to meet the requirement. Although my passion lies in design, they were not seeing it; the complexity of it, the challenge of it, and the innovation behind it. The students were not responding to the course materials and I was frustrated, knowing they were not prepared to conduct real-world design activities after 15 weeks in class. They believed that if they took a design model into the workplace they could follow it step-by-step and design effective solutions. I knew this was not the case and they would fail in the workplace. My students deserved better and the course had to change in a fundamental way.

Going All In

One of the first areas I tackled was the class context. Despite my pedagogical reservations, teaching the class online was non-negotiable so I decided to embrace this constraint instead of fighting against it. After two semesters of teaching this course through the university's LMS (Blackboard), I moved the course to a Google Site in conjunction with Google Applications. This opened up the possibilities of altering the teaching and learning opportunities. I created a page for each week of the course on the main Google Site, with the outcomes, instructional materials, assignments, etc. for that week leveraging Google's suite of apps to include reflective journals (via Google documents), peer groups (who interacted via Google documents, chats, and video-based hangouts to provide input on each other's work), and group assignments (drawing on these same tools). This Google-based LMS provided channels for communication that approximated face-to-face interactions

Figure 14.1 Google site for the course.

much more closely that what had been possible in Blackboard, particularly through the use of shared documents, chats, and hangouts.

Changing the Content

With a more workable online environment for the course in place, revamping the content was the next step. Nigel Cross's book on design thinking (Cross 2011), and discussions with designers outside of the field, helped me realize that teaching the "how" without teaching the "thinking" was fruitless. The required text became *Design Thinking* by Cross (2011), introducing design *before* even mentioning the term Instructional Design. For seven weeks students read about and watch design examples that have nothing to do with the ID field. From jewelry and wheelchairs to race cars and can openers, students are introduced to the diversity of design and how it influences all corners of life. Using Google Documents, they write prompted reflections every week about design in general, about their own experiences with design, and about their individual identity as a designer. One example includes a prompt asking students to describe something that they have designed (*not* instruction). They write about and send pictures of gardens, items they have designed to hold articles, a two-dog leash, etc. The purpose is for students to learn a little about design knowledge in general, the *designerly way,* and then to begin to use those principles to learn about instructional design. The prompts provide scaffolding for students, forcing them to look at design as a holistic activity, and to look at themselves as the arbiters of design who will have to deal with uncertainty and the challenges of the design space, before we move into the specifics of instructional design. When we do reach that point in week eight, the foundation they have in design thinking helps them

---

Assignments: Please complete these in the order listed.

1. Watch the design videos. In order to view these, simply copy the links below and paste them in your internet browser.

Home Products Designed With You in Mind

http://www.cbsnews.com/video/watch/?id=7366888n&tag=contentMain;contentBody
In this CBS News video you will see an overview of design described. Keep in mind that this is a video about **DESIGN**.

The Dazzling Jewelry of Van Cleef and Arpels

http://www.cbsnews.com/video/watch/?id=7366884n&tag=contentMain;contentBody
In this second CBS News video you will see design resulting in jewelry. Keep in mind that once again this is a video about **DESIGN**. Note the similarities this video has with the overall discipline of design.

2. Answer the **Journal Reflection Question #1.** in a Google document. Create a Google document and label the document with your LAST name and the course number as the title of your document, i.e. 6110_Baaki_Journal. You will use this **one** Google document for the entire semester. Each week's reflections and case studies will go above the previous week's reflection.

3. Read the Boling and Smith article and Chapter 1 of the Cross book, Design Thinking.

4. Answer the Journal Reflection Question 2 and 3 below in your created Google document.

Week 1 ends at 11:59 P.M. on Sunday, January 18.

IT 6110/LIS6350 Week 1 Journal Reflection Questions

1. What are your thoughts today about design based on watching the two videos?

2. According to Cross - "Everyone can and does design. We all design when we plan for something new to happen." Describe in detail a time when you designed something. How (if appropriate) was it - effective, efficient, creative, imaginative and/or stimulating?

3. Describe a time when you felt totally uncertain. Try to remember how that felt and the greatest challenges you faced because of the uncertainty. What did you do to handle it? Knowing that is part of being a designer is **always** dealing with uncertainty, how do you feel about being a designer?

Figure 14.2 Assignments from Week 1.

better understand and manage ID's particular complexities with more confidence, as well as the resources and understanding of how it relates to the big picture of design. Students begin to learn that they are designers first; the product they design is instruction or instructional experiences.

Each student shares their reflection journal with only me via Google documents, and I read each journal and respond and provide feedback in detail every week. This gives me the opportunity to ensure they have an understanding of design thinking *before* we introduce instructional design. I respond in depth to journals from each student, usually taking 16 hours to read, respond and provide feedback (the class allows for 25 students). Those first seven weeks are critical in helping students get into the right mindset about design and assisting them to *unlearn* anything they may have picked up along the way. Many students are frightened and unsure at first and positive and in-depth feedback is key in those first seven weeks. Supportive yet clear statements to guide them to begin thinking in the design mindset are critical. I typically see the growth by the 4th or 5th week, and by this point it is becoming clear which students "get it" and those that don't. For example, those who get it discuss the realization that they have to embrace uncertainty, that they are the mediators of the design space and that, using their precedents and the uncertainty they feel, they have the ability to innovate a better solution. Those students who need additional support talk about how they want a formula or a step-by-step process to design a solution.

Home products designed with you in mind

©SUNDAY MORNING

MAY 22, 2011, 11:07 AM | For more than 30 years, Smart Design has created signature designs for companies as diverse as OXO and Ford by employing a simple credo - design is about people, not things. Michelle Miller reports.

Figure 14.3 Screenshot from video assigned Week 1. CBS News.

Those who get it often state they don't necessarily like uncertainty, but will learn how to use this state as it is a key part in design, while those who need additional support are afraid of uncertainty and want to control it. Those are the students who need additional feedback, additional meetings with me via Google hangout and support from their peer groups. While most students embrace the design thinking approach because they see the big picture of design and its impact before we begin to learn about instructional design, some face trials with the shift into the designerly way of thinking. Those students are the greatest challenge and the greatest reward. Additional time and energy with them during the introductory course through additional design examples, discussions about design and its impact on day-to-day living, acknowledging their fears and answering their questions, results in a better understanding of design in general and the impact of design in their lives.

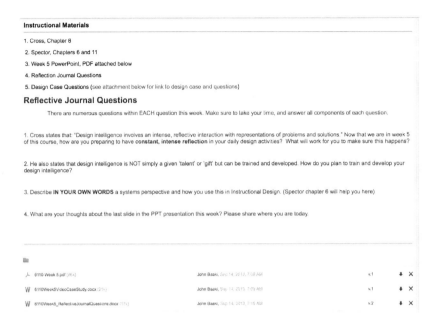

Figure 14.4 Assignments from Week 5. Note: Reflection question #4 referred to a slide that addressed uncertainty in design, so students were being asked to reflect on their own thoughts about uncertainty in design.

Introducing... Instructional Design!

During week eight of the course, we begin to delve into the specifics of instructional design. Students begin working with the *Foundations of Educational Technology* book by Spector (2012). This introduces students to the ID field and it is critical to help them create the bridge of design with the product they will design; instruction. Students begin working on ID case studies, starting with easier tasks (such as identifying constraints in an ID situation and mapping the relationship between these constraints), and then moving to more complexity (such as, here is a problem, how do you visualize the end solution?). Peer groups are formed at this point to support students' giving and receiving feedback; they communicate through a shared Google document and chats or hangouts as needed. For their final project, students are asked to outline an ID problem that they are interested in solving, and then I surprise them by giving them another student's problem and giving their problem to someone else to work on for the rest of the semester. In other words, one is now the designer and one is now the client. The students are forced to deal with uncertainty as they encounter a problem to be solved that they did not create and having to work with someone they do not know very well. The students then communicate via various Google apps to ensure the designer has a clear understanding of the potential learners, client needs, and situational constraints before they begin, as well as during several draft cycles. The designer and client meet with me so I can support them in resolving challenges and model questioning and real-time design sessions. We work in small teams while they use design principles, focusing on problem/solution throughout the rest of the semester. The instructional product students produce is detailed in a concept map that links context, learners, outcomes, instructional strategies, material resources, assessment, and evaluation. In addition, I continue with the individual journals to gauge how they are aligning design and instructional design. Again, rather than relying on an ID model such as ADDIE, students follow general design principles: identify a constraint, come up with a solution, see what that solution brings in terms of new constraints, solve those, and so forth. Institutional grading is based on their individual journals, peer review journals, case studies, designer, client and instructor meetings and the concept map with supporting documents that lead to the final submission.

Where Do We Go From Here?

The course continues to evolve each semester. Students are guided through personal discovery, especially in the first seven weeks when they journal about themselves and their beliefs, experiences and knowledge of design, with the aid of the Cross (2011) book. When the students move to the Spector book, which is quite different, we focus on making the connections with the designerly way and designing instruction. Weekly journals help identify student misconceptions while providing scaffolding in developing designer professional identity. The high points are their responses to the questions "What is design? What is instruction?" asked three times throughout the semester. Seeing their growth, how their definition of themselves as designers evolves as they attempt to design their own solutions, watching students design using the principles; accepting uncertainty at the least and embracing and using it at its best. The reflective journaling generates more engaged interactions with each student and provides me with the opportunity to get to know him or her on a very personal basis. When a student is struggling with a concept or challenged with a design problem, we can identify it and work to resolve it in large part because of this engagement. There are times when students try to stay in a structured box and not stretch themselves by using the constraints as tools to push themselves in a new direction. *But*, being involved and engaged with each student is the key to identifying and supporting them during those times. The commitment needed to teach this class in this way is at times overwhelming. Students are extremely engaged and hungry for feedback (they submit Sunday night by midnight, I read Monday and Tuesday), something I realized when one week I had to wait until Wednesday to read and provide feedback. Students were sending emails and chats asking if I was OK and if I had their Google Document. We are in this class together. The Spector (2012) book provides students with the needed ID terminology, but does not force them to use one model, something that is supportive of the goal of introducing design and instructional design to new graduate students. Students work in design spaces and try to identify those spaces over time; however they know that one space does not necessarily precede another space and that they will be in and out of each of these spaces on numerous occasions.

The design and development of this course is based on design theory, design knowledge, and the study of design from an interdisciplinary perspective and numerous years as a designer. Reading those in the ID field whose research and writing support design principles and a holistic approach to design (Smith and Boling 2009; Gibbons and Yanchar 2010, etc.) reinforces the decisions made each semester to persevere, even when the results are not ideal. Designers know that design is not a simplistic process; students need to see and embrace complexity right away so they are not naïve about designing. Although the notion of students in a physical studio appeared to be ideal, in the end this online design affords an intimacy a classroom may not have provided. The goal of this introductory ID course is to introduce design, ID, and to help students begin to identify and develop their professional identity. The online format aligns with those goals. Group design projects are not optimum for this format, but students aren't ready for that challenge in the early stage of their design identity development. Students

---

Week 14 & 15 (4/13/15 - 4/26/15)

What space are you in and where do you end up?

Thursday, April 9, 2015

We are down to the final two weeks. Everyone is moving along. Keep it going! Keep designing!

Now, design what ifs become design decisions. Design exploration becomes design commitment.

What space are you in? Where do you go from here? Here are my thoughts. Paste into a browser and enjoy!

http://www.screencast.com/t/H1KqgWSLbbB

Week 14 and 15 Outcomes

1. Embrace prototyping and testing - Communicate the core elements of solutions to others and learn what works and doesn't work to improve solutions.

2. Keep prototyping toward an Experience Design Prototype. (Week 14)

3. Give us something to **react** to and make it **rich**! (Week 14 and 15)

4. Reflect on your instructional design journey. (Week 14)

5. Complete an Experience Design Prototype. (Week 15)

Figure 14.5 Instructional message for Weeks 14 and 15.

Reflect on the following:

1. As you reflect back on your work on your instructional design project, what role has uncertainty played in the process for you so far?

   How have you responded to uncertainty? Has it influenced how you move among design spaces or other aspects of your process?

2. Knowing that you will be presented this week with an additional element for your final EDP, how do you feel about the uncertainty of that?

   How are you preparing to manage the unknown?

3. What have you learned about design in general and ID specifically this semester?

4. Go back to your previous responses during this semester on the "What is design?" question.

   What has changed in your definitions after completing this course and your ID project?

5. Go back to your previous responses during this semester on the "What is instruction?" question.

   What has changed in your definitions after completing this course and your ID project?

6. How do you see yourself as an instructional designer? What does it mean to you to be a designer?

   What kind of designer do you see yourself as? What goals do you have for yourself? What actions will you take to develop as a designer and reach those goals?

Figure 14.6 Reflection questions for Weeks 14 and 15.

work on a group design project in the follow-up course to this initial design course, with the intention that they will have begun to develop their design precedents and will have a richer experience in a group design project after the initial development of their own skills. In this first class students conduct weekly peer reviews, beginning in week eight when introduced to their individual design problems. This supports an exchange of ideas and concerns and provides students with the opportunity to give and receive design feedback. By using Google documents and Google chat students record their meetings, allowing me the opportunity to understand their thought process and to provide additional written feedback while each is working through the design problems. We also meet weekly in Google Hangouts, the designer, the client and me, to discuss their design projects, the constraints, and to brainstorm solutions. While hesitant at first, this has proven to be an effective means of communication; an opportunity to have a real-time visual discussion and provide feedback. Maintaining the focus of this course on the designer and design in general, and not be as focused on ID specifically, is challenging. Although students will gain specific ID knowledge and experience in follow-up courses, it is at times difficult for the students to think conceptually and holistically and not narrowly on systematic ID.

Design is not a black and white process and some students initially struggle with that realization. Watching each student try to live with uncertainty through very challenging journal questions and readings that seem to make no sense to them requires persistence and trust on the part of the students. Constant contact with each student is required, reading and responding to his or her journals and being available anytime on Google chat. The first four weeks or so are critical as students begin to change their design mindset. Change is difficult and some in the field are not fully committed to the design thinking approach across all coursework, so students may learn ADDIE in the evaluation course or the needs assessment course, forcing me to attempt to *undo* what they have been taught. At first it appears easier for a student to follow ADDIE rather than live in uncertainty and draw on precedents, principles and professional identity while designing. However, through patience, persistence and positive feedback I was able to give up ADDIE and so are they.

References

Cennamo, K. and Kalk, D. (2005) *Real World Instructional Design*. Belmont, CA: Wadsworth/Thomson Learning

Cross, N. (2011) *Design Thinking: Understanding how Designers Think and Work*. New York, NY: Berg

Gibbons, A. S. and Yanchar, S. C. (2010) 'An alternative view of the instructional design process'. *Educational Technology*, 50, pp. 16–26

Smith, K. M. and Boling, E. (2009) 'What do we make of design? Design as a concept in educational technology'. *Educational Technology*, 49, pp. 3–17

Spector, J. M. (2012) *Foundations of Educational Technology*. New York, NY: Routledge

15 A Case of User-Centered Design as Subversive Practice

Katy Campbell

Subversion

In a political context "subversion" has been characterized as a betrayal of nationalism. However, post-structuralists, among them feminists in all design professions, have more recently prescribed a very broad form of subversion. In this view - my view - subversion is directed at dominant cultural forces. Leslie Bow (2001) defines subversion as "'living at the borders', like metaphors of travel, migrancy, or the floating world, (exemplifying) the theoretical shift toward conceptualizing identity as fluid, shifting, continually negotiated and contextualized" (p. 25). Instructional designers in learning organizations often experience conflict working within the dominant, didactic, disciplinary expert culture of academia (Woo 2015), as do faculty members working multidisciplinarily, minority faculty, sessional instructors and those who, like me, work in marginalized fields such as continuing education and community engagement (Campbell 2008). Further, my colleagues and I have found that instructional designers who confront the long-prevailing, and normative, narrative of scientific design practice have been marginalized in their cultural communities (Schwier *et al.* 2004). This chapter tells a story of subversive practice in course design that ultimately failed to engage participants in the course. Throughout the experience of designing and teaching the course I felt betrayed and was left questioning the core values that inform my practice and identity.

The Background

There is no graduate program in educational technology in my faculty. Working over three decades in three different academic institutions, I have never had a physical academic ID community of colleagues, although I almost joined a distance university that had a master's degree and a certificate, and was developing a doctorate in distance education. So, I've always had to subvert the existing curriculum to teach design.

In my current faculty we do have a professional Master of Arts in Communications and Technology (MACT), which is the closest thing to an ID program. Now 15 years old, MACT is a cohort-based, blended design with two three-week spring institutes that bracket four online core courses.

Three electives and a capping project round out the program. The program examines sociocultural issues related to the use of communications technology, but not specifically learning technology. I thought I could tuck a design course into MACT, which after all is my home program, so I approached the program director with a proposal for an elective course.

Full disclosure: At that time my nose was seriously out of joint because, even though I was hired on tenure-track specifically for my ID background, I wasn't invited to contribute to the core curriculum of the degree in the first place (my role as ID scholar/practitioner related more to university-wide faculty development). At one point I was asked to develop several workshops for the authors/instructors of the core courses, and I worked really hard on creating those materials ("this is problem-based learning," "this is case-based learning"…). No one followed up with me and the courses were designed, so to speak, to fit text into the WebCT template. In other words, each course site contained a syllabus, a warning about academic integrity, a schedule, a list of readings and assignments and, if the instructor was courageous, a discussion forum. For the first ten years of the program, citing academic freedom, the director completely resisted any design conversation. During all that time the original authors/instructors were the only teachers of their particular courses and, as is common in universities, the core courses consisted of content that each academic was particularly interested in such as, for example, e-commerce.

I had the idea – dream? – that because the Faculty of Education had recently disbanded their educational technology centre and all that was left were a few courses in Educational Psychology, I could develop a certificate, focusing on design, from within the MACT program. My strategy was to design and embed three or four elective courses that *looked* like communications and technology, because what was design if not communication? I could suddenly, with a flourish, one day back them out of the MACT garage, already packaged up and ready to go. That was my master plan, but I kept it to myself because, although Education had made a clear statement in the indirect way that you do in a university, they weren't going to want me just "taking," or declaring, instructional design as a legitimate domain for the Faculty of Extension. Subversion has always been a useful strategy in faculties like Extension, and it has occurred to me more than once that subversion is a successful and even necessary approach for often-marginalized fields like instructional design.

Pedagogy and Subversion: Genesis

In my first academic position at the State University of New York (SUNY-Geneseo 1993-95) I became intrigued by Johnson and Johnson's cooperative learning model (c.f. Johnson and Johnson 1994) and was sold on the idea of teaching about cooperative learning *through* cooperative learning. This was my first class in my first tenure-track academic position. I had been hired in teacher education although I'd only taught for five years in a public school system and taught only French as a Foreign Language. I suspect that the Dean of the College of Education was so enamored of the narrative inquiry work of Jean Clandinin that she pushed for my selection because Dr. Clandinin was my doctoral supervisor (it was as close as the CoE was going to get). I floundered a bit – in fact, dreaded – teaching undergraduate courses in teaching methods: Not my area of expertise. But I approached the challenge as a designer would, or as my subverted pseudo-designer self would have worked with a faculty member in Education who had to design the course. The course, as a design, was beautiful. It was tight, incredibly well-resourced, cognitively scaffolded, paced appropriately, had interactive activities, included both formative and summative assessments, peer coaching, blah, blah, blah. But the students didn't like it. They panned it. They gave me middling ratings. One student actually said, "I don't want to learn to DO cooperative learning, I just want to learn how to teach with the model." Although I was flabbergasted, I realized that I had designed media, courses, experiences, for others but had never used them myself. In other words I was designing for a fictional, idealized me-as-teacher-educator. However, thanks to a graduate student, I did discover the Internet in 1993, and tried an experiment with an elementary school in rural New York, pairing up Grade 5 children in a rural school in Kentucky with my student teachers using an awful clunky thing called MIS. The technology rarely worked, but everyone was thrilled.

Around the end of my first probationary period at the college I accepted, sight unseen, a position in distance education at a community college in northern Canada. Distance education was no more my field than teacher education, but – what the heck – I was a designer! I could work with *any* discipline because I knew how to support learning. However, I encountered total resistance, even overt hostility, to developing a distance delivery capacity. All I accomplished was helping one person get a floppy disk working, although we visited half a dozen fly-in aboriginal communities to complete needs assessments that wouldn't likely be considered in curriculum redevelopment. I wondered where the resistance was located or, better yet, *why* resistance is always located in learning technology.

Back to MACT

Given these experiences I determined that my elective course would be a core design course (meaning what?) that I would disguise as "user-centered design." Since "becoming" a designer I had been most passionate about respecting diversity and widening access to learners who were excluded, marginalized, disenfranchised, vulnerable, etc. My research was about gender issues and learning technologies; more specifically about female faculty and their experiences with learning technology and design. I determined to really focus on the universal design aspect of user-centered design. Because I am a feminist, and was exploring theoretical frames that would be most comfortable for me, standpoint theory seemed to be a good basis for the course. Also, naturally, despite the antipathy with which my New York students had greeted experiential learning, I was going to do that again because I am a true-blue constructivist and, besides, deeply committed to the idea of positive social interdependence. But, this time, I would be much more sophisticated and explicitly deconstruct the course design for them as they were actually experiencing the design. This made lots of sense to *me*, naturally; as it turns out, not so much for them.

A gleam in my eye since 2000, the course was advertised for the winter of 2004: Nothing like a timeline to focus your mind. If I didn't get eight students the course would be cancelled. I decided to create the course anyway because I personally wanted to learn more about UCD. I started in the spring of 2003.

The intended audience for MACT was, and is, eclectic. The learning community, about two-thirds women, typically includes journalists, teachers, human resource types, public relations officers, fundraisers, directors of not-for-profits, artists of all types, web designers, writers, city planners, lawyers, telecommunications providers, educational technologists, entrepreneurs, health care providers and IT technicians (one or two people who thought they were going to learn about server technology). Of two dozen people there are always at least two international students. The average age is 35–45. To be admitted, each individual has to have had at least three years of experience in a related field. They don't want "theory," they are skeptical about research, they may not be sold on online learning, they have probably been out of formal learning environments for decades, and most of them work full-time. What they have in common is a conviction about, and resignation to, the nature of technology in their professional lives. Nobody wants to spend much time in a discussion forum; ironically most were locally based and developed their personal/professional supportive face-to-face communities.

I plunged into the user-centered design literature. I bought what I could find on Amazon and filled up binders with articles, musings, newsletters, bibliographies, etc. from the web. I looked for course descriptions at other universities. I read and downloaded everything Jacob Neilsen ever wrote. I learned what I could about UCD and then reframed it with instructional design. At this point I did not know what the course was going to look like. The only constraint was WebCT – i.e. I had to use WebCT. I wasn't all that thrilled about this, believing LMS are value-laden and ethnocentric in their designs, but I figured I could find a way to subvert that, or at least point it out to the students. Nevertheless, if I had to use a tool I was going to use it well, especially features that would increase interaction. For example, I discovered how to set up groups, and groups within groups. I wasn't sure I was going to use them, but "groups" was an available engagement tool and I was dabbling in communities of practice.

Through my reading and exploring I began to form my own construct of user-centered design that aligned comfortably with my constructivist epistemology, feminist perspective, and commitment to learning for social action. Design for democracy! For example, I kept thinking about universal design as standpoint theory. If I wanted students to design for users and not for themselves, I decided I had to bump them out of their middle-class Western perspectives (or whatever perspectives they did have). I was quite taken with the idea of personas. I wanted to work with personas in a real way. Remember, dear colleague, that I was trying to disguise an ID course as a UCD course, so I tried to steer away from using pedagogical-type language like "learner needs." Developing a critical eye was key, so that no one would leave the class blithely taking their own cultural assumptions for granted. What were their cultural assumptions? *That* was a good place to start. The course was going to look at user-centered design as a values-based approach to the design of information resources. So, the first activities were going to tease out their beliefs about how information should be presented, for example, for a 48 year old accountant (see Figure 15.1).

Sample
persona

Age: 48
Occupation: accountant
Personal: divorced, 2 children in
university
Income: owns home, income $75k/yr,
active lifestyle
Web use: productivity, financial apps,
minimal social media
Technical profile: competent user, 90%
at work, personal laptop, iPad, iPhone

Figure 15.1 Sample narrated PowerPoint slide Module 4: User profiling. Slide 11 with narration text: For example, your client wants to develop an online dating service. Your user research strategy included a user segmentation process in which you identified x key segments of the target user population: singles 27-34, and older adults 44-67. The latter segment contained several categories, including females who were widowed, and males and females who were divorced.

Here is a persona named Kelly (that's me, by the way).

First, though, I had lots of content but no design. What did I mean by "design?" I always have a hard time describing that, even to myself, although, when pressed, I talk about the gestalt that I imagine the Hollywood director needs or has to develop. She has to have read the script. How will she tell the story? What is the continuing scope of the screenwriter or author? Meet the producers. Talk about their vision – who was the audience? Whose perspective prevailed? How much money was there? What markets would the movie be released in? When? How long should it be? Was the movie written for a particular actor or was that open? Who had ultimate artistic authority? And so on. The director had to have a sense of Hollywood politics. What was the history of the relationship between the studio and the producers and the actors and the director? Was the director familiar with various technologies or techniques? Does the director have a signature style? Does the story require special effects? Who will make them? When are they needed? How much will they cost? Black and white or color? Will music play a role? How does the director interact with actors? What role does the scriptwriter have? How do the actors get along? Is one a die-hard "method" actor while the other just lets it flow over him? Will one or more endings get made? Will different versions be piloted? How will the director block out the scenes? What if there are cost overruns? And then, there's editing....

I sat down with a mind-mapping program called *Inspiration* and put "UCD is values based" in the center cloud. Then, in a neutral color, I rapidly recorded each idea I wanted to include. When I was sure I had "everything," I started sorting out subordinate and superordinate ideas. I changed the colors of the boxes accordingly. I moved the squares around the screen until I was able to see relationships. Then I started drawing connecting lines between the ideas; that way I could get a sense of the conceptual structure of the domain. When I was satisfied I hadn't missed any ideas, I stopped working on it for the day. I returned to the mind map in a few days and found that I had additional thoughts that had come to me unconsciously, or in turning over in my mind what I had read and mapped already, or my husband had suggested, or what had occurred to me after I'd recently tried to use a website effectively, or what barriers I had long encountered working with my faculty clients. I started a list of things that really offended me, or just irritated me, and a list of ideas worth liberating. This part of the design process was iterative and sometimes quite frustrating; but finally I had a picture of *my* meaning of UCD. This picture is represented in Figure 15.2.

Finally, I played with scaffolding the theories and practices of UCD. I was unhappy that the LMS required a modularized approach but, when I thought of each chunk as an aggregation of learning objects, I could live with it. In each module, or unit, I started with a narrated PowerPoint™ slideshow and posed an open-ended question to be discussed.

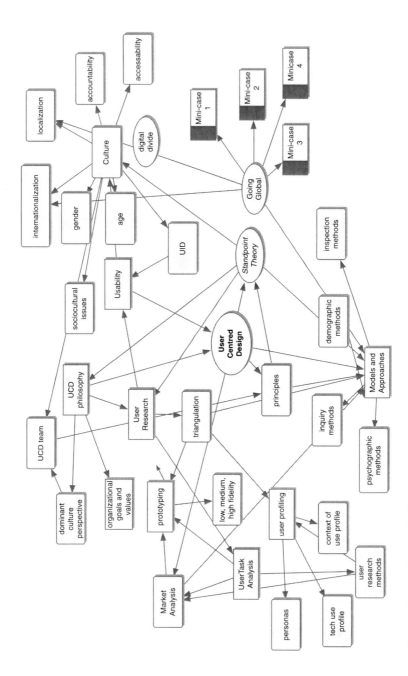

Figure 15.2 First UCD Mindmap 2003.

Table 15.1 Course description.

Online Winter Course January 2004
Research and Practice in the User-Centered
Design Process (EXT 597)
An elective course developed for the Master of Arts in
Communications and Technology (MACT) program
Course Description and Objectives
User-centered design (UCD) is a client or user-centered philosophy in which
   the individual is at the center of an iterative design process that encompasses
   multiple factors in the interaction between user and information product. UCD
   considers cognitive, sociocultural, political, and technological factors involved in
   defining user tasks and goals that drive the design and development of software,
   websites, information systems and processes - anything with which people
   interact. UCD is concerned with the usefulness, usability, desirability, legibility,
   learnability, accessibility and meaningfulness of an information product.
In this course, we will adopt the perspective of Universal Design (UD). Born
   in the late 1970s, UD emerged from architecture and addressed design
   issues related to the accessibility of facilities and services. Based on UD, the
   Instructional Design and the UCD fields overlap in their focus on the design of
   inclusive information/learning environments, in which the diverse needs and
   preferences of users provide the basis for design decisions.
During the course, you will learn about and apply UCD principles and practices to
   solve a real-world problem. Topics include:

- Standpoint theory;
- User profiling;
- User research models and methods;
- Usability;
- Sociocultural contexts affecting design.

I had included all the information needed to provide background for the
concept in the form of links, embedded media, interviews, puffs, and so on.
I planned three activities to be assessed – one to be completed individually
and one to be completed with a partner; the major activity was project-based.
Group interaction was also assessed. The learning guide, over which I *slaved*,
explained project-based learning (with additional readings – optional),
contained a personal learning planner and contract (for critical reflection), and
additional cases of UCD in other design fields. After some negotiation, I set
virtual and real-time office hours for each week. At the end of the 13-week
schedule I invited each learner to meet either personally or virtually with me
to debrief their experience; and discovered, once again, that they really
hadn't enjoyed the course. Could this be a case of the doctor diagnosing
herself and having a fool for a patient?

   I returned to the "studio," with two class participants as co-designers.
Together we tried to identify the design issues. We learned that the participants had not enjoyed the discussion forum. They were too busy to provide

timely interactions. They thought they had nothing to add. They felt intimidated. Many resented the attenuating tone - mine and that of several participants. The authentic "project", to use UCD practices and processes as a consulting team for a travel agency wanting a web presence, did not excite them. I was reluctant to revise the project because I had been creating and collecting travel agency objects for the learning object repository, including taped interviews, personas, scanned brochures, links to websites, chunks of video, travel advice and regulations from governments worldwide, online presentations from travel agents, TV commercials, exemplar sites, and research about consumer practices. I was exhausted. How could I do that for a range of project scenarios in time for the next iteration? I solicited ideas from my participatory designers. We revised the readings, the deliverables, the forms of assessment (see Figure 15.3). We decided to introduce a rubric and, in the third delivery, include self, peer and team assessments (see Figure 15.4). With some difficulty – technologically, temporally, and personally - I persuaded *real* travel agency owners to act as the clients and to participate in team presentations.

As an instructional design consultant, and sympathetic shoulder, I knew that learners involved in a pedagogical innovation would suspend disbelief for longer if the evidence-based design of the course was presented to them early, and if formative feedback from learner to teacher was facilitated at various times during delivery. This was in my playbook as a faculty consultant, partially because ongoing course evaluations tended to result in less extreme or "angry" course-end evaluations, a selling point for nervous faculty clients. My subversive goal was the development of reflective practice. If the strategy led to course design or teaching improvements, or less terrified faculty who might become pedagogical leaders, well... I developed what I considered a brilliant, and accessible, explanation of the course design and intended learning goals that I included in the online handbook and as an extra module in the course (see Figure 15.4). Referencing an earlier disastrous experience as a learner in a phenomenology course I had designed for the nursing program, however, I did recall that it struck me as terribly ironic (and embarrassing) that "what's sauce for the goose" isn't always "sauce for the gander." As a finishing touch I recruited two more learners and a colleague to pilot the new course design. As a designer, especially when working with interactive video, I was always able to "get started" when the opening scene rolled, visually, in my mind. I could *see* this course design, almost as if it were physically playing out in front of me. Let the show begin. However, instead of employing the best design practices in my repertory, within a month of the revised course launch two-thirds of the participants had dropped the elective, one complaining to the program director and another leaving me an astonishing email just oozing invective.

Three tries (2004-2006); no success. I was emotionally drained as a designer (obviously, I had always been a fraud and clients had been too

Table 15.2 Mini-case #1 rubric, 2005.

Assessment for Mini-case #1

The report, or proposal, for this mini-case should include:

- A complete description of your team;
- A compelling argument for a UCD process;
- A summary of the context for the report;
- A business plan with timelines, deliverables, resources needed, etc.

Criteria	Poor 0-2	Good 3-4	Outstanding 5
The problem identification and statement. Up to 5 points.	Neither implicit nor explicit reference is made to the problem that is to be examined. The problem is not valid. No indication of the importance of the topic to the authors' professional context.	Readers are aware of the overall problem, challenge, or topic that is to be examined. The significance of the problem or topic to the authors' professional context is not explicit.	The topic is introduced, and is relevant and significant. The groundwork is laid for the development of the argument and direction of the project. The topic has significance for the author.
Development of argument. Up to 8 points.	Major sections of pertinent data have been omitted. The topic is of little significance to the UCD field.	Pertinent data is included, but not covered in as much depth or insight, or as explicitly, as possible. Significance to UCD field is evident.	The appropriate data is covered in depth. Significance of topic to UCD field is unquestionable.
Inclusion of evidence. Up to 4 points.	There is little evidence offered to support the authors' argument. Appropriate sources and references are not included.	Evidence for the argument is presented clearly but may not support the issue as well as expected. Sources are included but may not be relevant, current, or significant.	The evidence for the argument is clearly presented, supports the argument, and is valid. Sources are cited when specific statements are made. The author has included the most current, relevant and important UCD sources.

(continued)

Table 15.2 Mini-case #1 rubric, 2005 (Continued).

Criteria			
Clarity and quality of writing. Up to 6 points.	It is hard to know what the writer is trying to express. Writing is convoluted. Misspelled words, incorrect grammar, and improper punctuation are evident. Many errors in citing references.	Writing is generally clear, but unnecessary words are occasionally used. Meaning is sometimes hidden. Paragraph or sentence structure is too repetitive. Some errors in citing references.	Writing is crisp, clear, succinct and compelling. The writer incorporates the active voice when appropriate. Excellent syntax, appropriate use of inclusive language. No spelling errors. Citations are consistently and accurately referenced (preferably in APA).
Synthesis of ideas and evaluation of results. Up to 5 points.	There is no indication the author tried to synthesize the information or make a conclusion based on the evidence under review.	The author provides concluding remarks that show an analysis and synthesis of ideas occurred. Some of the conclusions, however, were not supported in the body of the report. The hypothesis or research question is stated.	The author was able to make succinct, precise and insightful conclusions based on the evidence. Insights into the problem are appropriate. Conclusions are strongly supported in the report.
Communication of results. Up to 3 points.	Readers are not clear about the results or how they were arrived at. The form of communication was not appropriate to the problem. No connection to future action or research.	The problem and results are communicated appropriately. The author is able to address some questions related to the treatment of the problem, or the results.	The problem and results are communicated appropriately and innovatively. The author is able to satisfactorily address specific questions. Recommendations are made for future research or action.
Evidence of learning. Up to 4 points.	No evidence of critical reflection or new insight.	The author provides some evidence of critical reflection and personal insight.	The author critically reflects on the topic or issue in a way that demonstrates personal insight and transformation of previous views.

Table 15.3 Excerpt from student's self-assessment journal, 2006.

February 12, 2006

As a starting point, I'll use the questions that were posted in the WebCT discussion forum as a guideline to help capture my thoughts. I think I'll approach this as a work in progress, and continue to flesh out this document over the duration of the course.

Part 1

- What makes this a good case?
  - I think what makes this a good case is that it is something that we can personally relate to. We have all had some experience with business and pleasure travel, and have probably had at least some exposure to online presentation of travel information (accommodation choices, flights, researching local information, etc.).
  - It is an established industry that is changing because of increased connectivity and access to information that the World Wide Web affords.
  - An online presence enables a global audience and target market. This is an important premise to consider in terms of access, accessibility, and UCD principals.
- How did you go about developing it?
  - Information gathering included a number of sources:
    - Interviews with an individual from the travel industry, a "web-savvy" consumer of travel, ...
    - Our own research from relevant web sites such as government studies, other travel agencies, ...
    - Timely news items such as the AMA travel periodical "Westworld."
  - Discussion with team members.
- What problems did you encounter?
  - I think the biggest problem we had was to find a way to work together at a distance and bring our research findings and discussions into one place.
  - Settling on a work flow process and decision making process was also a problem.
  - Getting to know each other.
- How did you solve them?
  - A couple of team members proposed "technology solutions" that are geared towards group work in a virtual setting. Gaetano proposed Microsoft SharePoint, and I proposed the idea of a wiki. The group essentially self-selected an environment based on their initial impressions of the proposed solution.
  - Group decisions were made by considering the majority of opinion. So far, there has been nothing so contentious that a minority have felt the need to challenge the "majority decision."

---

polite to tell me), a teacher (I believed in project-based learning and participatory user-centered design), a colleague (this was embarrassing), and a person (they didn't think I was funny, they hated me, they pitied me, they felt betrayed; they wanted their money back). Interestingly, I felt resilient as a scholar: a guiding tenet has always been to "make everything work twice" and I had learned and shared through the usual academic and professional channels. Furthermore, I had remained true to my epistemological values, including relational practice. However, I took a six-month sabbatical during which I taught the course and then declined to contribute in the next term.

Contents

Title	Page
Introduction to the Course: Course Design.............	3
Learner Feedback and My Responses...................	6
Course Assessment..	12
The Project..	23
The UCD Proposal..	26
A Few Key Terms...	28
Tentative Schedule for 2006................................	30
Make a Project Plan..	32
Action Plan...	37
What is a User-Centred Design?............................	41
Who is the End User? Sociocultural Issues.............	43
Models and Approaches in User-Centred Design.....	47
User Task Analysis...	49
User Profiling..	53
Prototyping...	61
Usability (optional)...	64
Testing Methods..	69
Inspection Methods..	71
Inquiry Methods...	72
Develop the Instrument.......................................	73
Quality Review Checklist......................................	76
A Sample Usability Plan.......................................	87
Sample Interview Protocol: Potential Faculty Interview/Focus...	91
The Case of Accounting Re-design.......................	98
Resources..	102

2

Figure 15.3 Table of contents for the revised handbook, 2005.

The MACT Director asked a faculty member in Humanities Computing, who was working with metadata and learning objects, to teach the course going forward. It looked completely different, as my colleague had different values and expectations; it went well for a few years until he was lured away by another university. I didn't teach the course again.

Introduction to the Course: Course Design

This course has been designed to give you the experience of being part of a user-centered design team. The team will be constituted to include a range of experience/expertise identified by each course participant. For example, one of your team members may have experience in marketing, another may be an instructional designer, and so on.

The course has a <u>critical</u> theoretical and conceptual framework. In other words, in a global community we must be critical of the dominant culture approach we take in information design. The activities are designed with this intention – hopefully they will succeed in giving you a new, more critical perspective about your own practices.

Based on learner feedback (from 2005), the course is case-based, and includes both individual and team-based activities and related assessments. A case-based environment is meant to provide relevant meaningful experiences that simulate the complex problems of the real world (as much as possible).

Case studies teach abstract concepts from specific, concrete problems, and are especially effective for developing the judgment skills necessary to deal with the complex, difficult, contradictory situations in real life that some experts have called "wicked problems."

User-centered design <u>is</u> a messy field. For one thing, it is an aggregation of many fields including human-computer interface design, instructional design, information design, evaluation design, cognitive psychology, and marketing… There are no right or fixed answers in UCD, but there are good and better practices.

The case I have developed for this course is called *Going Glocal*. It is the story of a travel agency that has been living in the past. The current owners, a husband and wife team named the Zhaos, recognize that they must expand their market into new areas and for new audiences, but they need help in both understanding and implementing the process.

That is where UCD comes in. Here is an excellent opportunity for you to educate the Zhaos about the philosophy of UCD (client-centeredness; inclusiveness) and help them become more critical world citizens. That means educating yourself and your team members about the issues and challenges of "going glocal". *Glocal* is a term that tries to capture user needs and concerns at both a local and a global level.

3

Figure 15.4 Excerpt of the introduction to the course from the handbook, 2005.

Coda

This year I turn 60 years' old. A Dean for seven years, with five more in front of me, I've had little time to practice and even less for scholarship, although those are intertwined for me. Because my faculty was obliged to undertake a period of transformation and identity work in which I was deeply and passionately embedded, I have reflectively reframed my understanding of design through metaphor. Being explicit about how design thinking informs and contextualizes how I am as "Dean" has allowed me to dig deeper into metaphorical thinking, for example, design as feminist practice; academic leadership as design thinking. I wish I had had the benefit of deconstructing designs, real designs, problematic designs that "didn't work" at that time or for that group. Is there an optimal blueprint? Does design-as-science provide the truth about effective and engaging design? I don't know the answer to these and dozens of other questions, or how to describe design practice or even effectively communicate it. But I do believe in the reflective practitioner and that learning, especially self-learning, must always lead to social action. In the context of our faculty, our university, our uneasy place in sociopolitical times, "design as engagement scholarship" will be my next metaphorical exploration.

References

Aaron Marcus and Associates Inc. (2001) *Cultural Dimensions and Global Web Design: What? So What? Now What?* Available at: http://www.AMandA.com

Abras, C., Maloney-Krichmar, D. and Preece, J. (2005) 'User-Centered Design' in W. Bainbridge (Ed) *Encyclopedia of Human-Computer Interaction.* Thousand Oaks, CA: Sage Publications

Balka, E. (2001, March) 'Women users: Re-gendering technology: Analytic framework and theoretical challenges'. Work in Progress. Workshop, Institute for Advanced Studies in Science, Technology and Society, Graz, Austria

Bow, L. (2001) *Betrayal and Other Acts of Subversion.* Princeton, NJ: Princeton University Press

Campbell, K. (2008) 'In search of moral coherence: reconciling uneasy histories and identities'. *International Journal of Qualitative Methods*, 7(4), pp. 45–58

Cleary, Y. (2000) 'An Examination of the impact of subjective cultural issues on the usability of a localized website - The Louvre Museum website'. Paper presented at *Museums and the Web 2000*, University of Limerick, Ireland. Available at: http://www.archimuse.com/mw2000/papers/cleary/cleary.html

Dormann, C. and Chisalita, C. (2002) *Cultural Values in Website Design.* Presentation for the 11th European Conference on Cognitive Ergonomics ECCEII Catania, Italy, Sept 8–11, 2002

Gjoen, H. and Hard, M. (2002) 'Cultural politics in action: Developing user scripts in relation to the electric vehicle'. *Science, Technology and Human Values*, 27(2), pp. 262–281

Karvonen, K. (2001, August) 'Designing trust for a universal audience: A multicultural study on the formation of trust in the Internet in the Nordic countries'. Invited paper for publication in the *Proceedings of the First International Conference on Universal Access in HCI*, (UAHCI 2001), New Orleans, LA

Johnson, D. and Johnson, R. (1994) *Learning Together and Alone, Cooperative, Competitive, and Individualistic Learning.* Needham Heights, MA: Prentice-Hall

Keulartz, J., Schermer, M., Korthals, M. and Swierstra (2004) 'Ethics in technological culture: A pragmatic proposal for a pragmatist approach'. *Science, Technology and Human Values*, 29(1), pp. 3–29

Klein, H. J. and Kleinman, D. L. (2002) 'The social construction of technology: Structural considerations'. *Science, Technology and Human Values*, 27(1), pp. 28–52

Morse, K. (2003) 'Does one size fit all? Exploring asynchronous learning in a multicultural context'. *Journal of Asynchronous Learning Networks*, 7(1), pp. 37–55. Available at: http://www.aln.org/publications/jaln/v7n1/v7n1_morse.asp

Nielsen, J. (2000) *Designing Web Usability*. Indianapolis, IN: New Riders Publishing

Nielsen, J. (n.d.) *Use-it.com*. http://www.use-it.com

Schwier, R. A., Campbell, K. and Kenny, R. (2004) 'Instructional designers' observations about identity, communities of practice and change agency'. *Australasian Journal of Educational Technology*, 20(1), pp. 69–100

Shah, M. D. (2004) 'Accessibility improvement of multicultural educational web interface by using the User-Centred Design (UCD) approach'. *Proceedings of the 2004 Informing Science and IT Education Joint Conference.*

Simon, S. J. (1999) *A Cross Cultural Analysis of Web Site Design: An Empirical Study of Global Web Users*. Available at: http://marketing.byu.edu/htmlpages/ccrs/proceedings99/simon.htm

Walsham, G. (2000) 'IT, globalization and cultural diversity' in C. Avgerou and G. Walsham (Eds.) *Information Technology in Context* (p. 291). Burlington, VT: Ashgate

Vredenburg, K., Isensee, S. and Righi, C. (2002) *User-centered Design: An Integrated Approach*. Upper Saddle River, NJ: Prentice-Hall

Wenger, E. (1998) *Communities of Practice: Learning, Meaning, and Identity*. Cambridge, UK: Cambridge University Press

Woo, D. J. (2015) 'Central practitioners developing legitimate peripheral participation in a community of practice for changing schools'. *Australasian Journal of Educational Technology*, 31(2), pp. 164–176

16 Undisciplined and Out of Control

A Course in Systemic Design for First-year Undergraduate Students

Gordon Rowland

Introduction

> Tell me every thing that you can about the handle you used to open the door as you entered this classroom. Describe it to me as a designed system. What are its parts and how are they related? How does it connect with the larger system of the door? Who uses it, when, and how? Why is it placed where it is? How did it evolve from previous types of handles? What are its qualities, both good and bad? For example, how well does it function? How does it feel in your hand? Which hand or hands do you use to operate it?
>
> It's difficult to answer these questions just from memory, so let's try it. One by one exit the room paying close attention to how you operate the handle and how it feels.
>
> Now walk with me. Let's compare the handle to our classroom with the seven other types of door handles in this building. Which ones are better than others? Why? For whom? How can each be improved? What will happen to them when they are no longer needed?
>
> For next class – and for the rest of your life – examine every room you enter, every object you encounter, everything in the world as a designed system.

To tell the story of STCM 12300 Systems Thinking and Design, I will begin with a description of the context and a sense of where my ideas came from. Then I will describe the course and what I believe to be critical elements in teaching it. I will reflect upon design decisions that I made, and conclude with thoughts on where the course and approach may evolve.

Across these chapters of the story there are a number of recurring themes: learning by doing in authentic context; building on students' already sophisticated problem-solving abilities; shifting the instructor role from content provider to problem-solving facilitator; iterative development; and creative tensions.

Context

The course that I will describe is an undergraduate introduction to systemic design, taught in the School of Communications at Ithaca College. Ithaca College is a residential, comprehensive college in upstate New York. We have approximately 6,000 students, a large majority of whom are enrolled in our undergraduate programs. The college started as a music conservatory over a century ago and now includes four professional schools – business, communications, health sciences and human performance, and music – along with a school of humanities and sciences. The schools, and to a large extent the programs within them, have fairly independent curricula, although there has been a recent initiative to do some modest integration in a common core curriculum.

I have been a faculty member at the college since 1991 in a department that has gone through many changes over the past 40 years, evolving from Educational Communication (media development for education), to Corporate/Organizational Media (media design and production in all types of organizations), to Corporate Communication (adding the study of human communication to media), to Organizational Communication, Learning, and Design (clarifying that we teach more than public relations, when "corporate communication" came to imply that field), and recently to Strategic Communication (as a result of a merger with a program in integrated marketing communication). Currently, the Park School of Communications has over 1,600 undergraduate majors, and over 400 of them are in our department. Approximately 150 of these 400 students major in the program in which I teach, Communication Management and Design (CMD), and they concentrate their studies in corporate communication (a large majority) or communication design (historically an emphasis on workplace learning and performance). The course I will describe below is one of the early courses in the CMD core, which is a set of courses that introduces topics at the beginning, and integrates topics at the end of the curriculum.

History of the Course

When I arrived at Ithaca College I was assigned to teach an introductory course in Instructional Design. I taught three sections with 25 students in each, one in a large auditorium early in the morning, and two in a smaller classroom later in the day. I followed how the previous instructor, just retired, had taught the course for many years. I stepped through separate units matched to the chapters of a standard textbook, thus leading students through a linear design process: needs analysis, task analysis, objectives and criterion-referenced test items, strategy and media selection, and so on. Across the three sections, maybe half a dozen students discovered a passion for the topic, imagined future careers in corporate training, and found the approach effective. For the rest, and thus for me, it was near disaster. They had no interest in designing instruction, saw no relevance to their career goals, questioned why the course was required in their major, and did the minimum expected for the grade.

Learning from Failure

I had to immediately recognize several problems. First, I had been attracted to the position by what I saw as the power and logic of integrating various fields, including instructional design/technology, organizational communication, and media design and production, in a single program. I learned that this made sense to faculty, alumni, and working professionals, but not to students, particularly early in their academic careers. Second, I had thought that students in a Corporate Communication program (the program name at the time) would want to understand an important corporate function. As often as not, they appeared to have selected the program because of what it was not; they wanted to study communications at Ithaca College but not in the other available programs in cinema, photography, journalism, or television-radio. If they had a specific interest it was most often in advertising or public relations. Thirdly, the systematic, linear model of design seemed to them to squash all creativity. I may as well have been teaching mathematics, the avoidance of which, for many, was a selling point of majoring in communications. Finally, my teaching approach followed the pattern of nearly every other course they were taking - lectures, practice exercises, and small artificial projects. I was doing little to motivate them or to increase their interest in the topic. I needed to redesign the course, particularly to establish relevance, expand the context, and move away from the linear model.

Over the next several years, I made a number of changes. I added sources representing alternative perspectives to the text, then eliminated the text altogether. I shifted from a slow march through procedural steps to a rapid series of design projects, each more significant and sophisticated. Rather than present concepts and tools and ask students to apply them in simple exercises, I shared them only after students had engaged in designing and realized that they needed them. I moved from common to student-selected projects – client-based, and more and more authentic, whenever appropriate – and broadened the context from corporate training to all formal and informal education. I took a mastery approach to basics, giving them a study guide, a first exam, answers to the first exam, a second exam in areas they had previously missed, and so on. I ended the course with a design competition for a real client.

As the course evolved, I also began to add early units on systems thinking and design, separate from the context of instruction/education. Through examples and activities that were more concrete and related to students' everyday experiences, I found that I could get them engaged with seeing situations holistically, and much of the world around them as artificially constructed, before focusing on instruction. Instruction thus became a single context for design knowledge and skill that could transfer and be applied in many of their areas of interest. This generality was also consistent with my dissertation research, in which I had found great commonality between how expert instructional designers and designers in other fields approached solving problems. The redesign thus made a closer link to practice, and adopted strategies from design education in other fields, specifically more of a studio approach, based in activity and involving learning by doing in authentic context.

Simultaneous to this course redesign effort, and certainly informing that effort, I was attending conferences and engaging in collaborative inquiry with members of the International Systems Institute (ISI), particularly with Bela H. Banathy. I saw that I was just scratching the surface of systems science, design, and systemic design (the integration of the two), and I became convinced that (a) my students would benefit from deeper study of these areas, and (b) they were capable of doing so, in contrast, for example, to the typical teaching of systems science topics only in graduate studies. I convinced my department chair to let me develop and attempt a new course that would precede Instructional Design and that would explore systems thinking and design more generally.

The New Course

I offered the course for the first time experimentally (i.e., not approved as a permanent part of the curriculum). I chose the course number 123 to symbolize foundational knowledge, and I gave it the title "Undisciplined and Out of Control." That title came from conversations with Harold Nelson at my first ISI conference about the "undisciplined" nature of systems thinking and the "out of control" action of designing. Harold subsequently wrote an article with that title for a special issue of *Performance Improvement Quarterly* that I edited (Nelson 1994), and when I developed the course this became required reading.

The course was a great hit. So much so that it soon became a requirement in the program, and a sought-after elective by non-majors. Students saw that it not only helped them in subsequent courses but led them to see the world differently. I proposed it as a permanent addition to the college catalog, and approval was given on the condition that the name be changed. The students appreciated "undisciplined and out of control;" curriculum review committees had no sense of humor. It became "Systems Thinking and Design: Undisciplined and Out of Control," then ultimately just "Systems Thinking and Design."

Course Specifics

In designing the course I was guided by my instincts and experiences, somewhat by the literature on design education, and especially by my own research, which has consistently pointed toward learning by doing in

Table 16.1 Units and challenges.

Weeks	Unit	Challenge
1-3	1. Systems and designs in the world	Challenge 1
4-7	2. Systems thinking	Challenge 2
8-9	3. Designing	Challenge 3
10-12	4. Systemic design in the workplace	
13-14	5. Conscious evolution	

authentic context as a common theme in powerful/transformative learning experiences. Consequently, nearly all class sessions involve learning activities. There are very few lectures and no tests. The large majority of activities involve teams of three or four students, and I spend most of the class period working with those teams in a studio-like approach – for example, developing, sharing, and criticizing designs. The class meets twice a week for 75 minutes, for 14 weeks plus a final session during finals week. There are approximately 20 students in each section.

Course Units

The course is divided into five units: systems and designs in the world; systems thinking; designing; systemic design in the workplace; and conscious evolution (see Table 16.1). My original ideas did not include the connection to the workplace, but my colleagues insisted on it because they felt the context of professional work in communications was necessary for the course to be part of the Bachelor of Science in CMD curriculum. I have come to agree and to see the value in making the connections early.

For most units we follow a cycle: I introduce the topic area with an in-class activity(ies); students read a set of resources; then they complete a "challenge" (for example, a design project) (see Figure 16.1). The challenge involves doing research and generating ideas, at least one in-class critique by peers, evaluation for a grade, and reflection on feedback. I will describe each of these steps or learning events in more detail below.

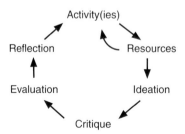

Figure 16.1 Cycle of learning events for each unit.

Learning Activities and Resources

Many class sessions involve learning activities. For example, to introduce the unit on systems and designs in the world, we take a field trip to explore the design of our own facility – starting with the door handles (described above), then the windows, signs, layout, and so on. I attempt to promote seeing every thing around them as a system that has been designed and that can be improved through further design. Another day students form teams and walk around campus photographing what they consider to be good and poor designs. We project the images on their return, discuss the qualities of design and begin to gain a sense of design criteria. Examples of other activities include: guessing the identity of a piece of music from only its pitches or rhythm, demonstrating the systems principle of emergence; developing systems models of one's typical and most powerful learning experiences, to explore the nature of complexity; mapping the causes and consequences of a major social issue across an entire side of the classroom, to appreciate intercon-nectedness (Senge 1990 referred to this as "the wall"); building a self-propelled car from a bag of random parts, to enhance creativity (and have some fun just prior to a college break); groups using different formal approaches to respond to the same design brief, to examine the influence of methods; and a series of roleplays that blend exposure to issues of workplace learning and performance with an introduction to professional consulting practices.

Students explore three or more resources for each unit, and these resources include books, book chapters, articles, films, videos, websites, and so on. I select one resource for each unit, and this is required; students select others from long lists that include both seminal and current sources. I ask students to summarize and connect resources, and to draw links in brief papers between major concepts in the resources and their concrete personal experi-ences. On the due date, each student shares an insight from the summary or links, and we discuss the topic in general.

Challenges

Beyond the resources and in-class learning activities, I ask students to take on three challenges – basically to do three design projects. The first involves redesigning some physical artifact in their environment. They select an object, primarily on the basis of it being something that has frustrated them in the past, carefully describe the object as a system and criticize it as a design, imagine multiple alternatives that would improve it, then select and argue for particular improvements. They share their work at classes before the due date and help each other generate ideas.

The second challenge, done with a partner, involves modeling a system from multiple perspectives. Students select a natural, designed, or human activity system and create graphic models that illustrate system parts and interrelationships. They defend their choice of perspectives and explain insights they gain through the process.

The third challenge, done in small teams and extending over units three through five, involves applying their design and systems-modeling skills to attempt to resolve a major social issue. They select a significant issue, explore it as quickly yet thoroughly as possible, model it from multiple perspectives, search for leverage points for action (for example, apparent root causes and/or points where action is most possible), imagine a wide range of potential actions, then select the options with the most potential and argue for their implementation.

I introduce the challenge this way with a quick activity:

> "Choose a significant issue that you think you could understand and to which you could propose potential solutions if you and a team of classmates had a month to work on it.... Now do it in 20 minutes."
>
> [After the twenty minutes] "Let's hear your ideas but, to make things interesting, I'm going to assign stakeholder roles to the other teams in the class. Their job will be to criticize your ideas from the perspectives of those stakeholder groups - like the Catholic church if your issue is teenage pregnancy, or the fruit and vegetable industries if your issue is immigration reform."

Students thus begin the challenge with deep understanding of two things: tackling a significant issue is going to take great effort; and they will need to think broadly about who has a stake in the issue and how their perspectives will need to be incorporated. At the end of the term, the teams present their projects to a panel of faculty members from different disciplines across campus, who offer criticism and select the "winner." We run the session as a serious but fun competition.

Final Paper

We debrief each challenge as papers are submitted and again as soon as I have provided written feedback. I encourage students to maintain reflective journals, and the insights in these contribute to a final individual paper that has three parts: a concept map of systemic design; an interview with a professional practitioner about how systemic design is or could be applied in his or her work; and a reflective essay on his or her potential contribution to conscious evolution. For each part, I offer alternatives, such as designing a new learning activity rather than creating a concept map for part 1.

Facilities, Grades, and Plans

The physical facility for the course is a flexible classroom designed with multiple surfaces – blackboards on two sides to accommodate large displays (for example, systems models), and poster board along one side for pinning up work. Importantly, we have trapezoidal tables and stackable chairs. These get reconfigured almost every session to accommodate different types of activities. The classroom technology is nothing special. Just a typical media complement of Mac and PC with internet access, computer/video projection, document camera, and so on.

I grade resource summaries/links to experience and challenges using explicit criteria - not any norm or curve. I count attendance within a contribution grade. Their contribution is important and includes helping other students succeed, especially through frequent critiques. All three challenges are presented to classmates at least once, and rich feedback is obtained, prior to due dates.

My class plans are quite specific and constitute what those in the training world would recognize as a complete Instructor Guide. This makes it more possible for others to teach the course, although it remains difficult to do so without experiencing the class sessions yourself. With that in mind, I helped a colleague learn to teach the class several years ago. For each and every class for a semester we talked over my plans, he observed my class meeting, I observed his, then we talked over what had happened. Subsequently, he did the same with a second colleague, so that three of us would be prepared to teach the course when one of us would take sabbatical or additional sections were needed.

Critical Elements of Teaching

There are a few things I have learned that are critical to remember in teaching the course. First, something that works well one time may be ineffective another, and each new class is a very different experience. For example, the issue that student teams choose to tackle in the third challenge has a significant impact on their enthusiasm and effort. Consequently, it is essential to be constantly present, engaged, listening and watching carefully. It is necessary to treat students with respect as individuals and as co-learners, and to be especially tuned in to their reactions at the outset. Students' common initial reaction to the class is "What the heck is going on?" so my enthusiasm has to sell the approach and give them the confidence that I know what I am doing and that the ride will be worth it. The strong reputation of the course goes a long way to helping them suspend their disbelief. However, one thing that educators might assume to be difficult is actually not at all. After the basic recognition that "this will be different," students do not find the adjustment to the approach of learning through activity in authentic contexts difficult. It strikes them as fun and, in a sense, a return to a more natural way of learning that disappeared at the school doors for much of their lives. Also, they appreciate the transformative character – learning to see the world differently. Beyond career goals, this is their unstated reason for attending college – that is, most of them come to the college wanting not just the skills for a job but to experience personal transformation. High points of the course are thus the frequent "a-ha" moments when students see applications not only in other courses but in their lives. I receive frequent notes from alumni about how the course changed the way they saw the world and how that has impacted them since. That's very rewarding. In fact, I cite those notes in the very first class session and it helps to set very high expectations.

Related to the point about being present, I have learned that the approach requires me to get off the stage, to listen and learn, and to be very conscious of what students need in the moment. Typically, we faculty members might "profess" in a class, that is offer our expertise simply because we have it and interpret our job as sharing it. In the approach to this class I have to set my ego aside and focus on what the individual student needs – more or less an adult version of skillful teaching of young children. Inseparable from this, the approach involves less emphasis on content coverage and more attention to problem solving. The goals and instructor roles have changed simultaneously, one as cause and consequence of the other.

Relating this to the pattern of how additional instructors have learned to teach the course, it is important for each of us to recognize that our own preparation as students and instructors is rarely sufficient for or well matched to the approach. It takes a major effort to learn to facilitate the activities and to take a different role, to a large degree because it is not something we have experienced in our own education, at least not at the college level. It is not even entirely consistent with how our role is defined in documents that are used in performance reviews (for example, tenure and promotion procedures). We have to believe in it.

Design Decisions

While I needed to make some initial decisions about overall course goals and structure, and these have remained fairly intact over the years, nearly all details of the course have evolved through an iterative process.

Reflective Teaching Journal

In particular, I have found it useful to keep and utilize a reflective journal. After every class session I write an entry about what worked and didn't work, why I think that was the case, and ideas for the next time I run the activity. I read the previous entry before the next class session to get my head back into where we were, and I read the entire journal when planning the next edition of the course. I started doing this very early in my teaching career, I have done it for each of the 200 or more courses I have taught since, and it has proven invaluable.

Theoretical and Practical Perspectives

Reviewing that journal, I recognize that my design of the Systems Thinking and Design course has been guided by a number of different theoretical and practical perspectives. First, I recognize that I have attempted to apply systemic design myself. I have seen the course as a whole, dependent on the interrelationships between many parts, and attempted to think holistically as I designed. For example, I have recognized that the goals, approach, and teaching style described above intertwine and affect one another, and seen how success of the overall approach has emerged simultaneous to the development of a teaching style that is aligned closely to it. Specifically, I have developed an ability to run learning activities well at the same time as developing the activities, not only as a subconscious side effect but as a conscious process of skill development.

Making another important link to the literature on systemic design, Banathy (1991) describes a necessary choice of primary systems level as one designs. In the case of education, the primary level might be governance, administration, instruction, or student experience. I have consciously chosen student learning experience as the primary system level, and this relates directly to the change of instructor role.

My research on powerful/transformative learning experiences (for example, Rowland 2013) has informed the course design as well. This research continually points toward the kinds of experiences I try to develop and facilitate. It is hard to separate this out. The research affirms and supports the direction I have been taking and, even though I have been as careful as I could to avoid the latter, the direction has likely influenced my research, for example the questions I ask and how I interpret data.

My journal also reveals that I have attempted to follow the logic of planned change in the content sequence. For example, the first challenge is to redesign a physical object or environment, well before we ever talk about communication and learning. This is more concrete. It pushes students to start seeing the artificiality of the world around them, and to think about how they can improve it. As Martin Luther King Jr pointed out, no social change can be accomplished until people believe that change is possible. I help my students see that they can change things around them. Then they can begin to discover relationships (systems thinking) and how they can enhance their creativity (to support design). As a result, areas that we study subsequently, like instructional design, are no longer strange contexts far from interest areas that led students to our program. They are applications of general concepts, principles, and processes.

In terms of theoretical bases, there are theories that are consistent with my approach, mostly those that follow from a constructivist epistemology, but the links to them have mostly been subsequent to design decisions. That is, heuristics associated with these theories have served more as checklists – what am I forgetting, or what does the theory suggest that I could incorporate into the design – than as prescriptions. An example would be some of the forms of guidance I provide in activities and challenges. I decided to emphasize hands-on activities – learning by doing in authentic context – then the literature on constructivist approaches gave me hints on ways to support learning in doing so. A more specific example would be the exploration of resources. As I described earlier, students select resources that interest them, write summaries and draw links to concrete personal experience. When they share insights that they have gained from this, rich conversations about the resources emerge. Through this process they are exposed to multiple views, and they negotiate the meaning of central concepts that we will apply throughout the remainder of the course.

Finally, my decisions have clearly been informed by a philosophy of undergraduate education – what I call liberal professional education (Rowland 2007). My perspective is that over the past two decades our curriculum has taken a turn to be more and more instrumentally oriented, that is focused on competence in specific entry-level jobs/tasks in communication. This is certainly important, especially given the costs of attending a private college. However, it needs to be strongly balanced by, and a part of, liberal education (for example, Katehi 2015). Equivalent job preparation is available at trade schools for far less, while our institution – a comprehensive college – is capable of doing something different and special. Systems thinking and design is a part of that, hence content and activities that go well beyond the communication context. The final unit of the course is about the conscious evolution of our species. Is that an important subject for a future professional and a citizen of the planet? Absolutely. Is it a direct outgrowth of systems thinking and design? Certainly. Is it a typical topic in communications management? No.

Next Steps

As the course has evolved, there have been a number of tensions that have impacted our efforts. These will continue to do so.

I have mentioned several already: the balance between liberal education and professional preparation; the uniqueness of transdisciplinary subject matter versus conformity to college expectations; and my personal development of a different teaching style, in tandem with a different approach, versus the need for others to teach the course.

The tension between content coverage and development of complex problem-solving capabilities is compounded by the recent demand for accountability. We must now write rather narrow student learning outcomes and demonstrate their achievement, primarily to satisfy external bodies (for example, accreditation boards).

Perhaps the greatest tension is the mixed blessing of success. Demand for the course is high and often goes unmet. Here I have considered a number of options. The expected and understandable response from administration is to increase class size. However, the activities are designed for approximately 20 students, and that size works very well. Following a common model in the sciences, a large lecture session with smaller labs might work. However, most activities would require a major redesign, and it is not clear who would teach the labs and what could be shifted and remain effective in large lecture sessions. We have a master's program, but the typical student in this program would not be prepared to facilitate a systems thinking and design lab, and one of the promises the institution makes to parents and students is instruction by faculty, not graduate assistants.

Adding to the demand, colleagues from a number of departments and programs on campus have approached me over the years to include the course in their curricula. The answer has been consistently no for programs outside of my school because there are too many of our majors who need the seats. (Also, for context if you are at a university, our teaching load has recently been reduced from 4-4 to 4-3, that is, to seven courses per year.) The answer was yes only once, for a program outside my department but within the school. The difference was not academic necessity or strength of rationale; it was political – a faculty vote on curriculum within the school. As you might infer, I would prefer a wider mix of students with different majors in the course. It is more enriching for everyone when that is the case.

One option that I have taken and that has proven very successful, though, is to offer a similar experience in another form. Through an internal grant, colleagues and I have developed four one-credit short courses on systems and design, and these are available to students in any major. Over the past five years we have offered more than 60 of these courses to over 1,000 students, with faculty members from all schools at the college participating (see Rowland *et al.* 2011). In these we have used a co-teaching model to scale the effort, and I believe one of our greatest successes has been helping the participating faculty think beyond their disciplines.

As a final thought, I recognize that the tensions described here have not always been negative. Rather, some have served as a source of creativity and led to broader benefits. For example, the inability to offer more sections of Systems Thinking and Design triggered the development of the short courses for all students, and this brought in many more faculty who otherwise would not have been involved. Ultimately, I believe we will be better served by adopting this attitude and looking for broad potential in such tensions. It is designerly to do so.

References

Banathy, B. H. (1991) *Systems Design of Education: A Journey to Create the Future.* Englewood Cliffs, NJ: Educational Technology Publications

Katehi, L. (2015, May 26) 'Liberal arts and our future'. *Huffington Post*. Available at: http://www.huffingtonpost.com/linda-katehi/liberal-arts-and-our-futu_b_7444758.html

Nelson, H. (1994) 'The necessity of being "undisciplined" and "out of control": Design action and systems thinking'. *Performance Improvement Quarterly*, 7(3), pp. 22–29

Rowland, G. (2007). *The Promise of Liberal Professional Education*. Available at: http://faculty.ithaca.edu/rowland/docs/Promise/

Rowland, G. (2013) 'Powerful learning experiences: What we have learned'. *Performance Improvement Quarterly*, 26(2), pp. 39–43

Rowland, G., Hamilton, J. and Morales, M. (2011) 'The IICC Project: Integration-Insight-Creativity-Character'. *International Journal of Designs for Learning*, 2(1), pp. 18–39

Senge, P. (1990) *The Fifth Discipline: The Art and Practice of the Learning Organization*. New York, NY: Doubleday

17 Design Thinking in Action

Perspectives on Teaching and Redesigning a Learning Design Studio

Michael M. Rook and Simon Hooper

Introduction

The Learning Design Studio (LDS) at the Pennsylvania State University is a studio-based course that provides students with opportunities to develop learning technologies - digital artifacts that can support, or even transform, how, when, and where teaching and learning take place. The Learning Design Studio is different from other studio-based courses in many Educational Technology programs. For example, those with an Instructional Design orientation emphasize the development of instruction to produce specific learning outcomes. In a sense, such approaches are more the application of rules to produce outcomes rather than a design approach to produce an ultimate particular (Nelson and Stolterman 2012).

In contrast, the goals for LDS are more closely aligned with Fallman's (2008) notion of Interaction Design and Papert's (1991) notion of Constructionism. Interaction Design combines three areas of study: design practice, design exploration, and design study. Design practice engages participants in design activities as part of a design team. Design exploration involves experimentation resulting in artifacts that reflect what is possible rather than what fits into an existing conception of current practice. The Interaction Designer experiments by producing multiple iterations to consider what is possible – what would be ideal rather than what fits. Design study involves engaging in the research base of design theory, methodology, history, and philosophy.

The Learning Design Studio follows a similar model to Idit Harel's Constructionist Software Design Studio, which orients students to "cultural, pedagogical, as well as technical support... to become software designers" (Papert 1991, p. 1). Constructionism is often described simply as learning through designing, constructing, or learning-by-making. We believe that one cannot simply teach technology, or creativity, or design, but that students must learn these things while engaged in the practice of building tools, learning from failures, and engaging in peer critique (Smith 2006).

It is interesting to reflect on how the teaching of LDS has evolved. Initially we sought to teach multimedia design and development. All students learned foundational web design and development skills: web programming (for example, HTML/CSS/HTML5, etc.), graphic and video design (for example, Photoshop; iMovie; etc.), and databases (for example, MySQL/PHP, etc.). However, as diverse students enrolled in LDS we realized that learning designers have varied technology skill needs, and that each student should develop facility and agency with the technologies they will encounter in their areas of expertise.

In LDS, we promote the notion that technology should be used to transform teaching and learning rather than to reproduce existing learning methodologies. The course emphasizes three separate but complementary components: design expertise, technology skill development, and design thinking. By participating in design activities and artifact creation, team members develop tacit knowledge and competence. Students engage in (and, hopefully, contribute to) the intellectual discipline of the field, and learn from the experiences of others in related fields.

In this chapter we investigate how we can achieve these goals. We present LDS from the perspective of the two current instructors who have influenced and taught the course since its inception in 2007. We outline the structure of LDS, describe our individual and combined perspectives and pedagogical approaches, and conclude with our vision for the future of LDS based on our current design challenges. Our goal is to provide a detailed case that can be used as a blueprint for creating or redesigning a learning design studio.

Overview

What is Learning Design Studio?

The LDS is a studio-based course that develops design- and software-development skills across four instructional levels. At the beginning of the course students select a level. Those in levels 1-3 establish a learning pathway – a personalized curriculum of technology modules that students choose to learn. The course is structured to allow a student to repeat the course up to four times, each time building a different learning pathway. A student who has already completed level 1 would select different technology modules and different course readings. Whereas levels 1-3 emphasize learning new design and development skills, level 4 involves using the competencies from the first 3 levels to plan and implement a solution to an educational problem (see Figure 17.1 for the current titles of each instructional level; read Hooper *et al.* 2015, for a detailed description and theoretical orientation of the LDS levels).

Historical Perspectives

The LDS began as an elective course in the Learning, Design, and Technology curriculum at Penn State in 2007. The second author, Simon,

Figure 17.1 The Spring 2014 LDS Homepage.

was the first course instructor. The first author, Michael, was a student in the first iteration of the course, and transitioned from student, to teaching assistant, to co-instructor between 2007 and 2014. During the Fall 2014 semester, Michael and Simon co-taught LDS. In Table 17.1 we outline both Michael's and Simon's individual experiences to provide context for the teaching of LDS.

Current Course Experience

A Day in Learning Design Studio

The LDS meets weekly for three hours in a technology-enabled teaching facility known as the Krause Innovation Studio. The Krause Innovation Studio classroom has state-of-the-art presentation capabilities, several breakout rooms, and diverse technology-based collaboration tools (see Figure 17.2). The classroom includes four tables with six chairs placed as if spokes in a wheel.

Table 17.1 Individual perspectives on LDS.

Michael (7 years of teaching experience)	Simon (33 years of teaching experience)
The notion of design that I have focused on in my teaching has been in the field of multimedia design for learning technologies at the K-12 and higher education levels. Although I have taught since 2006, I began teaching design on my own in the fall of 2008 as instructor of Instructional Design for Multimedia Technologies, a course almost identical to the first level of LDS. The course focused on the development of multimedia using current software environments such as Adobe Dreamweaver and Flash.	I have taught learning design in graduate programs at the university level since 1989 at two R-1 institutions. At the first university I taught in the department of Curriculum and Instruction. Most students attracted to the program had educational backgrounds; few had in-depth experience with technology. At my current institution fewer students have educational backgrounds, most have an interest in instructional or learning design but, once again, few have deep technology experiences.
During project time, I walked around the room and facilitated conversations with individual students about their work, their challenges, and possible ideas and/or solutions. Each time I taught this course, the course enrollment was under ten so the facilitation and individualized discussion worked nicely and allowed for productive work.	For several years I taught my students to develop interactive curriculum materials with Authorware. I also taught courses for teachers on integrating technology in their classrooms. Teachers would learn to use various multimedia design and development tools and consider what it meant to integrate technology into the curriculum. In the late 1990s I became interested in designing and developing more
Over the past few years I have transitioned from student of LDS to co-instructor of the course. As co-instructor, I found that I could offer support when it was clear that I was the expert in the topic at hand. This came into play with a discussion around installing a WordPress instance on a server and running the instance as a website.	interactive technology. Before 1995 there was little connection from multimedia products to the Internet - these were essentially independent environments, and they were not mixed. Moreover, the tools that existed provided little to support such connections. Then came Flash. Flash was a game changer because it allowed developers to create truly interactive experiences that went beyond asking questions and judging the accuracy
In my interactions with students, I have found that many of the problems I encounter have focused on scaffolding and feedback. Both Simon and I have had conversations in the past on if it is better to have students learn basic understandings of design first and then provide students with opportunities to scaffold each other while they engage with projects, or to start with projects immediately (even if students are lacking in basic understandings of design) and demonstrate scaffolding with the hope that students will learn to scaffold each other. This has been a chicken *vs.* egg challenge that I still do not have a great answer to. I know that in my time as sole	of a response or using drill and practice environments to test for knowledge comprehension. Flash also encouraged designers to consider the nature of the interface that was most suitable for the end user(s). For years I have "taught" interactive design. By that I mean I have used a structured curriculum to lead people to design and develop web-based technology. This is not the same as technology integration. Technology integration involves the use of existing technology in the classroom. Creating web-based technology involves design, and design is a completely different way of thinking.

Michael (continued)

instructor of the multimedia course, I wanted to provide my students with opportunities to learn from each other (through scaffolding) even if I did not provide it to them during the semester.

Looking back I see the potential value in a support network focused on peer assistance for students' challenges. To act upon this idea I started to think about a research program to understand the experience of peer assistance in technology application and development.

During my time co-teaching the course I surveyed students at the beginning of the semester to determine where design expertise resided and how I could help students use each other when they encountered issues in class. However, my proposed solution to this problem (that of finding the experts with different software tools and applications prior to starting development work) introduced new issues related to: 1) student expertise; and 2) challenges with online students. Students thought they knew more than their peers, yet described their own expertise as little to none. Also, students participating online did not have as much of an opportunity to assist peers as those in the resident (face-to-face) environment.

That said, I am enthusiastic about the potential of a studio-based course on producing quality learning designers. Often students come into a program having varied and diverse expertise, especially with a lack of expertise in designing and developing artifacts using software applications. A studio not only provides students with experience in developing their own solutions, but also offers opportunities to scaffold peers and form networks through which to provide feedback and design critiques.

Simon (continued)

I moved to the Pennsylvania State University in 2007 after teaching for 18 years at my previous institution. At that time I was becoming very interested in design and design thinking. I knew I didn't want to use technology as a way of increasing the efficiency of the current educational system, as I was never enamored with direct instruction or with Instructional Design. I saw the move as a way to reinvent myself. I started to ask myself questions about why I taught the way I taught and I began to think about how I could incorporate Inquiry into my teaching. I had also learned a lot about design through personal practice in consulting. I had discovered that making things taught me a tremendous amount, not only about how to become a better developer but also a better learning designer. Around that time I had many conversations with faculty at the University of Georgia who had incorporated a design studio into their Instructional Design curriculum. I was impressed with the enthusiasm their students displayed for the teaching approach and wondered whether I could do something similar - although I didn't want to simply replicate their model.

I also remembered conversations I had with students. They often told me how they wished they could have taken the same course with me multiple times. They explained that there was so much to learn that they would like to be able to retake the course, and they believed they would learn a lot by doing so. These students also told me that they loved my teaching style - all they needed was the permission to study what they really wanted to learn and the occasional prod to move them in the right direction. What they wanted was for me to "wind them up and let them go!"

Figure 17.2 The Krause Innovation Studio classroom at the Pennsylvania State University.

The space is very colorful to stimulate creativity. Small white boards, suitable for sketching and presenting, hang on rails along the walls. Each table includes electric outlets (for charging computers) and VGA cables to project up to six devices. The classroom includes five projectors and display screens, one at each table and a fifth for convenience. There is no obvious front of the classroom and there is ample room to move around. For many of these reasons, it is an ideal design space (read Rook *et al.* 2015 for additional information about the Krause Innovation Studio).

The LDS follows a consistent weekly format. Class begins with one of two alternating biweekly activities each lasting approximately 30 minutes. One, known as "What's Hot?", involves students using the Yammer social media space to post at least one new-technology idea before class. Postings are expected to address new technologies that support teaching and learning. We meet in a small, intimate, breakout area (see Figure 17.3) where students are invited (but not required) to introduce their posts. The activity is popular among students as it is an excellent way to keep up with emerging educational-technology innovations. The other activity involves students meeting in self-selected groups to discuss development on learning pathway projects. Students have requested opportunities to observe and discuss their project approaches on similar design activities with peers. Next, we move into the classroom for one of three activities: 1) discussions of course readings; 2) in-class design activities; and 3) project work.

Figure 17.3 The Breakout Area in the Krause Innovation Studio.

Discussions of course readings

Students are assigned to one of two (or sometimes three) reading groups. First timers read introductory articles about design and design thinking. Others read *The Design Way* (Nelson and Stolterman 2012), a more advanced (and conceptually complex) design text. Students who have completed both sets of readings are asked to select their own readings relevant to their individual project interests. All students are expected to have completed readings before class and to have either written a response or recorded a video-log summarizing the main points and stating a personal perspective. The first reading discussion is moderated by the course instructor, but students are assigned to lead subsequent discussions. Students frequently mention the value of these small-group discussions in post-course evaluations.

In-class design activities

Design activities occur four times each semester. Students are assigned to small heterogeneous-experience groups (so expertise is distributed) to work on design tasks. The activities often change each semester, but the general idea is that a design process is followed, and each group produces and presents an artifact reflecting the ideas produced from a group brainstorm. The first design task introduces design thinking, a design process created at

Stanford's d.School (as described in IDEO 2009, and Kelley and Littman 2001). We use this process because it provides students with an open-ended design process that is suitable for framing and thinking about design challenges. The process is similar to the advanced notion of design presented by Nelson and Stolterman (2012), who describe design thinking as a cognitive "model of design inquiry" (p. 7). Subsequent design activities emphasize using the design thinking process to address a series of design challenges.

Project work

The third activity involves each student working on self-selected technology-learning modules (although level 4 students do not work on technology modules: they work alone or in a small group on a self-identified design challenge). During project work, we often find students learning from each other, acting as more knowledgeable peers, and providing peer scaffolding.

At the end of the semester students give a presentation highlighting some aspect of the project(s) on which they have been working. We ask students to present using the Pecha Kucha format. Students find these presentations surprisingly difficult to perform, but when they are done well they are very powerful. For example, one student sang her final presentation.

Current Teaching Practice

Compared with traditional college teaching, the role of the LDS instructor changes considerably in content knowledge requirements, pedagogy, and assessment practice.

Content

Course content knowledge is challenging as the course is essentially four courses in one. Course instructors must not only understand how to use (and be aware of what can be accomplished with) technologies across a broad spectrum of educational contexts, they must understand design thinking, be familiar with multiple sets of course readings, and be able to help students with diverse development and programming issues.

Pedagogy

The pedagogical approach shifts between content delivery and providing students with guidance and structure. During project work students are asked to complete technology modules, often with the support of video-based tutorials such as those found on Lynda.com. During project work, we avoid leading students to pre-determined answers as we believe that novice designers learn best from guidance to help them grow from failure. The guidance we provide comes in the form of carefully timed nudges toward experiences or resources that produce the desired outcomes or help the students figure out answers to their problems. This ability to prompt and question is a valuable skill for an instructor to develop.

Another consideration in teaching LDS involves fostering creativity. Throughout the semester, students receive instructor and peer feedback. It is the instructor's role to establish a community of respect because students can be each other's biggest critics. The instructor should encourage students to avoid harsh criticism, which tends to stifle creative work and limit students' confidence.

Assessment

University policy requires that we assign letter grades although assigning grades is one of our least favorite activities in LDS. We believe that giving feedback is essential but that assigning letter grades to graduate students is not. Students need formative feedback that can be used to guide improvement rather than summative data that does little to improve personal progress. Grading is competency based. When possible, we establish skills/ standards that must be achieved. If students achieve a standard they receive full course credit.

Feedback comes from formative and summative evaluation generated by instructors, peers, or self, and design critiques known as desk crits. Instructors use desk crits (in which students present their work to small groups of peers) to provide formative feedback, and summative feedback on completed projects. It is imperative that desk crits provide constructive feedback that motivates students, especially considering students in LDS (who often come from non-design fields) frequently doubt their own ability.

Students often ask the instructors whether their work is of satisfactory quality (presumably to be able to get a good grade). There are at least two answers to the quality question. The first, which has become our tongue-in-cheek mantra is: "No it is not good enough, because design is never finished." The second is more complex, and more helpful. It involves guiding the student to generate insight into ways his/her work could improve. Sometimes that information will come from the instructor, and sometimes from a more knowledgeable other. Ideally, and eventually, it will come from the student. The longer a student spends in LDS, the less likely he/she will ask the quality question. It's not difficult to understand why students behave in this way as they have been conditioned, through repeated exposure in other university courses, to meet the external expectation(s) of a course instructor. However, when students "get it" they tend to become motivated and realize that project improvement is more about personal growth. Motivation in this case changes from engagement in course content to acquire a grade to engagement as "time to think, to dream, to gaze, to get a new idea and try it and drop it or persist, time to talk, to see other people's work and their reaction to yours" (Papert 1991, p. 3).

Current and Future Teaching Challenges

Online and Hybrid LDS

Our university has a long history with technology in education and a well-established presence and architecture for online course delivery. Given the reduced enrollments projected for residential masters courses and degree programs, many academic units are being encouraged to recruit students into online programs. Likewise, LDS is being redesigned for online delivery.

Design studios are typically taught face-to-face but we are trying to provide an experience for an online audience that reflects the conditions needed to design and develop effective online learning environments. Hirsh-Pasek *et al.* (2015) identified four learning pillars from literature in the Learning Sciences. To be educationally effective, online learning environments should be 1) active, 2) engaged, 3) meaningful, and 4) socially interactive. That is, learners should be involved in their learning experiences, they should be engaged in the content they are learning, the learning experiences should produce learning that is personally meaningful, and there should be high-quality interaction and collaboration among peers. Additionally, learners should receive sufficient guidance to support exploration, discovery, and rapid recovery from failure. Although targeted at children's app design, similar conditions are likely to be relevant for online learning courses and for adults as well as for children.

Parts of the course are expected to be relatively straightforward to replicate in the online environment. For example, we have a curriculum in place that requires students to select the technology modules they want to complete. Learning resources are provided in various formats; students learn the technologies and then demonstrate their understanding on related design and development activities. However, those involving the establishment of collaborative relationships for peer assistance (as are required for completing the design activities, providing design critiques, and for analysis of course readings) are anticipated to be challenging.

Students who meet residentially work in small groups on design activities. For example, we present scenarios from educational settings and ask students to design software apps or other technologies. Likewise we believe that discussing course readings is important. Discussion establishes an environment in which students can check their understanding, experience multiple perspectives on complex issues, and explore the implications of what they have read. Such discussions are difficult to nurture in face-to-face settings, but even more complicated in online settings. Indeed, online students do not necessarily meet at the same time or in the same place.

We have found it difficult to establish an online collaborative environment that affords different forms of communication during the design process, and even harder in an online environment is establishing the type of face-to-face community that evolves over the course of a semester. We have much to learn about how to how to establish a community of practice (Wenger 1998) comprising both residential and fully online students. Our challenge is to determine how the array of existing and emerging tools can support communication and collaboration to facilitate the design process. In the future, we anticipate multiple attempts to rethink community. Thus, we are engaged in an iterative process of designing versions of the class for hybrid and distance delivery.

LDS Anytime, Anywhere

The Krause Innovation Studio affords opportunities for residential students to meet and collaborate face-to-face, allows fluid movement between groups during design activities, supports prototyping through use of multiple whiteboards and other surfaces, and can be used by students to work on individual projects. That said, the Studio doors are closed outside regular hours; LDS students typically have access to the spaces during regular class hours and for limited time periods during the rest of the week. One of our long-term goals is to establish a space that LDS students can use 24-hours a day and 7-days a week. It would be interesting to study how a 24-hour space dedicated to LDS could change the course and community dynamics.

We also plan to rethink the digital space. We would like to establish a setting that enables asynchronous group interactions that span semesters. We would like the LDS digital environment to be a self-sustaining community in which current students can interact with group members, share digital artifacts, and communicate with previous LDS students. In such a system, a previous LDS student could rejoin the community and complete a new module. LDS might shift from a traditional course to a competency approach that current and previous students can access anytime and anywhere.

Scaffolding Novices

We've identified three teaching challenges in LDS focused on scaffolding novices: establishing best practices; choosing an educational problem; and providing design support.

Best practices

In many fields (for example, architecture design, industrial design), there are agreed-upon examples of great designs that novices can study. In learning design and the design of learning technologies, this perspective is lacking. We do not have agreed-upon examples of digital artifacts that are transforming educational practices. Such examples could provide novices with informed understandings of design exploration. Also, these examples could include detailed descriptions of the design process and thinking during the production of an artifact. Over the next few years, we hope to begin a conversation that calls for the creation of such a list of great designs in learning design.

Educational problems

We have not been able to get students in the early levels of LDS to identify an educational problem on which to work. We believe that novices often find such a goal to be intimidating. We hope to scaffold this activity by developing a framework that guides students on how to find an appropriate project on which to work for a full semester. We intend to generate examples of sample projects that can be used by students who cannot find their own projects. Working on authentic projects is likely to help students to apply design thinking in their project designs, and will make it easier to determine which technologies to learn to use to support project development.

Design support

As mentioned in Michael's individual perspective (see Table 17.1), there is significant value in providing a support network for students as they encounter design challenges and failures. We are interested in understanding how we can use digital tools to support struggling students. This will become a future tension and commitment in our work as we seek to provide students with 24/7 access to design support through instructor, previous student, web, or peer assistance.

Final Thoughts

While teaching LDS has been a worthwhile pursuit, it is not without challenges. In addition to what we have already identified, LDS takes a considerable amount of time to teach and involves continual and iterative redesigns. That said, the amount of effort pales in comparison to the joy and satisfaction that comes with being an instructor of a learning design studio. We hope this chapter has expressed this enjoyment and motivates others to consider teaching or redesigning a studio-based course.

References

Fallman, D. (2008) 'The interaction design research triangle of design practice, design studies, and design exploration'. *Design Issues*, 24(3), pp. 4–18

Hirsh-Pasek, K., Zosh, J. M., Golinkoff, R. M., Gray, J. H., Bobb, M. B. and Kaufman, J. (2015) 'Putting education in "educational" apps: Lessons from the science of learning'. *Psychological Science in the Public Interest*, 16(1), pp. 3–34

Hooper, S., Rook, M. M. and Choi, K. (2015) 'Reconsidering the design of a learning design studio' in B. Hokanson (Ed.) *The Design of Learning Experience: Creating the Future of Educational Technology*. New York, NY: Springer-Verlag

IDEO (2009) Human centered design toolkit (2nd Ed.). Available at: http://www.ideo.com/work/human-centered-design-toolkit

Kelley, T. and Littman, J. (2001) 'The art of innovation: Lessons in creativity from IDEO, America's leading design firm'. New York, NY: Currency Books

Nelson, H. G. and Stolterman, E. (2012) *The Design Way: Intentional Change in an Unpredictable World* (2nd Ed.). Cambridge, MA: MIT Press

Papert, S. (1991) 'Situating constructionism' in I. Harel and S. Papert (Eds) *Constructionism* (pp. 1–11). Norwood, NJ: Ablex

Rook, M. M., Choi, K. and McDonald, S. P. (2015) 'Learning theory expertise in the design of learning spaces: Who needs a seat at the table?' *Journal of Learning Spaces*, 4(1), pp. 1–13

Smith, B. (2006) 'Design and computational flexibility'. *Design Creativity*, 17(2), pp. 65–72

Wenger, E. (1998) *Communities of Practice: Learning, Meaning, and Identity*. New York, NY: Cambridge University Press

18 What is Studio?

Katherine S. Cennamo

Introduction

The term "studio," while socialized as a common pedagogical term in traditional design contexts, has emerged as a much looser construct when applied to other disciplines. In traditional design disciplines such as architecture, a studio class may meet for four hours a day, three days a week, in the studio space where all students have individual desks available to them around the clock. In this architecture context, students are presented with a design challenge that is intentionally brief and open-ended – the "design brief." They then participate in design tasks under the supervision of a professor who holds periodic critique sessions in multiple forms. Students are enculturated into the ways of architecture through exploring design problems, receiving feedback on their work, and subsequently developing their designs in an iterative fashion. As they present their design work in public critiques, students learn to communicate using the vocabulary of the discipline, and develop both their skills and identity as designers (for example, Dannels 2005). Studios in traditional design disciplines such as architecture are not without problems (see, for example, Gray and Smith, this volume, Chapter 19) but, nonetheless, aspects of the traditional design studios have been adopted in various forms.

Even a cursory review of educational literature, however, quickly reveals that the construct of studio means different things to different authors, depending on the academic and professional cultures in which they live and work. The studios described in this book represent an equally broad view of studio, illustrating a wide variety of studio formats. Although the studio mode of teaching has indisputably been applied broadly, to build a deeper theoretical and practical understanding of how to teach in the studio mode, it is important to address a core question left largely unaddressed in the literature – what is studio?

In this chapter, I will briefly review the history of the academic design studio, discuss characteristics of studio-based instruction and the ways in which it might vary, and examine how the culture in which the academic design studio is situated impacts its implementation. I hope this framework will give you a way to think about the design cases presented in the remaining chapters.

Historical Views of the Studio

The studio approach in European and North American design programs has a long tradition. The studio, as it was first introduced, had roots in the common apprenticeship-driven training of artisans, which stretches back millennia in craft history (Nelson and Stolterman 2012; Schön 1985). To follow the example presented previously, the earliest training approaches for students hoping to work as architects came in apprenticeships, at first in workshops and then, by the early nineteenth century, in architectural firms and drafting rooms in more formal educational spaces.

This apprenticeship model of the master craftsman and their student developed into the atelier-based system at the École des Beaux-Arts in France during the early nineteenth century (Cret 1908; 1941), allowing for a greater number of students than the traditional apprenticeship model. The atelier system followed the intent of the apprenticeship system but at larger scale, allowing ateliers or professors to lead groups of students throughout their professional training in painting, sculpture, and architecture. The ateliers promoted the "exchange of advice, help and criticism among the students," and were primarily responsible for the development of their students over multiple years of education (Cret 1941, p.11). The school also provided pedagogical structure for all students, including the issuance of competitions for design projects and the formation of design juries, or panels of experts, to judge the results of the submitted projects (Cret 1941).

By the mid-nineteenth century, two European models for training designers in more formal, standardized educational settings, instead of in strictly apprenticeship models, were of increasing influence: the German network of polytechnic schools and the French École des Beaux-Arts, based on the atelier model. Engineering programs, some of which pre-date the first formal architectural program in the United States, tended to adopt the German model, while other more traditional artistic disciplines followed the French model. When the first architectural programs were established in the United States, they were often associated with architects who had themselves studied in France at the École, and who thus brought with them the traditions and practices associated with the French model.

By the late-nineteenth century, the French model – and its associated design studio – was the dominant approach to architectural education in the United States. The French model was further refined through influences from the German Bauhaus in the early-twentieth century, especially after the dissolution of the Bauhaus in the 1930s as a result of the rise of Nazi Germany. The Bauhaus tradition brought an influx of modernist and functionalist thought, while relying on a more structured system of teaching design (Wick 2000). The core Bauhaus curriculum linked foundational courses and the study of materials and nature, leading to mastery of a specific type of design (see Figure 18.1). The organization of this design curriculum once

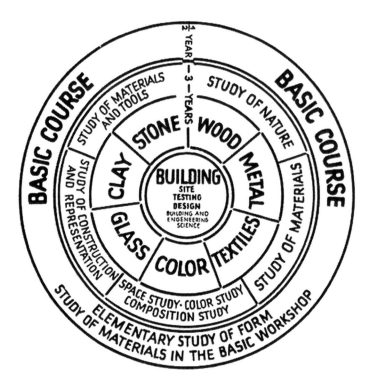

Figure 18.1 Diagram of the Bauhaus curriculum, as designed by Walter Gropius.

again increased the number of students who could be taught at any one time, and decreased the importance of the atelier system creating, rather, a thinking or philosophy of design on the school level, rather than primarily on the instructor or atelier level.

Studio-based learning remains the dominant form of education in architecture and a wide range of design disciplines such as engineering, interior design, and graphic design. In many, the studio is the "signature pedagogy" of the discipline (Shulman 2005). Yet, as noted in the opening to this chapter, the implementation of the studio – including essential instructional methods, learning environments, and patterns of student interaction – varies widely among individuals, institutions, and academic disciplines.

Features of the Studio

Clearly, when discussing studio approaches across academic disciplines and programs, there needs to be a way to talk about the differences and similarities among studio cultures – some way to acknowledge that studios might look different and still be "studios" in a more transdisciplinary sense. Toward that goal, Shaffer's (2007) ethnographic study of an architecture studio at the Massachusetts Institute of Technology (MIT) may provide a useful starting point. Based on his observations, Shaffer described the studio as a "coherent system" where *surface structures, pedagogical activities*, and *epistemology* interact to create a unique and immersive learning environment. The framing of studios in terms of these elements, as identified by Shaffer, can provide a way to discuss studios and how they might vary across contexts (Brandt *et al.* 2013).

Surface Structures

Surface structures include the easily identifiable physical and logistical components of a studio: the designed learning environment, presence and type of furniture, time blocks for access, materials or tools that are available, formal curricula and assignments. As defined by Shaffer (2007), surface structures are "the physical, temporal, material, and social context of action and interaction" (p. 103). Specific examples typical in traditional studios include the propensity toward extensive meeting time, availability of dedicated workspaces or lockers for each student, presence of a community space for presentation and gathering, and the affordance of multiple materials for modeling, prototyping, or sketching. It is the surface structures that are most evident when observing a studio in action.

Beyond the physical space, studios also have been implemented in virtual environments. Efforts to integrate technological tools to support features of extant physical spaces, including collaboration, sharing of work, and critique by peers and instructors (Blevis *et al.* 2008; Lotz *et al.* 2015), are ongoing and include explorations of the pedagogical implications of teaching and learning design in such virtual studio spaces (Kvan 2001).

Pedagogical Activities

Shaffer (2007) defines pedagogical activities as "the recurrent participant structures of roles and actions that organize activity in the studio" (p. 103). Schön (1987) refers to the studio pedagogy as centered on *learning-by-doing* and *reflection-in-action*, where design expertise is built over time through engagement in immersive, authentic activities and regular reflection both *on-action*, retroactively, and *in-action*, in the moment.

Critique is often cited as the primary pedagogical activity that motivates both reflection on-action and in-action (Schön 1987). While certain design disciplines emphasize certain forms of critique more than others (for example, summative formal design juries in architectural education), a wide range of critique forms are commonly found in design education (Oh *et al.* 2012), which are further categorized in descending order of formality and public accessibility by Hokanson (2012) into: formal (for example, design juries), seminar/group (for example, pinups), desk, and peer.

As a unique characteristic of the design studio and a central feature of the studio signature pedagogy, the critique serves not only as a means of assessment but also as a more holistic and developmental activity in which students test the coherence or communication of a design idea (Dannels *et al.* 2008). Klebesadel and Kornetsky (2009) underscore the primacy of critique noting that through "effective critique, students can and do learn theory, create arguments, and situate the performance or artwork into social, ethical, or political perspectives" (p. 116). This communication between students and instructors bridges design activity and developing design expertise, aiding in the formation of a professional design identity (for example, Dannels 2005; Gray 2013a).

As a primary form of developing design expertise, the communication patterns of the discipline, and one's identity as a designer, critiques are of value both to those who listen-in and those who are the subject of critiques (Cennamo and Brandt 2012). Through meta-discussions of concepts, behaviors, and skills, direct modeling and coaching of design-thinking, and explicit prompts and instructions, the studio instructors establish the participant roles and norms of both the studio classroom and the design discipline into which the students aspire as they respond to students' work (Cennamo *et al.* 2011).

While reflection, critique, and engagement in authentic design activity can be formal pedagogical practices that, in their implementation, are concurrently shaped by relationships of peers and the orientation of a studio culture or learning community, peer mentoring and collaborative design among group members can extend the reach of pedagogical activities (for example, Gray 2013b; 2014) and encourage individual and group discovery outside the confines of a formal studio meeting times.

Epistemology

In this context, epistemology refers to beliefs about what constitutes "knowing" and how that knowledge is constructed in the studio classroom. In Shaffer's study, he defined it as "ways of deciding what constitutes a legitimate architectural claim. That is, the conceptual and intellectual warrants that validate activity" (2007, p. 103). In looking beyond the architectural classroom, the epistemology of the studio reflects the core beliefs of a discipline, classroom, studio facilitator, and group of design students, and emerges as a cluster of emergent normative qualities that define ways of being and acting in a specific disciplinary context (Brandt *et al.* 2013). "Different communities of practice (for example, different professions) have different epistemologies: different ways of knowing, of deciding what is worth knowing, and of adding to the collective body of knowledge and understanding" (Shaffer 2003, p. 5). For example, Brandt *et al.* (2013) reported very different conceptions of what constituted "good design" when comparing an industrial design and a human-computer interaction (HCI) studio classroom. Whereas the industrial design studio demonstrated a reflective practice paradigm, in which the uniqueness of the design problem was examined through multiple design solutions subjectively analyzed in the design critique, the HCI studio course applied a problem-solving paradigm that valued a logical, step-wise analysis of the design problem and the empirical data of usability. Other epistemological differences arise in considering the role of instructor as "studio master" or "co-constructor of knowledge;" the purpose of critique as primarily oriented towards assessment or socialization into the profession, or the relation of academically-focused project work to future professional expectations.

Studio and Practice Communities

When seeking to categorize elements of a complex environment such as a studio, I acknowledge the risk of oversimplifying the relationships among studio components and offer these categories not to oversimplify but, instead, to provide a language that can examine what makes a studio what it is. Any analysis of the studio must acknowledge *discipline-specific* tools, practices, and beliefs, as well as *studio-specific* surface features, pedagogy, and epistemology.

It is important to consider how the academic design studio, in all its complexity, can be situated in, and prepares students to become members of, the larger professional community (Brandt *et al.* 2013). The activities students – and instructors – undertake in the studio depend, in part, on the discipline of design. This process starts with the purpose of design (for example, products for industrial design, interactions or experiences for HCI, instruction or learning for instructional design), and then moves outward to encapsulate the tools and practices for achieving that purpose. Numerous tools or methods are unique or characteristic of a particular design discipline: the production of blueprints or physical models in architecture, production of various prototypes or wireframes in HCI, and the creation of paper prototypes, design documents or specifications in instructional design. Just as studios are situated in a particular academic community, they are also situated in, and prepare students to become part of, a particular professional community of practice.

Interactions and Affordances

When examining what makes a studio, it is important to look beyond the surface structures of long hours, project-based assignments, critique sessions, and dedicated desk space, to better understand the pedagogy and epistemological understanding afforded or constrained by the methods through which students study design within their discipline. According to Greeno (1994), "an affordance relates attributes of something in the environment to an interactive activity by an agent who has some ability" (p. 388). As an example, consider the findings from a project in which my colleagues and I collected and analyzed over 100 hours of videotaped course activities and course documents from studio classes in architecture, industrial design, and HCI (Cennamo and Brandt 2012; Brandt *et al.* 2013). Based on our analysis, we found that the time available for studio-based instruction created tensions between pedagogical control *vs.* flexibility.

The architecture and industrial design classes met for four hours at a time, three days per week. The instructors intentionally drafted their syllabi to be flexible and responsive to the needs of the students. In one instance, the industrial design instructor was having difficulty with the sophomore students not being innovative and not evolving in their work on a project. She noted in her journal: "I decided to use a method of iteration that I had used before with juniors as a way of giving structure and a deadline, which is often so much more valuable than time. Students were asked to develop 10 concepts for their [projects] on 10 pieces of paper. They were to bring these to the next class. We spent much of the next week going through these concepts pinned up on the wall." This scenario is representative of what was observed in this studio environment: flexibility worked at both a pedagogical level (to address the development of a particular classroom of students), and at an epistemological level. The extended time blocks available to the architecture and industrial design faculty allowed for the inclusion of activities during class that encouraged active experimentation and iteration. Moments in the curriculum, planned and spontaneous, in which students and faculty collaborated together in a common design problem, not only developed the students' facility with the design process, but also enhanced students' epistemological understanding of the studio and professional norms.

In contrast, the HCI classes met for approximately two and a half hours per week. Time constraints resulted in the HCI instructors holding a high level of pedagogical control over the studio practices. Student critiques were often timed for pragmatic rather than pedagogical purposes. At these universities, these single courses were the only exposure to HCI that most computer science students had. Hence both HCI instructors used lectures to ensure coverage of key principles within the discipline. The course requirements and time limits made it difficult to rely primarily on the projects, associated critiques, and peer mentoring for revealing principles of importance. Although they lacked the luxury of ample space and time, the HCI instructors dealt creatively with the constraints to develop a similar set of affordances. For example, the HCI instructors carefully orchestrated the sequence of projects so the succession of the assignments and the iterative exercises made efficient use of the limited time in the compressed nature of the university quarter system. The assignments incrementally increased in complexity until the final project, which required students' awareness of programming and design at multiple levels.

The way in which studio is enacted can vary by discipline and academic program, often bounded by logistical concerns, epistemologically grounded notions of how knowledge is built and communicated, and past experiences in implementing or participating in traditional art and design studios. Yet decisions made in one aspect of the studio impact others. Consider the decision to assign individual or group work as a way to demonstrate the interaction between components in a generative way. In this case, the structure and requirements of the project is the primary pedagogical activity that encourages or directs students to form teams or work in prescribed ways. A shift in this pedagogical activity may affect other studio components. The surface features of the studio may be adapted to facilitate group work – tables may be moved together, meetings may become the norm rather than individual, solitary work, and collaborative design activities (for example, brainstorming, affinity diagramming) may dominate the student's physical experience of the studio. The epistemological underpinnings of the studio may evolve, particularly in studios that have previously valued individual work as a primary measurement of academic progress; team evaluations and assessments may be necessary, norms of competition between students may be realigned, and the pedagogy may value "soft skills" relating to collaboration as highly as an individual's tool or design knowledge.

Affordances of surface structures also provide, or enable, opportunities for both physical function and social interaction as perceived by both the instructor and the students. The presence of designed artifacts – either in process or completed – can further illustrate this interaction among studio components. The designed artifacts reinforce the expected behaviors of the studio and can serve as a close-at-hand source of design precedent within the field of design (Oxman 1990; Vyas and Nijholt 2012). The designed artifacts serve as a boundary object where the physicality of the artifacts communicates the normalcy of their presence in the space (i.e., surface features); the utility of these artifacts is felt by students and professors in academic and professional terms (i.e., pedagogical activities that cross between academic and professional contexts); and the value of this form of knowledge is understood and respected as a norm of the discipline in this context (i.e., an epistemological belief). So, while actions or interactions are not directly attributable to surface features, particular surface structures may enable certain learning benefits.

Commonalities Across Studios

If studios are situated in disciplinary communities of practice and academic communities, studios can and do vary in their surface structures, pedagogical activities, and epistemologies, and decisions made regarding one component impact the others, then what is *essential* for a studio? What is common across implementations?

To begin with, a *design studio must be focused on design problems*. Design problems are "wicked problems," characterized by a virtually infinite number of possible solutions, and are not tractable or solvable in their initially defined state (Rittel and Webber 1973). In this way, studio-based learning differs from problem-based learning or project-based learning (PBL) approaches. Although PBL *can* involve design problems, the pedagogy of PBL often focuses on narrowing or constraining the solutions through the process. As Monson (2008) noted, when solving a design problem: "the path of problem to solution maintained or increased possibilities rather than diminished them" (p. 10). In the language of Schön (1987), designers must learn to "…put things together and bring new things into being, dealing in the process with many variables and constraints, some initially known and some discovered through designing" (p. 42). Within the studio learning environment, students do not learn a body of content knowledge and then apply it but, instead, they learn *about* design while *doing* design (Lawson and Dorst 2009; Nelson and Stolterman 2012). Content acquisition is not separated from the practice of applying it; students increase their expertise as designers by engaging in design activity and reflecting on their design moves both in the moment (i.e., reflection-in-action) and after a design activity is complete (i.e., reflection-on-action) (Schön 1987). Design students are thus positioned to become practicing members of a professional community of practice with a design discipline – being and becoming a designer.

Looking Back, Looking Forward

The meaning that individuals hold for studio differs, depending on the academic and professional cultures in which they live and work; the chapters in this book are no exception. The studios described illustrate a wide variety of studio formats. Yet, they are linked by the belief that the studio method is of value in preparing design professionals.

As you read and reflect on the cases in this book, consider how the authors have used the surface structures of their studios to enable certain pedagogical activities, guided by their personal and disciplinary epistemologies. Notice how they interact to create a dynamic learning environment in which the students of design can develop their skills and identities through their experience of the studio culture. How are projects displayed for review? Do students work individually or in groups? How are the pedagogical activities enabled or restrained by the surface structures? Also, what do these activities reveal about the instructor's beliefs about how knowledge is constructed in their discipline? Consider, too, how the studio participants are prepared for their role in the studio classroom. Because the studio experience can be initially challenging for students, instructors and students must actively work to establish the rights and duties of the studio environment (Cennamo *et al.* 2011; Gray 2013a).

As you examine the numerous manifestations of studio in this book, note how the configurations of surface structure, pedagogy, and epistemology provide affordances (Gibson 1977; 1979) that are worthy of consideration when adapting the studio method. As you consider ways to incorporate the studio experience into your courses, you will also need to consider questions such as: What are the tools in which my students must become proficient? What activities will best prepare my students for the realities of their design practice? What is the epistemological foundation upon which I stand?

Acknowledgements

As with many long-term collaborations, in the end it is often difficult to determine to whom the manuscript belongs. I gratefully acknowledge the contributions of Colin Gray, who actively contributed not only his ideas and feedback on previous drafts, but several excellent segments of text that he graciously allowed to remain in this final version. I am grateful also to Kennon Smith for her contributions to prior versions. Although Colin and Kennon ultimately chose to develop a separate chapter, without a doubt, this chapter would have been very different without their contributions. I also would be remiss if I did not acknowledge my long-term collaborator Carol Brandt for her intellectual contributions to the research that is described herein. Thanks to all.

References

Blevis, E., Lim, Y. K., Stolterman, E. and Makice, K. (2008) 'The iterative design of a virtual design studio'. *Techtrends*, 52(1), pp. 74–83

Brandt, C. B., Cennamo, K., Douglas, S., Vernon, M., McGrath, M. and Reimer, Y. (2013) 'A theoretical framework for the studio as a learning environment'. *International Journal of Technology and Design Education*, 23(2), pp. 329–348

Cennamo, K. and Brandt, C. (2012) 'The right kind of telling: Knowledge-building in the academic design studio'. *Educational Technology Research and Development*, 60(5), pp. 839–858

Cennamo, K., Brandt, C., Scott, B., Douglas, S., McGrath, M., Reimer, Y. and Vernon, M. (2011) 'Managing the complexity of design problems through studio-based learning'. *Interdisciplinary Journal of Problem-based Learning*, 5(2), Article 5. Available at: http://docs.lib.purdue.edu/ijpbl/vol5/iss2/5

Cret, P. (1908) 'The École des Beaux Arts: What its architectural teaching means'. *Architectural Record*, 23, pp. 367–371

Cret, P. P. (1941) 'The École des Beaux Arts and architectural education'. *The Journal of the American Society of Architectural Historians*, 1(2), pp. 3–15

Dannels, D. P. (2005) 'Performing tribal rituals: A genre analysis of "crits" in design studios'. *Communication Education*, 54(2), pp. 136–160

Dannels, D., Gaffney, A. and Martin, K. (2008) 'Beyond content, deeper than delivery: What critique feedback reveals about communication expectations in design education'. *International Journal for the Scholarship of Teaching and Learning*, 2(2), pp. 1–16

Gibson, J. J. (1977) 'The theory of affordances' in R. E. Shaw and J. Bransford (Eds) *Perceiving, Acting and Knowing: Toward an Ecological Psychology*. Hillsdale, NJ: Lawrence Erlbaum Associates

Gibson, J. J. (1979) *The Ecological Approach to Visual Perception*. Boston, MA: Houghton Mifflin

Gray, C. M. (2013a) 'Factors that shape design thinking'. *Design and Technology Education*, 18(3), pp. 8–20

Gray, C. M. (2013b) 'Informal peer critique and the negotiation of habitus in a design studio'. *Art, Design and Communication in Higher Education*, 12(2), pp. 195–209, doi:10.1386/adch.12.2.195_1

Gray, C. M. (2014) 'Living in two worlds: A critical ethnography of academic and proto-professional interactions in a human-computer interaction design studio'. (Unpublished doctoral dissertation)

Gray, C. M. and Smith, K. M. (forthcoming) 'Critical views of studio education' in E. Boling, R. A. Schwier, K. Campbell, K. M. Smith and C. M. Gray (Eds) *Studio Teaching in Higher Education: Selected Design Cases*. New York, NY: Routledge

Greeno, J. G. (1994) 'Gibson's affordances'. *Psychological Review*, 101(2), pp. 336–342

Hokanson, B. (2012) 'The design critique as a model for distributed learning' in L. Moller and J. B. Huett (Eds) *The Next Generation of Distance Education: Unconstrained Learning* (pp. 71–83). Boston, MA: Springer

Klebesadel, H. and Kornetsky, L. (2009) 'Critique as signature pedagogy in the arts' in R. Gurung, N. Chick and A. Haynie (Eds) *Exploring Signature Pedagogies: Approaches to Teaching Disciplinary Habits of Mind* (pp. 99–120). Sterling, VA: Stylus Publishing

Kvan, T. (2001) 'The pedagogy of virtual design studios'. *Automation in Construction*, 10(3), pp. 345–353

Lawson, B. and Dorst, K. (2009) *Design Expertise*. Oxford, UK: Architectural Press

Lotz, N., Jones, D. and Holden, G. (2015) 'Social engagement in online design pedagogies' in *LearnxDesign: The 3rd International Conference for Design Education Researchers and preK-16 Design Educators (Vol. IV)* (pp. 1643–1668). Aalto, FI: Aalto University

Monson, C. (2008) 'Studio-based learning as pedagogic research: A case study of inquiry between architecture and education' in *2008 Annual Conference of the Association of Collegiate Schools of Architecture*. Last accessed 23 January 2010. Available at: https://www.acsaarch.org/files/conferences/teachers/2008/monson.pdf

Nelson, H. G. and Stolterman, E. (2012) *The Design Way: Intentional Change in an Unpredictable World* (2nd Ed.). Cambridge, MA: MIT Press

Oh, Y., Ishizaki, S., Gross, M. D. and Yi-Luen Do, E. (2012) 'A theoretical framework of design critiquing in architecture studios'. *Design Studies*, 34(3), pp. 302–325, doi: http://dx.doi.org/10.1016/j.destud.2012.08.004

Oxman, R. (1990) 'Prior knowledge in design: A dynamic knowledge-based model of design and creativity'. *Design Studies*, 11(1), pp. 17–28

Rittel, H. W. J. and Webber, M. M. (1973) 'Dilemmas in a general theory of planning'. *Policy Sciences*, 4(2), pp. 155–169

Schön, D. A. (1985) *The Design Studio: An Exploration of its Traditions and Potentials.* London, UK: RIBA Publications Limited

Schön, D. A. (1987) *Educating the Reflective Practitioner: Toward a New Design for Teaching and Learning in the Professions.* San Francisco, CA: Jossey-Bass

Shaffer, D. W. (2003) *Pedagogical Praxis: The Professions as Models for Learning in the Age of the Smart Machine.* WCER Working Paper No. 2003-6. Madison, WI: University of Wisconsin-Madison, Wisconsin Center for Educational Research

Shaffer, D. W. (2007) 'Learning in design' in R. A. Lesh, E. Hamilton and J. J. Kaput (Eds) *Foundations for the Future in Mathematics Education* (pp. 99–125). Mahwah, NJ: Lawrence Erlbaum

Shulman, L. S. (2005) 'Signature pedagogies in the professions'. *Daedalus*, 134(3), pp. 52–59

Vyas, D. and Nijholt, A. (2012) 'Artful surfaces: An ethnographic study exploring the use of space in design studios'. *Digital Creativity*, 23(3-4), pp. 176–195, doi:10.1080/14626268.2012.658522

Wick, R. (2000) *Teaching at the Bauhaus.* Ostfildern-Ruit: Hatje Cantz Verlag

19 Critical Views of Studio

Colin M. Gray and Kennon M. Smith

The studio remains a cornerstone of design education in the United States and is common in a wide range of design disciplines, including graphic design, interior design, product design, studio art, and architecture, among others (Hetland *et al.* 2007; Klebesadel and Kornetsky 2009). Studio experiences are seen in these disciplines as having critical value in providing students with authentic contexts for making complex judgments, exploring divergent paths, developing non-routine solutions to ill-structured problems, and encouraging tool mastery (Schön 1985). The success of these approaches, coupled with the ways of thinking and acting nurtured in these settings, suggests that studio approaches might be beneficially adopted or adapted in a variety of fields that have not traditionally utilized a studio pedagogy, yet require a similar acquisition of a complex array of knowledge and skills.

While studio is ubiquitous, enjoying almost universal acceptance as a signature pedagogy in many creative fields, the acculturation encouraged through studio learning is often coupled with an inadvertent reproduction of studio norms – both positive and negative – often with little awareness on the part of students and instructors responsible (Brandt *et al.* 2013; Gray 2014). In this chapter we wish to provide a more nuanced view of studio pedagogy, exploring critical views that have emerged within traditional understandings of studio, and fostering the exploration of critical evaluations of studio as it expands into disciplines that do not have a history of studio learning.

Criticality and Design Education

The center of studio learning - the critique - was portrayed by Donald Schön in the seminal text, *The Reflective Practitioner* (1983). Schön's view of the studio was centered on a desk critique, where he narrated the development of a design through the stereotypically paternalistic eyes of the male instructor, Quist. In this image of reflective practice, Schön describes a highly individualistic and socially isolated learning environment, picturing only the interactions between a novice student and expert instructor, ignoring virtually any other external influences or peer socialization that would commonly be found in a studio classroom (Webster 2008). While this one-on-one interaction between instructor and student is a popularly espoused view of studio, a number of scholars have assessed studio education in a more critical way, particularly in the context of architectural education, where critique practices have evolved over multiple centuries (Cuff 1991). While we cannot thoroughly review all scholars who have addressed studio pedagogy in a critical way, we will outline some common approaches and theoretical frames that have been productively used to explore the normative and epistemological dimensions of the studio in the past.

A critical focus on architectural education began in the 1980s, linking concerns of studio culture and the non-neutrality of such education with similar efforts being made at this time in the critical theory and critical pedagogy traditions (Dutton 1987; 1991). Following this trajectory, several scholars expanded on the normative commitments that are bound up in the studio environment, providing a more in-depth understanding of the often patriarchal and domineering "boot camp" student experience. Willenbrock (1991) used a critical lens to explore the student experience of the undergraduate studio environment, commenting on the power dynamics of critique culture, which particularly privileged the male voice, echoed by Webster (2008) almost two decades later. The same year, Anthony (1991) published an extensive volume documenting the competition and often harmful power relationships that were common across a range of architecture programs, and which led to a critique culture that was frequently driven by fear, intimidation, and bullying at the expense of student wellbeing and agency.

These critical approaches to essential components of the studio, such as the "crit," were buttressed by the importation of critical and social theory, explicating how the studio culture was sustaining itself over time and the constitutive norms that were responsible for the character of the studio. The work of Pierre Bourdieu, and particularly the construct of *habitus*, was introduced to the design pedagogy literature by Stevens (1995), and drawn on by Crysler (1995) in conjunction with the critical pedagogy perspective offered by Giroux, referencing Freire and others. *Habitus* and its relationship to related critical traditions allowed for a richer discussion of a negotiated experience, where privilege and power play a significant role in who is able to affect the studio culture and who is represented. This critical framing of design education allows for a broader exploration of the social climate that is created by the instructor through the selection of pedagogical techniques and learning environments – an inherently power-laden event (Anthony 1991; Crysler 1995). In addition, this perspective generatively complicates the learner role, moving from a primarily homogenous and passive view of the learner – privileging certain types of students and outcomes to the detriment of others – to a more democratic relationship that moves beyond unidirectional transmission of knowledge (Gray 2013; Stevens 1995). While there has not been a sustained investment on the part of the design education community in continuing to develop a specific critical vocabulary, more recent publications have built upon ideas common in critical pedagogy and critical theory in the past decade, informing investigations of issues such as power, equity, and agency in studio culture (for example, Oak and Lloyd 2014; Webster 2006; 2007), including a more in-depth understanding of how socialization in the studio environment is fostered through peer interactions (Gray 2013; 2014; Webster 2008).

Underlying Structures of the Studio

Recent theoretical frameworks of the studio include space for normative commitments that are tacitly reproduced (for example, Shaffer 2003; Brandt *et al.* 2013), often using the label of "epistemology" to describe beliefs about how knowledge is conveyed. However, these frameworks do not generally account for or link to the critical tradition that has been established in the studio pedagogy literature. While there is value in identifying the "habits of studio" that are conveyed to students through studio learning experiences, without documenting the power-laden and normative dimensions of the epistemological fabric the studio culture being reproduced can easily be hidden and give privileged access only to instructors.

The critical dimensions of epistemology can be traced back in the critical architectural literature (and even further to the critical pedagogy literature more broadly; for example, Freire 1970/2000) to a concept known as the *hidden curriculum* (Snyder 1971). The hidden curriculum encapsulates structures of the educational system such as "the ideology of knowledge and the social practices which structure the experiences of students and teachers" (Dutton 1991, p. 167), encompassing the implicit norms and values of working within a given discipline that are largely communicated through tacit and hegemonic means. In practical terms, the epistemology of the studio can promote harmful power relationships (see the Anthony 1991 discussion of design juries), while at the same time encouraging ethically-responsible design behaviors. However, no matter what curriculum is "designed," there is almost inevitably a disjuncture between the planned curriculum and what is experienced by students (Dutton 1991; Gray 2014). Willenbrock (1991) points out a number of disconnects in architectural education, including latent sexism, unjustified use of power in assessment of work or in student-professor communication. An evaluation of the epistemological structures of the studio that takes into account a critical perspective allows such issues to be raised, not to "point the finger" at professors for not doing a good job, but to promote active and continuous communication and reflection on the "organism" of the studio, to ensure it resolves issues that arise in a responsible manner.

When left unexamined, the epistemological structures of the studio can be complicit in unintentionally reproducing undesirable characteristics relating to power, sexism, or cultural insensitivity, not only affecting the learning environment of students, but also students' future professional identity. Brandt *et al.* (2013) observed that the studio served as a bridge between academic and professional communities of practice, identifying ways in which certain disciplines encouraged a stronger academic orientation (for example, human-computer interaction) while others encouraged a more centered orientation between academic preparation and professional practice (for example, industrial design). While this construction of the studio bridge allows for a helpful conversation about the nature of professional identity formation and the functioning of the studio in promoting this formation process, without including the student voice or understanding the power relationships that circumscribe the orientation of the studio bridge, we risk reproducing studio norms without examining the commitments they represent. For example, in a recent critical ethnography conducted by the first author in an HCI studio environment, students oriented the studio bridge much closer to practice, even while the instructors assumed an orientation towards the academic community (Gray 2014). This analysis demonstrates the fluidity of such theoretical constructs, and the value that critical perspectives on studio learning can offer, particularly in more richly defining the agency and capabilities of studio learners (Gray 2015; Gray and Howard 2015).

Concerns Regarding Studio Education

In the process of weighing the potential advantages of adopting a studio approach to learning, and in deciding the best ways to apply such approaches in their own classrooms, instructors would be well-served by understanding some of the persistent concerns that have been raised by other instructors and scholars embedded in disciplines that have a substantial history of using a studio approach. In order to better understand some of these issues, a review of literature (Smith and Young 2013) was conducted. Sources for this review were gathered both systematically (an examination of titles spanning 2000-2012 in the journals *Design Studies, Journal of Interior Design,* and *Journal of Architectural Education*), and opportunistically (through snowball techniques and searches identifying key texts such as Boyer and Mitgang 1996). Key concerns emerging from this review can be summarized with the four following questions:

1. Are the traditionally resource-intensive approaches to studio sustainable given contracting budgets and increasing accountability faced by many academic programs?
2. Do studio approaches tend to support students in gaining the knowledge, skills, and attributes they will need for successful professional practice?

3. Do studio approaches tend to promote a culture conducive to healthy work/study practices, open communication, and productive interpersonal relationships?
4. Do studio approaches provide enough flexibility to promote greater diversity among students, and thus eventually feed into professions that have been traditionally non-diversified?

While it might be surprising given the "good press" studio approaches often receive, for each of these questions there are voices in the reviewed literature that respond with a resounding "No." At the same time, voices on the other side of each debate might challenge the validity of such conclusions outright, minimize the importance of such concerns, or argue that the benefits of current studio approaches outweigh unavoidable (even if unfortunate) drawbacks. A full examination of arguments from both sides of each issue is beyond the scope of this current chapter, but we do wish to briefly outline some of the main concerns being raised, and to point the reader to useful paths in following up on specific points of interest. It is hoped that by so doing, instructors interested in exploring studio approaches can be forewarned of some of the pitfalls that others have experienced in the context of this approach.

Before examining each of these issues, the reader is asked to keep in mind two caveats as they consider the difficulties that have been reported by some embedded in traditional studio settings. First, in nearly every case, the issues and concerns raised by specific authors are not due to necessary or required aspects of studio, but to the ways studio has been enacted in specific contexts. Implementing a studio approach does not have to automatically lead to the types of outcomes discussed below, but there may be essential aspects of studio pedagogy that can leave participants vulnerable to specific patterns of negative experiences if they are not adequately recognized and safeguarded against. Second, with perhaps very few exceptions, the authors reviewed in this study were not advocating that studio approaches be jettisoned or otherwise avoided. Instead, they were overwhelmingly friendly critics who cared deeply about, and were often working or teaching within, the framework of design studios. In most cases they seemed to be writing to encourage an evolution of studio pedagogy in light of changing circumstances and acknowledged shortcomings, not its replacement. The attitude seems primarily to be that of a doctor diagnosing an illness and prescribing treatment to support the patient in returning to a healthier state of being. Thus, while some criticisms may sound dire, they should be considered carefully in the context of the overall success of the studio approach.

1. Resource Intensive

Studio models in traditional art and design education are quite resource-intensive when compared with approaches such as lecture-based courses.

In these studio models, students typically have access to classrooms with large work surfaces and, in some cases, have 24/7 access to their own personalized work area in a dedicated room. Studio courses commonly have low teacher/student ratios, with ideally no more than 15 students per instructor, and these courses often meet for long periods of time.

In a time of increasing pressure to minimize physical resources and costs at many institutions, studio instructors and studio programs face pressure to reevaluate the costly aspects of traditionally structured studios (van der Waarde and Vroombout 2012; Wilkin 2000). Some critics have issued calls for better understanding of the learning processes and objectives in traditional studios in an effort to increase the efficiency of studio education (Akin 2002; Oxman 2004; Rapoport 1984). For others, key structures that have characterized traditional studio education (for example, student/teacher ratios, prolonged engagement in on-site studios) are being questioned more directly (Jeffries 2007; Lotz *et al.* 2015). These questions are particularly significant as scholars question how or if design studios might be conducted in web-based, distance education settings.

2. Supporting Acquisition of Knowledge, Skills, and Attributes

As one might expect in any discipline, there are ongoing debates within the fields of architecture and interior design regarding how to prioritize time and other resources, especially as limitations in these areas can preclude optimal coverage of each and every objective. Within this debate, several speculate that some required courses in the overall design curriculum receive insufficient attention because studio courses tend to consume so much of the students' work time, demand such long out-of-class hours to complete projects, and are given so much emphasis. The studio consumes so much effort, compared with the other topics and modes of learning experienced as part of design studies, that students are left with little physical or mental energy for other courses (which are sometimes unattended or are given short shrift by students) or for potentially valuable extra-curricular experiences (Kellogg 2004; Rapoport 1984; Teal 2011). This situation is particularly ironic since many of the other courses in a traditional design curriculum are intended to support and enhance a student's ability to perform within the studio. In their comprehensive review of the state of architectural education, Boyer and Mitgang (1996) concluded, "Because of their exceptionally heavy workload, most students find it difficult to participate in activities that make for a well-rounded college experience" (p. 92). These scholars argued for greater interdisciplinarity stating, "Making the connections, both with the architecture curriculum and between architecture and other disciplines on campus, is, we believe, the single most important challenge confronting architectural programs" (Boyer and Mitgang 1996, p. 85).

Others suggest that even though studio is a rich context for learning to grapple with complex problems, it has tended to emphasize creative aspects of design (especially the visual or aesthetic qualities of the final product), while downplaying the importance of competencies such as codes, mechanical systems, and other considerations that are of great importance in the building design industries (Akin 2002; Buchanan 1989; Pizarro 2009). This tendency not only leaves some students with limited technical knowledge, but may also engender the false impression that all graduates will spend the majority of their professional time engaged in the generative aspects of design work (Boyer and Mitgang 1996; Koch *et al.* 2002), downplaying the importance of technical aspects or discouraging students who excel in such aspects from continuing in the field.

3. Promotion of a Studio Culture

For many years there has been an underlying concern that studio traditions have developed into a system of tacit expectations and practices that works counter to the students' well-being. These concerns coalesced after the tragic death in 2000 of an architectural student who was killed when he fell asleep at the wheel while returning home after two all-nighters in the studio. In response, the American Institute of Architecture Students (AIAS) launched a campaign to investigate studio culture, resulting in a series of professional meetings and publications focused on evaluating studio traditions and practices (Koch *et al.* 2002). The accrediting body for architecture programs (NAAB) added a new condition for accreditation, requiring programs to reevaluate the studio culture at their institutions.

Key concerns related to studio culture have included issues of student work habits and of communication and relationships among students and between students and faculty. Specifically, some critics have questioned the wisdom of setting standards requiring such long engagement with projects and fostering a culture that celebrates and rewards extreme work habits (Koch *et al.* 2002; Lunz 2001), with Fisher (1991) summing up key concerns by asking, "When do we cross the fine line between hard work and exploitation?" (p. 9). Other writers reported concerns that studio culture too often leads to competition between students, a tendency for students to become protective of their own ideas and reluctant to share them with others, or for students to struggle with cooperation and collaboration (Anthony 1991; Glasser 2000; Shih *et al.* 2006). As Koch *et al.* (2002) noted, "Too often, design in schools is seen as a solo and heroic effort, although this is rarely the way that architects practice. In many studios, students guard ideas and view their classmates as competitors" (p. 6).

Additional concerns have focused on the evaluation of students' work. A key point of contention has been the long-held tradition of public critiques (often called juries in their most formal instantiations) used to give feedback on student work, and the negative consequences that may arise if jurors are unrestrained in criticism which sometimes borders on public humiliation (Akin 2002; Anthony 1991; Willenbrock 1991). The difficulty in managing public critique is sometimes compounded for students because traditional studio systems have not always been conducted in a way that makes evaluation criteria transparent (Anthony 1991; Boyer and Mitgang 1996; Kellogg 2004; van der Waarde and Vroombout 2012; Webster 2007; Willenbrock 1991). This can lead to significant difficulty as students try to understand feedback they receive from jurors or studio instructors, and as they begin to learn how to evaluate the quality of their own work.

4. Encouragement of Diversity

The fields of architecture and interior design have struggled with developing professional bodies that accurately reflect the societies they serve. This has been especially notable in terms of both culture and gender. While this situation may be slowly changing, in the United States architecture is a profession disproportionately composed of men, while interior design is disproportionately composed of women. Minority populations tend to be under-represented in both fields. The ongoing lack of diversity in the architectural profession has raised ongoing alarms (Anthony 2002; Charles 2005) with relatively little change.

A number of scholars and researchers have noted patterns in studio pedagogy that might actually reinforce and perpetuate these and other imbalances, thus working against stated goals of greater diversity and inclusivity. Specifically, scholars have raised concerns over the Euro-centric focus of precedents drawn upon (Asogo 2001; Kucko *et al.* 2005), and the ways in which the jury system might be particularly discouraging for under-represented groups (Anthony 1991; 2002). Scholars have also raised concerns over the ways in which studio pedagogy, in specific implementations, might systematically discourage students with particular learning styles (Kvan and Jia 2005) or personality types (Wilkin 2000). For example, Roberts (2006) noted that students with what he terms "wholist" learning styles tend to have many strengths that are needed in professional practice, but that they may disproportionately self-select out of the field in the early years of their architectural education, due to patterns often arising in traditional studios.

Conclusion

As is true with many pedagogical approaches, any of the components of studio-based instruction can foster a positive or negative experience, depending on how they are implemented within the particular culture of a given academic discipline and institution. For example, some authors have noted that the studio setting can encourage competition and discourage teamwork.

Koch *et al.* (2002) explained, "In many studios, students guard ideas and view their classmates as competitors" (p. 6). Yet other authors have noted the camaraderie that develops in such a space (for example, Arvola and Artman 2008). One student interviewed by Cuff (1991) commented that "the long hours of work in a common studio space forged us into a close knit group of men and women who were marked by our dedication, endurance and talent" (p. 118). Thus, we offer a summary of these challenges as part of a critical view of studio learning so that you, as reader, can be alert to potential challenges that have been observed in disciplines with a long history of studio-based learning. As you review the chapters in this book, it would be prudent to note particular ways in which the authors have sought to negate potential negative impacts and encourage equity in the studio.

References

Akin, O. (2002) 'Case-based instruction strategies in architecture'. *Design Studies*, 23(4), pp. 407–431

Anthony, K. H. (1991) *Design Juries on Trial: The Renaissance of the Design Studio*. New York, NY: Van Nostrand Reinhold

Anthony, K. H. (2002) 'Designing for diversity: Implications for architectural education in the twenty-first century'. *Journal of Architectural Education*, 55(4), pp. 257–267

Arvola, M. and Artman, H. (2008) 'Studio life: The construction of digital design competence'. *Digital Kompetanse*, 3(2), pp. 78–96

Asogo, A. O. (2001) 'A model for integrating culture-based issues in creative thinking and problem solving in design studios'. *Journal of Interior Design*, 27(2), pp. 46–58

Boyer, E. and Mitgang, L. (1996) *Building Community: A New Future for Architecture Education and Practice*. Princeton, NJ: The Carnegie Foundation for the Advancement of Teaching

Brandt, C. B., Cennamo, K., Douglas, S., Vernon, M., McGrath, M. and Reimer, Y. (2013) 'A theoretical framework for the studio as a learning environment'. *International Journal of Technology and Design Education*, 23(2), pp. 329–348, doi:10.1007/s10798-011-9181-5

Buchanan, P. (1989) 'What is wrong with architectural education? Almost everything'. *The Architectural Review*, 185(1109), pp. 24–26

Charles, C. B. (2005) 'Ageless hope: A report card on access and equity in architecture education and practice'. *Journal of Architectural Education*, 58(3), pp. 53–54

Crysler, C. G. (1995) 'Critical pedagogy and architectural education'. *Journal of Architectural Education*, 48(4), pp. 208–217

Cuff, D. (1991) *Architecture: The Story of Practice*. Cambridge, MA: MIT Press

Dutton, T. A. (1987) 'Design and studio pedagogy'. *Journal of Architectural Education*, 41(1), pp. 16–25

Dutton, T. A. (1991) 'The hidden curriculum and the design studio: Toward a critical studio pedagogy' in T. A. Dutton (Ed.) *Voices in Architectural Education: Cultural Politics and Pedagogy* (pp. 165–194). New York, NY: Bergin and Garvey

Fisher, T. R. (1991) 'Patterns of exploitation'. *Progressive Architecture*, 9

Freire, P. (1970/2000) *Pedagogy of the Oppressed*. New York, NY: Continuum

Glasser, D. E. (2000) 'Reflections on architectural education'. *Journal of Architectural Education*, 53(4), pp. 250–252

Gray, C. M. (2013) 'Informal peer critique and the negotiation of habitus in a design studio'. *Art, Design and Communication in Higher Education*, 12(2), pp. 195–209, doi:10.1386/adch.12.2.195_1

Gray, C. M. (2014) 'Living in two worlds: A critical ethnography of academic and proto-professional interactions in a human-computer interaction design studio'. (Unpublished doctoral dissertation). Indiana University, Bloomington, IN

Gray, C. M. (2015) 'Critiquing the role of the learner and context in aesthetic learning experiences' in B. Hokanson, G. Clinton and M. Tracey (Eds) *The Design of Learning Experience: Creating the Future of Educational Technology* (pp. 199–213). Switzerland: Springer, doi:10.1007/978-3-319-16504-2_14

Gray, C. M. and Howard, C. D. (2015) '"Why are they not responding to critique?": A student-centered construction of the crit' in *LearnxDesign: The 3rd International Conference for Design Education Researchers and preK-16 Design Educators* (pp. 1680–1700). Aalto, FI: Aalto University

Hetland, L., Winner, E., Veenema, S. and Sheridan, K. (2007) *Studio Thinking: The Real Benefits of Visual Arts Education*. New York, NY: Teachers College Press

Jeffries, K. K. (2007) 'Diagnosing the creativity of designers: Individual feedback within mass higher education'. *Design Studies*, 28(5), pp. 485–497

Kellogg, C. (2004) *The Studio Culture Summit: An Overview Report*. Washington, DC: American Institute of Architecture Students (AIAS)

Klebesadel, H. and Kornetsky, L. (2009) 'Critique as signature pedagogy in the arts' in R. Gurung, N. Chick and A. Haynie (Eds.) *Exploring Signature Pedagogies: Approaches to Teaching Disciplinary Habits of Mind* (pp. 99–120). Sterling, VA: Stylus Publishing

Koch, A., Schwennsen, K., Dutton, T. A. and Smith, D. (2002) *The Redesign of Studio Culture: A Report of the AIAS Studio Culture Task Force*. American Institute of Architecture Students

Kucko, J., Prestwood, L. and Beacham, C. (2005) 'The Consortium for Design Education: A model for internationalizing interior design programs'. *Journal of Interior Design*, 31(1), pp. 25–37

Kvan, T. and Jia, Y. (2005) 'Students' learning styles and their correlation with performance in architectural design studio'. *Design Studies*, 26(1), pp. 19–34

Lotz, N., Holden, G. and Jones, D. (2015) 'Social engagement in online design pedagogies' in *LearnxDesign: The 3rd International Conference for Design Education Researchers and preK-16 Design Educators (Vol. IV)* (pp. 1643–1668). Aalto, FI: Aalto University

Lunz, B. (2001) 'At what price'. *Crit*, 51, pp. 24–25

Oak, A. and Lloyd, P. (2014) '"Wait, wait: Dave, your turn": Authority and assessment in the design critique' in *Proceedings of DTRS 10 Symposium*. West Lafayette, IN: Purdue University

Oxman, R. (2004) 'Think-maps: Teaching design thinking in design education'. *Design Studies*, 25(1), pp. 63–91

Pizarro, R. E. (2009) 'Teaching to understand the urban sensorium in the digital age: Lessons from the studio'. *Design Studies*, 30(3), pp. 272–286

Rapoport, A. (1984) 'Architectural education: There is an urgent need to reduce or eliminate the dominance of the studio'. *Architectural Record*, 172(10), pp. 100–103

Roberts, A. (2006) 'Cognitive styles and student progression in architectural design education'. *Design Studies*, 27(2), pp. 167–181

Schön, D. A. (1983) *The Reflective Practitioner: How Professionals Think in Action.* New York, NY: Basic Books

Schön, D. A. (1985) *The Design Studio: An Exploration of its Traditions and Potentials.* London, UK: RIBA Publications Limited

Shaffer, D. W. (2003) *Portrait of the Oxford Design Studio: An Ethnography of Design Pedagogy* (WCER Working Paper No. 2003–11). Madison, WI: University of Wisconsin-Madison, Wisconsin Center for Educational Research

Shih, S. G., Hu, T. P. and Chen, C. N. (2006) 'A game theory-based approach to the analysis of cooperative learning in design studios'. *Design Studies*, 27(6), pp. 711–722

Smith, K. M. and Young, B. L. (2013, February) *Design Studios: Developing a Framework for Evaluating their Place in a Twenty-first Century Profession.* Presented at the Interior Design Educators Council Annual Conference, Indianapolis, IN

Snyder, B. R. (1971) *The Hidden Curriculum.* New York, NY: Alfred A. Knopf

Stevens, G. (1995) 'Struggle in the studio: A Bourdivin look at architectural pedagogy'. *Journal of Architectural Education*, 49(2), pp. 105–122

Teal, R. (2011) 'Foundational history: An integrated approach to basic design, history, and theory'. *Journal of Architectural Education*, 64(2), pp. 37–45

van der Waarde, K. and Vroombout, M. (2012) 'Communication design education: Could nine reflections be sufficient?' *Visible Language*, 46(1/2)

Webster, H. (2006) 'Power, freedom and resistance: Excavating the design jury'. *International Journal of Art and Design Education*, 25(3), pp. 286–296

Webster, H. (2007) 'The analytics of power: Re-presenting the design jury'. *Journal of Architectural Education*, 60(3), pp. 21–27

Webster, H. (2008) 'Architectural education after Schön: Cracks, blurs, boundaries and beyond'. *Journal for Education in the Built Environment*, 3(2), pp. 63–74

Wilkin, M. (2000) 'Reviewing the review: An account of a research investigation of the 'crit.' in D. Nicol and S. Pilling (Eds) *Changing Architectural Education: Towards a New Professionalism* (pp. 100–107). London, UK: Spon Press

Willenbrock, L. (1991) 'An undergraduate voice in architectural education' in T. A. Dutton (Ed.) *Voices in Architectural Education: Cultural Politics and Pedagogy* (pp. 97–119). New York, NY: Bergin and Garvey

20 Emergent Views of Studio

Colin M. Gray

Introduction

In the past two decades, many disciplines that have historically taught in traditional lecture formats have increasingly sought to incorporate active learning pedagogies – as a way to increase retention, strengthen the "STEM pipeline" and improve student learning outcomes. In this process of curricular augmentation (or in some cases, transformation), it has become commonplace to adopt instructional innovations from other disciplines, often with little understanding of the original context of the instructional approach – resulting in a fragmentary adoption of instructional practices that are more holistically conceived and practiced in the originating discipline. When viewing this appropriation through the lens of Shulman's *signature pedagogies* (2005), it is evident that the origins of problem-based learning in medical rounds, exploration of case law in law classrooms and critique in art and design studios all have some resonance in contemporary approaches to active learning. But rather than a signature pedagogy being adopted in a wholesale or monolithic manner, many instructional techniques from diverse sources are being brought together in a sort of bricolage. The adoption of studio practices has resulted in a similarly fragmentary pattern of adoption, which I seek to describe in greater detail in this chapter.

I use the term *emergent* to describe the recent adoption, appropriation, or transfer of instructional practices from a source domain (in this case, studio practices from traditional art and design disciplines) to a new domain where these practices were not previously utilized. In the case of studio, the practices of hands-on learning have been reflected in experiential learning for decades, while the introduction of "wicked problems," reflective action, construction of prototypes, and critique or other forms of formative evaluation have been introduced in conjunction with problem- and project-based learning more recently. In this chapter, I will document broad patterns of adoption of studio in three disciplinary contexts: 1) engineering education, 2) computer science and human-computer interaction (HCI), and 3) instructional systems design (ISD). My goal is not to provide comprehensive coverage of the changing views of studio in each disciplinary context, but rather to demonstrate the diversity of "studio" as an instructional approach in non-traditional design disciplines – an entry point to viewing the appropriation of studio practices, and the epistemological commitments that this appropriation represents.

Disciplinary Approaches to Adoption

The fluid practice of studio may not be able to be pinned down in a universal model or theory, but studio nevertheless appears as a well-integrated whole. Shaffer's (2003) model of the studio offers a view of a "holistic experience" – an experience that is, in some sense, indivisible, but yet can be analyzed through the lenses of surface features, pedagogical activities, and epistemological commitments. *Surface features* are the physical, readily apparent elements of what comprises a studio environment, such as large work tables, natural light, or dedicated work areas for each student. *Pedagogical activities* describe the instructional landscape of the studio, including activities such as critique, real-world problems, iteration, and prototyping. *Epistemological commitments* are perhaps the most difficult to locate, yet these commitments serve as the tacit "hidden curriculum" of how a student's progress is judged, what kinds of behaviors are rewarded and, ultimately, what the discipline values and/or rewards. Taylor (2008) recognizes a similar confluence of factors in what emerges as "studio," noting: "...research indicates positive effects on student learning when studio classroom space is combined with active learning pedagogy, but the research does not separate the effect of the space from the effect of the pedagogy or address the effect of the space on teaching" (p. 217). This holistic view of the studio involves a fusion of physical or virtual learning environment, instructional experience, and enculturation into a discipline, recognizing that these types of integrated aesthetic learning experiences are always already being enacted in classroom instruction – yet often without awareness of the holism that binds these elements together.

When studio practices (like critique, for example) are incorporated into a new disciplinary context, they are adapted through the epistemological lens of the new discipline. In fact, in the process of developing this chapter, I identified the entry points of studio into these non-traditional disciplines and noted that, in several cases, the "translator" who introduced studio into the new discipline was the only reference for what comprised "studio" from then on. Thus, the complexity and variety of studio as it exists across traditional art and design disciplines as diverse as painting, graphic design, architecture, fashion design, and industrial design is compressed – with only a single strand or pedagogical feature of "studio" – perhaps critique – remaining when it is brought into a new discipline. These translations of studio from source to appropriating discipline are elaborated below. This process of translation or adoption is rife with epistemological commitments, yet the introduction of studio has rarely been undertaken with a full knowledge of the "holistic experience" studio can offer, much less the ways in which epistemological orientations of the originating and receiving discipline might differ. For example, an instructionally-oriented epistemological commitment in architecture might be the individual interpretation of a design problem, while in human-computer interaction the ability to collaborate effectively may be most highly valued. But, on a deeper level, epistemological commitments might also define a pattern of legitimacy for students' design rationale – what it means to think "as an architect" versus a product designer or a structural engineer. In this way, one can view the appropriation of studio as being driven by the epistemological orientation of the discipline adopting studio as a mode of instruction, the history of pedagogical practices within that discipline, and the awareness of and definition of "studio" as it may relate to existing traditional or non-traditional forms of studio education.

To see this quality of appropriation at work, I will follow the adoption of studio in three broad disciplinary contexts, attempting to locate the origin of that studio integration, the parts of studio that were incorporated (and from what original art and design disciplines), and the resulting legacy of studio in that discipline.

Engineering Education

Studio education was first adopted by physics educators in an explicit way at Rensselaer Polytechnic Institute in the early 1990s. At this institution, Jack Wilson recognized the poor passing rates in introductory physics courses – required for many engineering and science degree programs – and brought together a diverse group of experts in course innovation to construct a new learning experience. Interestingly, while the move away from the lecture format was clear (Cummings 1999; Wilson 1994), the origin of the "studio" label is not described; the commitments of the new *studio physics* were to "reduce the emphasis on the lecture, to improve the relationship between the course and laboratory, to scale up the amount of doing while scaling back the watching, to include team and cooperative learning experiences, to integrate rather than overlay technology into all of the courses, and above all to do so while reducing costs!" (pp. 519-520). In a later description of the studio physics approach at MIT, Belcher (2001) outlines the purpose of the studio classroom as "merg[ing] lecture, recitation, and hands-on laboratory experiments into a single common experience" (p. 60). In both of these cases, there is a strong emphasis on the physical arrangement of the classroom, with six architects consulting on the project at Rensselaer in creating the original small-group configuration of tables and chairs.

The SCALE-UP (Student-Centered Active Learning Environment with Upside-down Pedagogies) project began at University of North Carolina in the late 1990s, drawing on the success of studio physics at Rensselaer and

MIT (Saul *et al.* 2000). This program, which adopted many studio-like surface features such as round tables for group work and collaborative, project-centered activities, was created for classrooms of 100 or more students, which would have typically been taught using a lecture format. Over 200 sites nationwide now use the SCALE-UP format, or similar formats such as IMPULSE (Pendergrass *et al.* 2001) for classroom instruction in a wide range of STEM fields; these have become almost synonymous with active learning and "flipped" classroom instruction in an engineering context, particularly in first-year engineering experiences. However, it is still relatively uncommon for these classrooms to be referred to as "studios," and the distinctions between studios, labs, and other forms of active learning are still diffuse.

In an engineering design context, Little and Cardenas (2001) at Harvey Mudd College are considered pioneers of the studio approach, with their programs serving as an integrated example of project-based learning and studio interaction as a way to improve engagement and learning outcomes. As with the SCALE-UP model of instruction, the term *studio* here implied surface features that encourages collaborative group work, but these educators also drew on a broader set of instructional practices and outcomes, in this case based on the introduction of the architectural studio into the engineering education literature by Kuhn in 2001. This seminal article by Kuhn represents the primary translation of studio into the engineering discourse, outlining characteristics of the architecture studio such as: complex, semester-long projects; rapid and extensive iteration of design solutions; formative critique by peers, instructors, and outside visitors; study of design precedent to inform design solutions; and the imposition of constraints to find satisfactory design solutions.

Since these publications in the early 2000s, the concept of studio has become relatively mainstream in engineering education, although it is used less commonly than problem-based learning (PBL), active learning, or other common student-centered pedagogical approaches (see further discussion in Cennamo, 'What is Studio?', Chapter 18, this volume). However, studio is still used as a descriptor for instructional approaches that are closely allied with traditional design disciplines, such as the development of socially conscious collaborative spaces at Arizona State University (Lande 2012), or an interdisciplinary design studio taught at University of Georgia in collaboration by art education and engineering faculty (Sochacka *et al.* 2013). Outside of the mainstream of engineering and technology education, Exter *et al.* (2015) have adopted the studio model as one of two "strands" that form the core of an undergraduate transdisciplinary program. In this competency-based program, student-directed learning is encouraged through regular critique and reflection in the design studio, while formal mentoring allows students to set goals for the competencies on which they choose to focus.

Human-Computer Interaction and Computer Science

Studio pedagogy has emerged in computer science and HCI education as a way of encouraging collaborative learning, focusing attention on how students transition disciplinary knowledge from theory to practice. As Reimer and Douglas (2003) explain in an HCI context: "The problem is we have been trying to teach design without getting our hands dirty" (p. 192). As early as 1990, Terry Winograd made the case for HCI design education, calling for the use of a studio model to reflect the complexity of real-world design. Since his keynote address, design has emerged as a primary concern within the HCI community (Fallman 2003), reflecting the highly complex, wicked challenges that human interaction presents in relation to rapidly shifting technologies.

The computer science community has focused on a call for professionals to collaborate and communicate effectively with stakeholders. To address this need for authentic learning experiences that maximize opportunities for collaboration, Hundhausen *et al.* (2008) introduced the concept of studio to the computer science education community, drawing on the architectural studio to describe a pedagogy focused on collaborative learning, construction of personalized solutions, and the presentation of these solutions through design critiques. This initial effort to introduce a studio approach attempted to reprioritize ways of thinking about computing from learning specific programming languages toward focusing students' attention on *representation construction* ("visual and verbal representations of the computing concepts, algorithms, or processes under study") and *representation presentation and discussion* ("students present their representations for discussion and feedback from their peers as well as the instructor") (Hundhausen, *et al.* 2008, n.p.). Later work by Carter and Hundhausen (2011) incorporates Schön's view of the architecture studio into their studio model, structuring their instructional activities around critique – including evaluation of student work through critique, engaging students in critiquing each other's work, and viewing critique as revolving around the artifacts that students have created. While Hundhausen and colleagues focus their attention on the larger pedagogical structure needed for incorporating a studio-based approach, Greenberg (2009) describes a more targeted transition from a lecture-based to studio-based course, requiring students to design in class within predefined "interaction domains." In this hybrid environment with relatively limited class periods, students use sketching and idea exchange with peers to construct and iterate their projects; then they receive feedback and document their design processes through summative design critique and creating learning and professional portfolios.

Since Winograd's early work at Stanford incorporating a studio model to teach HCI courses, the modern wave of studio approaches to HCI education appear to have occurred in parallel with a broader "turn to design"

(Blevis *et al.* 2007; Faiola 2007). Reimer and Douglas (2003) represent a relatively early example of transitioning from Winograd's vision of an engaged, hands-on approach to doing HCI design, with these authors learning about studio through extended observation of an architecture program, and applying their findings in the construction of a new HCI studio course. They concluded that the studio format comprised teaching primarily through the design crit, "learning by doing" in a hands-on environment with extended class hours, where students were active learners that used instructors as a coach or expert resource, and using design processes taken from professional practice to reflect on and represent their work practices.

Blevis *et al.* (2008) extend many of these same understandings of studio into the digital domain, using a *virtual design studio* to foster collaboration between students in the absence of any physical studio space – finding ways to support a sense of studio culture (Blevis *et al.* 2007) even without some of the surface features that were common in traditional architecture studios. Siegel (Boling *et al.* 2013) describes a similar balancing of surface feature constraints in the same master's program, where he created an immersive educational experience for first-semester HCI design students using the classroom time for instruction in a non-studio context, while tacitly relying on external spaces where students actually did the work of design. Gray (2013a, 2013c) has described in greater detail the ways in which students enact critique as a form of socialization, encouraging their professional identity formation as UX or HCI designers in a non-classroom HCI studio environment. In this environment, Gray (2013a) found that students expanded on the summative critiques they were given in instructor-led classroom environments, actively engaging in peer critique and creating a *studio culture* in a communal non-classroom studio environment. The communication and representational skills learned in this environment were found to have a significant impact on their development of design thinking, and on their conceptions of what comprised design in an HCI context (Gray, 2013b).

Instructional Systems Design

The learning studio approach at University of Georgia is likely the oldest example of a fully-integrated, multi-level studio model in instructional design and technology (Clinton and Rieber 2010). In this sequence, which began in 1998, students interacted across multiple levels of expertise, working on individually-selected as well as external client-driven projects in a shared lab space. This approach to studio was driven by changing notions of what "design" entails in an IDT context and how this changing view of design impacted instructional approaches, drawing from an architecture studio for inspiration. Rowland *et al.* (1992) first discussed the ways in which design should be learned in IDT, drawing on Schön's notion of reflective practice to reorient learning to include more hands-on, application-oriented learning experiences. This approach was echoed by Ertmer and Cennamo (1995) a few years later, with these authors advocating for the introduction of apprenticeship-like experiences that focused on setting appropriate problems to be solved, providing formative feedback throughout the design process, and allowing opportunities for regular reflection and situated learning. While these instructional approaches were framed through the lens of *cognitive apprenticeship* rather than studio pedagogy, many of the suggestions about how instructional designers should be taught mirror the core commitments of studio, even while they are suggested through the language of learning and instructional theory.

The research of Boling and various co-authors represents the longest continuous study of studio pedagogy in IDT, and likely in any non-traditional design discipline outside of engineering. Boling has documented the evolution of her studio approach for almost ten years, as a single course on instructional graphics has increasingly taken on elements of the printmaking and fine art studio environment in which she was originally trained (Boling, 'How I Learned, Unlearned, and Learned Studio Again', Chapter 7, this volume). Early in this sequence of studies, Exter *et al.* (2009) identified the ways in which students learned to understand the value of critique, including acting on critique they received in iterating on their design projects - moving through mechanical, practical, conceptual, and integrative stages. Later work documented the evolution of instructional strategies and the appropriation of specific elements of studio, such as the desk crit, to meet program needs and enhance the learning of students (Boling and Smith 2010; 2014). This evolution of instructional techniques often resulted in the gradual and intentional introduction of studio elements, such as precedent materials (Boling *et al.* 2015), pin-up critiques, and a specific focus on representational techniques, often based on low-fidelity sketching (Boling and Gray 2015).

While Boling represents perhaps the most intensive, albeit small-scale, studio experience, other IDT educators have also used a studio model successfully and, arguably, in a more central position in the IDT curriculum. Tracey and Grzebyk (2014) describe their approach to designing instructional products for real-world clients in a team-based learning environment, which includes critique-like elements, authentic projects, and a focus on problem-finding and iteration. Hooper *et al.* (2015) have adopted an inter-disciplinary approach to what they refer to as *learning design*, bringing together instructional design, interaction design, and computer science in an immersive, multi-level studio environment that shares many characteristics with the original UGA studio. Tracey and Boling (2014), as part of a broad overview of instructional design education, echo the findings of these early studio adopters, calling for broader and deeper implementation of real-world design activities to support student learning. Drawing on literature from the broader design research community, they situate studio education as one outgrowth of viewing ISD as a field of design, rather than one of science. Many of the chapters in this volume demonstrate this shifting view, either explicitly or implicitly.

Conclusion

As I have demonstrated through this brief review across several disciplines, the adoption of studio within new disciplinary contexts is complex, even while the factors that bring about this adoption are relatively consistent. Studio pedagogy has been linked with effective, hands-on learning in traditional art and design contexts – creating a learning environment where students can address complex, real-world problems to develop skills and modes of thought required for effective performance. Adoption of specific pedagogical features across these disciplines has been uneven, with engineering disciplines particularly focusing closely on the appropriation of surface features. In computer science (CS) and ISD education, the disciplinary shift towards design – and the resulting adoption of studio – has resulted in questioning conventional wisdom about the primacy of theoretical or conceptual frameworks. In CS, this has resulted in an increased focus on conceptual structures of programming, with less focus on the specific programming language learned (Hundhausen *et al.* 2008). In ISD, by contrast, the studio approach has increased the focus on real-world design processes, moving away from the historic emphasis on fixed, or even flexible, design process models (Tracey and Boling 2014). While critique is often cited as the heart of the studio pedagogy, its use in these emergent studio contexts is remarkably scattered. While all "translators" that introduced studio to these varied disciplines focused heavily on critique as a primary method of teaching (Clinton and Rieber 2010; Kuhn 2001; Reimer and Douglas 2003), formative critique appears to be less consistently adopted, particularly in engineering and HCI education contexts, and this affects the type of studio culture enacted there. Even in disciplinary contexts where critique is valued, there are systemic issues that must be addressed in order to build up students' conceptual models about how critique should impact their work (Exter *et al.* 2009), and to assemble the kinds of precedent artifacts that must be present to stimulate student learning (Boling *et al.* 2015).

The rhetoric that surrounds the adoption of studio practices is complex; use of the term "studio" in the literature appears to take on a generic quality after its introduction into a discipline. For instance, after the first use of *studio physics* at Rensselaer in the 1990s, studio was used from then on to refer to that specific disciplinary appropriation of studio in the physics education and engineering context, rather than returning to any touchstones from art or design. This lack of transdisciplinary understanding and application of studio practices – linked to studios of the past in many diverse contexts – tends to privilege the *surface features* of the studio (likely because they are physically available, specifiable, and visible), reorienting pedagogical practices only within the scope of disciplinary norms, and often appearing to ignore the historic epistemological underpinnings of surface and pedagogical features entirely.

I hope this chapter provides an awareness of the ways in which studio has been appropriated into new disciplinary contexts, and encourages reflection regarding the epistemological commitments that result from the adoption of studio practices. For instance, encouraging students to iterate on their design solutions, but not providing space in the curriculum for this behavior to occur without significant time penalties, sets up a contradiction or tension between the epistemological commitment to continuously improve designs based on new information and the necessity of completing projects within the academic term. Because conceptions of studio education are often drawn from the architecture studio only, it is important to recognize the diversity of traditional art and design studios - and the even greater diversity that may be found currently in emergent studios. None of these enactments of studio are perfect or "correct," regardless of their origin, and there is no need to judge them against some canonical standard. The point to focus on is the often invisible fusion between the physical characteristics of the learning environment, the instructional strategies that are adopted in it, and the disciplinary context - all of them implying a set of epistemological commitments that form a rich, holistic view of the studio experience.

References

Belcher, J. W. (2001) 'Studio physics at MIT'. *MIT Physics Annual*, 1, pp. 58–64

Blevis, E., Lim, Y. K., Stolterman, E. and Makice, K. (2008) 'The iterative design of a virtual design studio'. *TechTrends*, 52(1), pp. 74–83

Blevis, E., Lim, Y.-K., Stolterman, E., Wolf, T. V. and Sato, K. (2007) 'Supporting design studio culture in HCI' in *Proceedings of CHI '07: Extended Abstracts on Human Factors in Computing Systems* (pp. 2821–2824). New York, NY: ACM Press, http://dx.doi.org/10.1145/1240866.1241086

Boling, E. and Gray, C. M. (2015) 'Designerly tools, sketching, and instructional designers and the guarantors of design' in B. Hokanson, G. Clinton, and M. W. Tracey (Eds) *The Design of Learning Experience: Creating the Future of Educational Technology* (pp. 109–126). Switzerland: Springer Verlag, http://dx.doi.org/10.1007/978-3-319-16504-2_8

Boling, E. and Smith, K. M. (2010) 'Intensive studio experience in a non-studio master's program: Student activities and thinking across levels of design' in *Proceedings of the Design Research Society Conference*, Montréal, Canada

Boling, E. and Smith, K. M. (2014) 'Critical issues in studio pedagogy: Beyond the mystique and down to business' in B. Hokanson and A. Gibbons (Eds) *Design in Educational Technology* (pp. 37–56). Switzerland: Springer, http://dx.doi.org/10.1007/978-3-319-00927-8_3

Boling, E., Gray, C. M. and Smith, K. M. (2015) 'Studio teaching in the low-precedent context of instructional design' in *Proceedings of LearnxDesign: The 3rd International Conference for Design Education Researchers and preK-16 Design Educators.* Chicago, IL: School of the Art Institute of Chicago

Boling, E., Siegel, M. A., Smith, K. M. and Parrish, P. (2013) 'Student goes on a journey; stranger rides into the classroom: Narratives and the instructor in the design studio'. *Art, Design & Communication in Higher Education*, 12(2), pp. 179–194, http://dx.doi.org/10.1386/adch.12.2.179_1

Carter, A. S. and Hundhausen, C. D. (2011) 'A review of studio-based learning in computer science'. *Journal of Computing Sciences in Colleges*, 27(1), pp. 105–111

Clinton, G. and Rieber, L. P. (2010) 'The studio experience at the university of Georgia: An example of constructionist learning for adults'. *Educational Technology Research and Development*, 58, pp. 755–780

Cummings, K. (1999) 'Evaluating innovation in studio physics'. *American Journal of Physics*, 67(S1), p. S38, http://dx.doi.org/10.1119/1.19078

Ertmer, P. A. and Cennamo, K. S. (1995) 'Teaching instructional design: An apprenticeship model'. *Performance Improvement Quarterly*, 8(4), pp. 43–58

Exter, M., Dionne, R. and Lukasik, C. (2015) 'Design of a learner-centered seminar-/studio-based polytechnic institute' in B. Hokanson, G. Clinton and M. Tracey (Eds) *The Design of Learning Experience: Creating the Future of Educational Technology* (pp. 139–154). Switzerland: Springer Verlag

Exter, M. E., Korkmaz, N. and Boling, E. (2009) *Use of Critique in an Instructional Design Course: Perceived Value and Impact on Students' Design Thinking*. Paper presentation at the Annual Meeting of the Association for Educational Communications and Technology, Louisville, KY

Faiola, A. (2007) 'The design enterprise: Rethinking the HCI education paradigm'. *Design Issues*, 23(3), pp. 30–45

Fallman, D. (2003) 'Design-oriented human-computer interaction' in *Proceedings of the SIGCHI Conference on Human Factors in Computing Systems* (pp. 225–232). New York, NY: ACM Press

Gray, C. M. (2013a) 'Emergent critique in informal design talk: Reflections of surface, pedagogical, and epistemological features in an HCI studio' in *Critique 2013: An International Conference Reflecting on Creative Practice in Art, Architecture, and Design* (pp. 341–355). Adelaide, South Australia: University of South Australia

Gray, C. M. (2013b) 'Factors that shape design thinking'. *Design and Technology Education*, 18(3), pp. 8–20

Gray, C. M. (2013c) 'Informal peer critique and the negotiation of habitus in a design studio'. *Art, Design & Communication in Higher Education*, 12(2), pp. 195–209, http://dx.doi.org/10.1386/adch.12.2.195_1

Greenberg, S. (2009) *Embedding a Design Studio Course in a Conventional Computer Science Program*. Report 2007-870-22, Department of Computer Science, University of Calgary, Calgary, Alberta, Canada

Hooper, S., Rook, M. M. and Choi, K. (2015) 'Reconsidering the design of a learning design studio' in B. Hokanson, G. Clinton and M. Tracey (Eds) *The Design of Learning Experience: Creating the Future of Educational Technology* (pp. 63–76). Switzerland: Springer Verlag

Hundhausen, C. D., Narayanan, N. H. and Crosby, M. E. (2008) 'Exploring studio-based instructional models for computing education' in *Proceedings of the 39th SIGCSE Technical Symposium on Computer Science Education* (pp. 392–396). New York, NY: ACM Press, http://dx.doi.org/10.1145/1352135.1352271

Little, P. and Cardenas, M. (2001) 'Use of "studio" methods in the introductory engineering design curriculum'. *Journal of Engineering Education*, 90(3), pp. 309–318, http://dx.doi.org/10.1002/j.2168-9830.2001.tb00610.x

Kuhn, S. (2001) 'Learning from the architecture studio: Implications for project-based pedagogy'. *International Journal of Engineering Education*, 17(4/5), pp. 349–352

Lande, M. (2012) 'Work in progress: Making room: Creating design spaces for design practice' in *Proceedings of Frontiers in Education Conference* (pp. 1–5). Piscataway, NJ: IEEE, http://dx.doi.org/10.1109/FIE.2012.6462347

Pendergrass, N. A., Kowalczyk, R. E., Dowd, J. P., Laoulache, R. N., Nelles, W., Golen, J. A. and Fowler, E. (2001) 'Improving first-year engineering education'. *Journal of Engineering Education*, 90(1), pp. 33–41, http://dx.doi.org/10.1002/j.2168-9830.2001.tb00564.x

Reimer, Y. J. and Douglas, S. A. (2003) 'Teaching HCI design with the studio approach'. *Computer Science Education*, 13(3), pp. 191–205 http://dx.doi.org/10.1076/csed.13.3.191.14945

Rowland, G., Fixl, A. and Yung, K. (1992) 'Educating the reflective designer'. *Educational Technology*, 32(12), pp. 36–44

Saul, J. M., Deardorff, D. L., Abbott, D. S., Allain, R. J. and Beichner, R. J. (2000) 'Evaluating introductory physics classes in light of the ABET criteria: An example from the SCALE-UP project' in *Proceedings of the American Society of Engineering Education*. New York, NY: ASEE

Shaffer, D. W. (2003) *Portrait of the Oxford Design Studio: An Ethnography of Design Pedagogy* (WCER Working Paper No. 2003–11). Madison, WI: University of Wisconsin-Madison, Wisconsin Center for Educational Research

Shulman, L. S. (2005) 'Signature pedagogies in the professions'. *Daedalus*, 134(3), pp. 52–59

Sochacka, N., Guyotte, K. W., Walther, J. and Kellam, N. N. (2013) 'Faculty reflections on a steam-inspired interdisciplinary studio course' in *2013 ASEE Annual Conference* (pp. 23.597.1–23.597.27). Available at: https://peer.asee.org/19611

Taylor, S. S. (2008) 'Effects of studio space on teaching and learning: Preliminary findings from two case studies'. *Innovative Higher Education*, 33(4), pp. 217–228, http://dx.doi.org/10.1007/s10755-008-9079-7

Tracey, M. W. and Boling, E. (2014) 'Preparing instructional designers: Traditional and emerging perspectives' in J. M. Spector, M. D. Merrill, J. Elen and M. J. Bishop (Eds.) *Handbook of Research on Educational Communications and Technology* (pp. 653–660). New York, NY: Springer, http://dx.doi.org/10.1007/978-1-4614-3185-5_52

Tracey, M. W. and Grzebyk, T. Q. (2014) 'Engaging multiple teams to design a blended learning course'. *International Journal of Designs for Learning*, 5(1), pp. 12–24

Wilson, J. M. (1994) 'The CUPLE physics studio'. *The Physics Teacher*, 32(9), p. 518, http://dx.doi.org/10.1119/1.2344100

Winograd, T. (1990) 'What can we teach about human-computer interaction?' (Plenary address) in *Proceedings of the SIGCHI Conference on Human Factors in Computing Systems* (pp. 443–448). New York, NY: ACM Press

About the Contributors

Elizabeth Boling, *Indiana University*
Elizabeth Boling, MFA in Studio Performance Printmaking, is Professor of Instructional Systems Technology and Associate Dean for Graduate Studies at Indiana University Bloomington (IUB). She spent ten years as illustrator, interface designer and development manager for educational software, five with an early startup producing computer-based instruction and five with the in-box documentation group at Apple Computer, before joining the IUB faculty to teach media design, instructional design, visual design and doctoral foundations. Her current scholarship focuses on design theory, practice and pedagogy from the perspective that design is a distinct mode of knowledge, thought and action. She leads a doctoral research group investigating conceptions of design and design practice, and is the founding editor of the *International Journal of Designs for Learning*, a peer-reviewed publication dedicated to increasing access to rigorous precedents in teaching and learning designs.

Katy Campbell, *University of Alberta*
Dr. Katy Campbell has served as the Dean of the Faculty of Extension at the University of Alberta since 2007. Born and raised in Edmonton, Alberta, she received her PhD (1994) in Instructional Studies from the University of Alberta. In 2008 she led the development of a new Faculty academic plan identifying engagement scholarship as its domain, leading to the development of graduate certificates and degrees related to social action, for example, Master of Arts in Community Engagement.

Prior to joining the University of Alberta Dr. Campbell was Assistant Professor at the State University of New York, *Ella Cline Shear School of Education*, Geneseo (1993-1995) and a distance education specialist at Keewatin Community College in northern Canada (1995-1996). An instructional designer and narrativist, she works within a feminist post-structural theoretical framework, examining the socially constructed nature of instructional design in higher education and cross-cultural settings. She is primarily interested in questions of cultural identity (especially gender), agency, and social change.

Katherine S. Cennamo, *Virginia Tech*
Katherine Cennamo is a Professor and Chair of Learning Sciences and Technologies at Virginia Tech. As a former video producer, teacher, and practicing instructional designer, she has over 30 years' experience in the design and development of instructional materials for corporate, education, and non-profit sectors. Through numerous funded projects, publications, presentations, instructional materials, and teaching activities, she has disseminated knowledge of instructional strategies based on established theories of learning, illuminated the nature of instructional design practice so that scholars and designers alike better understand their work, and applied this knowledge to the preparation of future instructional design professionals. In 2005 she joined a multidisciplinary design studio as an educational consultant and began her investigation of how the studio environment facilitates and sustains creative thought. Currently, her research and service activities focus on fostering critical and creative thinking skills in K-12 and higher education environments.

Gregory Clinton, *The University of Georgia*
Gregory Clinton received his PhD in Instructional Technology in 2007 from the University of Georgia, where he now serves as senior lecturer in the Learning, Design, and Technology program. He is also the Instructional Design and Development (IDD) coordinator and conference chair for the annual IDD@UGA conference. He conducted his dissertation research on the role of creativity in instructional design and development, and he continues to study creativity, social connectedness in online environments, connectivism, and the role of technology in society. Dr. Clinton's varied background includes a bachelor's degree in Music Composition (1980) and a master's degree in Special Education (1996), both from the University of Georgia. He has been working in the instruction technology field since 1993. Prior to joining the Learning, Design, and Technology faculty, he served as the Instructional Multimedia Project Manager at UGA's Center for Teaching and Learning.

Fred M. Duer, *Temple University*
Fred M. Duer heads the design program at Temple University in Philadelphia after having taught at Indiana University and Kansas State University. His professional designs range from summer stock for The Monomoy Theatre to opera for Opera Delaware. His regional theater credits include: Illinois Shakespeare Festival; Indiana Repertory Theatre; Utah Festival Opera; Texas Shakespeare Festival; Theatre Aspen; Colorado Shakespeare Festival; The San Diego Repertory Theatre; The Pasadena Playhouse; and Off-Broadway at The Criterion Center. Fred was a resident designer at The Old Globe Theatre for five years and, as a founding member, designed 11 productions for The Shakespeare Festival/Los Angeles over a 22-year period. As a television production designer, Fred designed the sets for: *The Fresh Prince of Bel-Air;*

In The House; Saved By The Bell: The New Class; and *City Guys.* He was nominated for an Emmy Award for *The Pat Sajak Show* on CBS in 1989.

Andrew S. Gibbons, *Brigham Young University*
Andrew S. Gibbons completed his doctorate in Instructional Psychology at Brigham Young University in 1974. For 18 years he worked in industry as a director of large-scale instructional system design projects, including work on simulation design and other innovative forms of computer-based instruction. In 1993 he accepted a faculty position at Utah State University in the Department of Instructional Technology, where he remained until 2003. At Brigham Young he was appointed Department Chair, which position he held until August 2014.

Dr. Gibbons' current research focuses on the architecture of instructional designs. His latest book, *An Architectural Approach to Instructional Design* (Routledge 2014), brings together the concept of design layers, design languages, and modularity. Gibbons has published a domain theory of Model-Centered Instruction, and is currently studying the use of layers, languages, and modularity as tools for creating instructional systems that are adaptive, generative, and scalable.

Colin M. Gray, *Purdue University*
Colin M. Gray is an Assistant Professor at Purdue University in the Department of Computer Graphics Technology, and a Faculty Fellow in the Educational Research and Development Incubator. He holds a PhD in Instructional Systems Technology from Indiana University Bloomington, a MEd in Educational Technology from University of South Carolina, and a MA in Graphic Design from Savannah College of Art & Design. He has worked as an art director, contract designer, and trainer, and his continued involvement in design work informs his research on design activity and how it is learned. His research focuses on the role of student experience in informing a critical design pedagogy, and the ways in which the pedagogy and underlying studio environment inform the development of design thinking, particularly in relation to critique and professional identity formation. His work crosses multiple disciplines, including engineering education, instructional design and technology, design theory and education, and human-computer interaction.

Brad Hokanson, *University of Minnesota*
Brad Hokanson is a Professor in Graphic Design at the University of Minnesota. He has a diverse academic record, including degrees in art, architecture, urban design, and he received his PhD in Instructional Technology. He teaches in the area of creative problem solving and has published research in the fields of creativity and educational technology.

He has recently completed research on the relationship between creativity and achievement in school children, comparing measured creativity with standardized achievement scores. He is now running his third massive online course on creativity for the University of Minnesota. Previous courses each enrolled over 52,000 learners.

He is President-Elect of the Association of Educational Communication and Technology. Visits to Buenos Aires support his Argentine tango habit.

Simon Hooper, *Pennsylvania State University*
Simon Hooper is a Professor of Learning, Design, and Technology at Penn State with research interests in design, learning analytics, and e-assessment. His teaching examines educational software design and his research focuses on design for electronic assessment systems. He is an experienced Internet researcher having conducted several software design projects involving thousands of participants. During the past ten years he has worked on projects to develop electronic assessment systems for American Sign Language (ASL) instruction (i.e. Avenue: ASL), to monitor literacy development for deaf and hard-of-hearing children in K-12 schools (i.e. Avenue: PM), and to design a web-based intervention on AIDS education.

Theodore J. Kopcha, *The University of Georgia*
Theodore J. (TJ) Kopcha received his degree from Arizona State University in 2005 and has worked at The University of Georgia since 2010, where he now serves as an Associate Professor of Learning, Design, and Technology. TJ is a former secondary mathematics instructor who has over a decade of experience with teaching and consulting in both higher education and K-12 settings, including research and evaluation projects. His work employs educational design research (EDR), which attempts to blend high quality scholarship with practical solutions to educational problems. In 2011 the American Association of Colleges of Teacher Education (AACTE) nationally recognized the innovative nature of his work in preservice teacher education, which was largely developed and studied through educational design research (EDR). TJ's current interests bring EDR perspectives to study the role of complexity thinking in the design of learning environments and research-based approaches to professional development.

Marit McCluske, *University of Illinois - Urbana-Champaign*
Marit McCluske is a visiting lecturer in the Graphic Design Program at the University of Illinois. She recently received her MFA in Graphic Design from the University of Minnesota. She is an award-winning educator, and was a teaching assistant for many sections of Creative Problem Solving over the course of two years. She teaches classes in design, photography and drawing, and also continues a practice as an interactive designer, photographer, and illustrator.

Her research and creative work explore the perceptive connections between auditory, visual, and tactile design elements, and how they can be used in interaction design to develop creativity, problem solving and other cognitive skills. Her current work integrates design theory with cognitive and educational psychology to develop meaningful sensory interaction through emerging technology, applied in learning environments.

Jill B. Pable, *University of Florida*
Jill Pable, PhD, FIDEC, ASID is a Professor in the Interior Design Department at Florida State University. She holds BS and MFA degrees in Interior Design and a PhD degree in Instructional Technology with specialization in architecture. She is the author and co-author respectively of *Sketching Interiors at the Speed of Thought* and *Interior Design: Strategies for Teaching and Learning.* She has served as national president of the Interior Design Educators Council and is a Fellow of IDEC. Included in the list of 30 Most Admired Design Educators in the United States in the 2015 annual DesignIntelligence rankings, her research focuses on the design of environments for the disadvantaged. She is the originator and project lead for *Design Solutions for Homelessness,* a research-informed online resource for architectural designers and organizations creating facilities for homeless persons. She believes that design can make life more interesting, fulfilling and humane.

Lloyd P. Rieber, *The University of Georgia*
Lloyd Rieber is a Professor in the Department of Career and Information Studies at The University of Georgia. He is also the past-Director of Innovation in Teaching and Technology for UGA's College of Education. He received his PhD from the Pennsylvania State University in 1987 and is a former classroom teacher. He has over 50 international and national publications, including two books in the area of computer graphics and interactive digital media. He is interested in designing learning environments based on visualization, accessibility, and constructivistic philosophies, with special emphasis on play theory. He has received four outstanding practice awards for his design work from the Association for Educational Communications and Technology (AECT).

Michael M. Rook, *Pennsylvania State University*
Michael M. Rook is a contributor to ongoing Krause Innovation Studio research at Penn State. Between June 2014 and August 2015 Michael was the Postdoctoral Scholar of the Krause Innovation Studio, during which he co-taught Learning Design Studio and conducted research on the design and affordances of learning spaces. Michael currently is a Science and Technology Policy Fellow at the American Association for the Advancement of Science, where he is placed in the Office of International Science and Engineering at the National Science Foundation in Arlington, Virginia. His research and teaching interests include peer technological support, future learning spaces, studio-based pedagogy, the role of culture in developing learning technologies, and design and computational thinking and fluency. He is an experienced developer of learning technologies having designed and

developed tools to support teachers, learners, and researchers in formal and informal learning contexts.

Gordon Rowland, *Ithaca College*
Gordon Rowland, Professor of Communications in the Roy H. Park School of Communications at Ithaca College, teaches courses at the undergraduate and graduate levels in such areas as systemic design, critical issues in organizations, collaboration and innovation, and workplace learning and performance. He is author of three books and over 50 book chapters and articles in the areas of systemic design, performance improvement, and design education.

Richard A. Schwier, *University of Saskatchewan*
Richard Schwier is Professor Emeritus in the Educational Technology and Design program at the University of Saskatchewan, where he developed and taught blended graduate courses in the theoretical foundations of educational technology and design, and in instructional design. His current research interests and extant scholarship include the catalysts and emphases of virtual learning communities, and the growth of professional identity and social change agency in instructional design. He also served as the Head of Curriculum Studies and the Coordinator of Graduate programs in Educational Technology and Design, and as the principal investigator in the Virtual Learning Communities Research Laboratory.

Martin A. Siegel, *Indiana University*
Martin Siegel is a Professor of Informatics, Education, and Cognitive Science at Indiana University, Bloomington. Within the School of Informatics and Computing, he is the Director of Graduate Studies. Prior to serving in this position, he served as the founding Director of the Human-Computer Interaction Design Program, the Executive Associate Dean of the School, and the Chair of the Informatics Department. From 1991-1999 he was the Director of Research and Development at the Center for Excellence in Education. Marty is among a group of pioneers in online learning, beginning with his work in the 1970s on the PLATO system. At the University of Illinois he was the Assistant Director of the Computer-based Education Research Laboratory (CERL) and Head of the Curriculum and Applications Group. In 1988, he was Microsoft's first Faculty Fellow. His current research focuses on the design of digital learning environments, slow change interaction design, and design pedagogy.

Kennon M. Smith, *Indiana University*
Kennon M. Smith, PhD, is an Associate Professor in the Interior Design program at Indiana University Bloomington. She completed undergraduate work in Design, and graduate work in Art History and Instructional Systems Technology. Her research is in the area of Design Studies, with an emphasis on comparative design – examining similarities and differences within and between design disciplines. She is particularly interested in the pathways by

which design education practices challenge or reinforce the traditions of such disciplines.

Monica W. Tracey, *Wayne State University*

Monica W. Tracey is an Associate Professor of Learning and Performance Systems in the College of Education at Wayne State University. Her teaching and research focuses on theory and design-based research of interdisciplinary design including design thinking, designer reflection and designer decision-making. Tracey has worked for over 29 years in design and on numerous design projects. Her work includes designing internationally and across disciplines. She has over 30 publications on her research and practice of instructional design including a Brown Book Award-winning co-authored book, book chapters and refereed journal articles. She has taught design in higher education since 1999 and serves on the editorial board for *Education Technology Research and Development* and for the *International Journal on Designs for Learning*. Tracey is currently the Co-Principal Investigator on a five-year R25 NIH Grant titled *Integrated Course in Biology and Physics of Radiation Oncology.*

Jay Wilson, *University of Saskatchewan*

Jay Wilson is an Associate Professor and Head of the Department of Curriculum Studies at the University of Saskatchewan. He is the Graduate Chair for the Curriculum Studies and Educational Technology and Design programs. He has extensive teaching experience in the area of technology and its application to learning and instruction. He is frequently called upon to consult in the areas of multimedia production, presentation skills, and delivery of professional development. His program of research centers on skill development in educators, experiential learning, and design studio learning environments. Jay's teaching has been recognized locally, nationally, and internationally in many ways including the University of Saskatchewan Master Teacher Award (2015), University of Saskatchewan's Outstanding New Teacher Award (2010), the Society for Teaching and Learning in Higher Education D2L Innovation Award (2012), and as an Apple Distinguished Educator (2011).

Index

Pages numbers in *italic* refer to figures and tables.

accountability 133, 155, 232
accreditation standards 105–7
acculturation 260
action 13
active learning 271, 272, 273–4
activities: disconnect between
    expectations and 61
activity-centric: studio as 9–13
ADDIE 196, 197
advanced design course 147–8
affective attributes: grading 111
affordances 253–5, 257
Alexander, C. 142
Allan, Gerry 187
American Institute of Architecture
    Students (AIAS) 266
anger 8
Anthony, K.H. 261
anxiety(ies) 8, 34, 49, 135
Appelman, Bob 90, 91, 92
Applied Theories of Instructional Design
    152–63; beginnings 153–4; context
    155–6; guided beliefs and course
    goals 154–5; learning to teach/
    teaching to learn 162; public critiques
    and iterative practice 156–9; teaching
    as iterative practice 159–62
apprenticeship model 249
apprenticeship-like experiences 277
architectural design 155
architectural profession: lack of diversity
    in 267
architectural studio 248, 249; in
    computer science 275; critical
    focus on 261; disconnects in 262;
    epistemological commitment 273;
    student workload 265; tension

between pedagogical control and
    flexibility 254
artefacts 140–1, 255
assessment: continual 16–17; creative
    problem solving course 193;
    instructional design course 28–9, 35;
    interior design course (FSU) 110–11,
    111–12; lake studio course 126;
    Learning Design Studio 243–4; user-
    centered design course 213, 214, 217,
    see also grading; performance review
assignments: creativity problem solving
    course 183, *see also* projects
Association for the Development
    of Computer-based Instructional
    Systems - ADCIS 39
asynchronous communication/
    interaction 32, 34, 245
atelier system 249
Attribute Listing method 185–6
authentic learning 132, 275
authentic learning environments 30
authenticity: instructional design course
    25, 29, 30, 34, 36; interior design
    course (FSU) 11; systems thinking
    and design course 222, 226, 232
author perspectives 5
authoring tools 44

Banathy, Bela H. 225, 231
Bauhaus tradition 249–50
Beck, J. 74
behavioural change programs 76
Belcher, J.W. 273
belief 184
best practices 245–6
'Big Project' studio 10–11

Blaaw, G. 142
Blackbaud 78
BlackBoard Collaborate® 22
blended groups 15, 16, 22, 36
Blevis, E. 276
blogs/blogging 126, 127
Bloom, B. 138
Boling, Elizabeth 8, 9, 10, 12, 16, 18, 88–100, 141, 142, 277
boundary objects 255
Bourdieu, Pierre 261
Bow, Leslie 206
Boyer, E. 265
brain writing 185
Brandt, C.B. 253, 263
Briggs, Leslie 138
Brooks, F. 142

Campbell, Katy 6–7, 7, 13, 17, 18, 19, 206–20
Cardenas, M. 274
Carter, A.S. 275
case studies 4
Cennamo, Katherine S. 8, 13, 14, 17, 19, 152–63, 248–57, 277
challenge(s) 8; creative problem solving course 187–91; interior design course (FSU) 112–13; scenic design course 176–7; systems thinking and design course 226, 227–8, 231
Chuck Close project 57
Clandinin, Jean 208
clarity 8
class critique 157–8
class discussions 42, 112, 124, 156, *160*
class meetings 25–6, 28, 32, 226
class plans 229
client contracts 25
client feedback 35, 63
client meetings 26, 202
client reports 26
clients: interior design studio 67–8
Clinton, Gregory 5, 17, 37–59
co-learners 229
co-responsibility 98
co-teaching 233
coach analogy 159
cognitive apprenticeship 49, 277
coherent system: studio as a 251–3
cohort model 49, 52–3
collaboration 107–9, 176, 245, 276
collaborative design 252, 255
collaborative learning 275

collegiality 111, 124, 130
color 173–4
comfort zones 8, 166, 179, 184, 191, 192
commitment 9, 132, 135, 145–6, 202
commonalities across studios 255–6
communication 248, 252; asynchronous 32, 34, 245; effective 167, 183; interior design course (FSU) 112; in the learning design studio 245; RDSC course 84; talking about artwork 175–6; video-based 15, 22, 25, 34; visual 112, *see also* discussion(s); interaction(s)
communities of practice 245, 252–3, 255, 263
community building 130, 134
community engagement 13
compelling activities 12
compelling emotions 9
competence 232
competition 168, 261, 266
complexity 12, 60, 69, 70, 71, 141, 187, 192, 197, 201, 203, 227, 253, 255, 272, 275
computer platform issue 65–6
computer science 275, 277, 278
computer-based instruction 139, 140, 144, *see also* educational multimedia design
concept boards 115–16, 118
concept guidance 122
concept maps 202, 228
concept selection 113
concept/concept development 101, 105, 113–15; current approach to teaching 115–18; ongoing questions and struggles with 118–22
confidence (instructor) 13, 33, 162
confidence (student) 69
confusion 8
'Constructionist' Software Design Studio 235
constructive feedback 126, 130, 135, 243
constructivism 209, 231, 235; concept generation 114; educational multimedia design course 43; interior design course (FSU) 101, 102; technology 37–8
consultant role (student) 50–1
content 13, 14, 33
content knowledge 256

context 13
context-sensitive approach 32
control 33, 162
cooperative learning 207, 208
core content 14
Corporate Communication program 224
corporate partners 75
cost pressures 15
Council for Interior Design Accreditation (CIDA) 105
counselor role 8
course readings: educational multimedia design course 46; Learning Design Studio (LDS) 241
'create the design' box (ISD) models 143
creative ability 191
creative identity 129
Creative Problem Solving course 180–94; assessment 193; belief in creative capability 184; central concept 182; differents 12, 184, 186–7, 187–91, 192; enthusiasm for 180; evolution of 191–2; habits 186–7; nature of the course 182–3; skills 185–6; students 184; studio format 181; teaching 193–4
creativity 181, 224, 231, 233; conflict of comfort zones with 8; fostering, in LDS 243; hurdles blocking 174–5; interior design course (FSU) 112, 114
critical pedagogy 261, 262
critical theory 261, 262
critical thinking 170, 176
criticality 260–3
critique 271; applied theories of instructional design course 157–8; computer science education 275; creative problem solving course 190; 'crowdsourcing' approach to 119–21; disciplinary adaptation 272; in emergent studio contexts 278; as a form of socialisation 276; forms 251–2; instructional design course 28–9, 34; interior design course 63; lake studio course 126; and reflection 251; student understanding of the value of 277; student-directed learning 274; on subjective nature of concepts 121, *see also* desktop critiques; group critique; public critiques
critique culture 261
Cross, Nigel 198, 202

'crowdsourcing' approach to critique 119–21
Crysler, C.G. 261
Cuff, D. 268
cultural assumptions 210
curve balls: RDSC projects 80

deadlines 169, 172
deconstruct (concept learning) 115
dedicated studio space 15
defensiveness 111, 113
demonstrations 63
design: evolution of instructional design 141–2; moral and social issues 19; separation of skills and 169, 170, 174; terminology 141, 142
Design Age 149
design agency 82
design cases: assembling and arranging the collection 5–7; curator role 4–5; purpose and value 4; writing 1–2, *see also individual cases*
design challenges *see* assignments; challenges; projects
design education: criticality and 260–3, *see also* instructional design
design elegance 46, 47
design expertise 251, 252, 256
design exploration 235, 246
design fields 142
Design Foundations course 102, 103, 105, 119
design judgement 69
design knowledge 149
design languages 141–2
design mindset 199
design problems 256
design studies 142
design support 246
Design Thinking 198
design thinking 16, 76, 198–9, 220, 241–2, 276
The Design Way 241
designers: meetings with practicing 34; understanding needs of 84
desktop critiques 260; educational multimedia design course 44, *45*, 47; interior design course (FSU) 16–17, 108, 110; interior design course (Indiana University) 62, 68; Learning Design Studio 243
differential responses 16–17, 68

differents *see* Do Something Different
  (DSD)
digital artwork 172, 173
digital graphics 110
ding 12, 170–1
disciplinary approaches: adoption of
  studio 272–8
discipline-specific tools 253
discomfort 8
disconnect: between expectations and
  actual activities 61
discovery 9, 105, 202, 252
discussion(s): instructional design course
  28–9, 32; lake studio course 127;
  learning design studio course 240,
  241, *see also* class discussions; meta-
  discussions; online discussion; panel
  discussions
distance education 208, 265
diversity 267, 279
Do Something Different (DSD) 12,
  184, 186–7, 187–91, 192
documentary assignments 10, 12, 92, 93
dormitory project 118
Dorst, K. 142
Douglas, S.A. 275, 276
drafting 168, 172, 174
Duer, Fred M. 5, 8, 11, 12, 13, 16, 18,
  164–79
dynamic learning environments 256

'eat something different' challenge 187
École des Beaux-Art 249
EDIT 6190: The Constructionist
  Course 40–7; first time experience
  41–5; second time experience 45–7
educational experiences: sharing with
  students 70
educational multimedia design
  37–59; balance between freedom
  and required experiences 51;
  curriculum change 52; EDIT 6190:
  The Constructionist Course 40–7;
  managing expectations 47–8; origins
  37; recent challenges 52–3; sample
  projects 54–9; a student's perspective
  42–3; theoretical influences on the
  EDIT design studio 37–40; TJ
  Kopcha's approach to 46–7; as a work
  in progress 54
educational problems: scaffolding
  identification of 246

Educational Technology 138, *see also*
  lake studio course
effective communication 167, 183
effective learning environments 244
emergent studio 5, 17
Emma Lake Kenderdine Campus 127–9
emotional dimension 7–9, 34, 49, 135
empathy 184
engineering education 273–4
enjoyment 35, 36, 48, 96, 97, 102, 107,
  122, 172, 177, 213
'enjoyment in design' 9
enthusiasm 9, 43, 81, 162, 180, 229, *239*
epistemological commitments 272, 273
epistemology 153, 252–3, 255, 257,
  262–3
Ertmer, P.A. 277
ETAD 879 126–30
ethical dilemmas 19
Euro-centrism 267
European (studio) models 249–50
evaluation *see* assessment; critique
evolution of instruction design:
  revolutionary phase 137–8; rise of
  design 141–2; rise of new artefacts
  140–1; rise of tools 139–40, *see also*
  functional-layer approach
excitement 9, 36, 94, 104, 128, 131,
  133, 214
exclusive-use spaces 64
exhaustion: from studio 7
expectations *see* student expectations
experience-within-an-experience 10
experiential learning 8, 209, 271
experimentation 235
expertise (teaching): acknowledging
  boundaries of 71
Exter, M. 274, 277
extrinsic motivation 49

face-to-face groups 15, 16, 22, 36, 127–8
face-to-face workshops (ETAD) 126,
  127, 134
faculty meetings: at UGA 40
failure: learning from 224–5, 242; of
  Studio approach 51
fairness 131
Fairweather, Peter 139, 144
Fallman, D. 235
fast-paced assignments 10, 11
feedback: creative problem solving
  course 192; differential nature of

16, 17; instructional design course 35; instructional systems design course 277; Instructional Technology program 199; interior design course (FSU) 109; interior design course (Indiana University) 63, 69–70; lake studio course 126, 130, 131, 135; Learning Design Studio 243; public critiques 266–7; RDSC course 75; theatrical scenic design course 175, 178; user-centered design course 214
fierce conversations 84
First Semester Review (Studio 1) 103
first timers: Learning Design Studio 241
first timers (UGA) 41–5; managing expectations of 47–8
flexibility 17, 35, 130, 159, 254
flipchart pages 157
flipped classrooms 274
Florida State University (FSU): interior design course 101–22
formal mentoring 274
formative feedback 109, 214, 243, 277
Forney, Jared 85
Foundations of Educational Technology (Spector) 201, 202, 203
frame-based systems 140
France 249
free-riding 35
freedom 17, 51, 104, 107, 121, 130, 131, 133, 176, 178
Freire, P. 261, 262
frozen simulations 144
functional-layer approach 143–4; commitment to 145–6; impact on teaching of basic design 144–5
funding 133

Gagné, Robert 137–8, 141
'gallery worthy' artwork 175
gender neutral language 20
Germany 249–50
Gibbons, Andrew S. 9, 13, 14, 15, 18, 46, 139
Glaser, Robert 138
Google Applications 197
Google Chat 204
Google Docs 34, 197, 198, 199, 201, 203, 204
Google Drive 22
Google Hangouts 22, 34, 200, 201, 204

Google-based LMS 197–8
grading: educational multimedia design course (UGA) 38; instructional technology program 202; interior design course (FSU) 110, 111–12; lake studio course 130; Learning Design Studio 243; scenic design course 175; systems thinking and design course 229
Gray, Colin M. 8, 9, 257, 260–8, 271–9
Greenberg, S. 275
Greeno, J.G. 254
group critique 10, 47, 75
group design 11
group discovery 252
group exercises 111, 183
group interaction (asynchronous) 245
group projects 11
group responsibility 155
group work 11, 156–7, 186, 244, 255, 274
Grzebyk, T.Q. 277
guidance 16, 242–3

habit to vary 186
habits: and creativity 186–7
habits of studio 262
habits of thought 13
habitus 261
hand art work 172, 173
hands-on learning 110, 232, 271, 276–7, 278
Harel, Idit 235
Harvey Mudd College 274
HGTV mindset 102
hidden curriculum 19, 262, 272
Hirsh-Pasek, K. 244
Hokanson, Brad 5, 8, 9, 11, 12, 13, 180–94, 252
holistic studio experience 272, 273
honesty 8, 68, 131
Hooper, L. 277
Hooper, Simon 9, 12, 16, 235–46
human-computer interaction (HCI) studio 275–6; critique 278; epistemological commitment 273; problem-solving paradigm 253; studio bridge 263; tension between pedagogical control and flexibility 254–5, *see also* Rapid Design for Slow Change
Hundhausen, C.D. 275

hybrid studio 275
hypermedia project 57–9

'I feel ...' statements 13, 29
ideas: belief as stemming from experiences
    and exposure to 184; critique and
    testing of 252; methods for generating
    185–6; openness to 176; protectiveness
    of 266; time for developing 172;
    translation of 101, 121
identify (concept learning) 115
illustration 170
immersion in studio 7
immersive learning environments 251
impromptu teaching 128
IMPULSE 274
in-class wall areas 108
in-class work sessions 172
in-house showcase (UGA) 53
Indiana University 30; interior design
    studio 60–72; Rapid Design for Slow
    Change 73–86
individual accountability 155–6
individual assessment 35
individual projects 11–12
industrial design studio 253, 254
information analysis 105
input (instructor) 17
Inspiration 211
instructional design 14, 277; evolution
    of 137–42; as a systematic, scientific
    endeavour 89, *see also* studio/studio
    approach
instructional design course (in authentic
    ID context) 21–36; assessment
    and critique 28–9, 35; authentic
    learning opportunity 30; authentic
    and self-directed learning values 29;
    client meetings and deliverables 26;
    considerations for the future 34–6;
    instructor's life 32–3; messy and
    socially significant projects 31–2;
    project management 29, 30–1, 35–6;
    stressor 35; student workload 32, 35;
    students in 21–2; studio space 34–5;
    teaching and learning in 33–4; on
    time, on budget, beyond expectations
    and without a net 22–6
instructional design course (studio
    learning experience) 88–100; course
    development and studio unlearned
    90–1; students 30; studio class 91–2;
    studio re-learned 98–100; teaching 92–8

instructional design and technology
    (IDT) 153
instructional systems design: studio
    adoption 276–7, 278
instructional systems development 92,
    138, 143, 144, 148
Instructional Technology Program 195–
    205; changing the content 198–201;
    class context 197–8; initial changes
    196–7; introducing instructional
    design 201–2; origin of 195–6
instructor-led critique 34
instructors 1; 'Big Project' studio
    10–11; challenges for, at UGA 47–51;
    counselor role 8; creative problem
    solving course 190; differential
    responses to students 16–17;
    emotional dimension of studio 8, 9,
    135; epistemological differences 253;
    evolution toward a studio technique
    143; instructional design course
    32–3; interior design studio (Indiana
    University) 68–9, 71–2; 'lake studio'
    course 123–5; 'Many Projects' studio
    11; quasi-therapist role 16; RDSC
    course 81–3; responsibility 13; scrutiny
    of 17; systems thinking and design
    course 230, *see also* student-teacher ratio
integrity (project) 10
intelligent simulation 140–1, 143, 144
interaction(s) 253–5; between students
    11, 111, 126, 134, 245; with students
    7, 68, 202
interaction design 235, 277
Interaction Design Project (IDP) 73, *see
    also* Rapid Design for Slow Change
interactive models 141
interconnectedness 227
interdisciplinarity 141, 142, 148, 203,
    265, 274, 277
interior design: lack of diversity in 267
interior design course (Florida State
    University) 101–22; class procedures
    109–12; constructivist learning 101,
    102; course context and student's
    prior experiences 102–4; evolution
    of the course 104–7; four-year
    curriculum *102*; improvements
    through extended collaboration
    107–9; ongoing questions and
    struggles with concept 118–22;
    teaching and learning concept
    development and application 113–16;

time management and other student challenges 112–13
interior design studio (Indiana University) 60–72; background context 60–1; becoming a studio teacher 68–71; crafting the projects 66–8; description 61–4; making and defending a studio environment 64–6; student workload 63
interpret and justify (concept learning) 115
Interservice Procedures for Instructional Systems Development (IPISD) 138
interventions (instructor) 17, 69–70
intrinsic motivation 51
introductory courses: instructional design 154, 196, 223; interior design 61; workshops, software skills 44
intuition/intuitive design 154, 155
iteration/iterative practice 11, 158–9, 159–62, 254
Ithaca College 223

justify (concept learning) 115

Klebesadel, H. 252
knowledge: acquisition 266; construction 114, 252, *see also* content knowledge; design knowledge; epistemology; past knowledge
Koch, A. 266, 268
Kopcha, Theodore J. 5, 17, 37–59
Kornetsky, L. 252
Krause Innovation Studio 237–40, 245
Kuhn, S. 274

lake studio course 123–36; active aspect of 9; administration 133; community engagement 13; design studio instructing 130–2; ETAD 879 126–30; funding 133; instructor 123–5; projects 134, 135; teaching 125–6; theoretical features 132–3; timeline, themes and milestones *130*; uncertainties 135
laptops 65–6
large projects 9–10
layer thinking *see* functional-layer approach
learner role 261
learning: creative problem solving course 12; educational multimedia design course 44; emotional dimension 8; from failure 224–5, 242; instructional design course 28, 29, 32–3; interior design course (FSU) 102; interior design course (Indiana University) 70; in the learning design studio 242; RDSC course 80
learning activities: systems thinking and design course 226, 227, 231
learning by doing 8, 102, 222, 225–6, 232, 251, 256, 276
learning community 52, 131, 152, 209, 252
learning context 13
learning design 277
Learning Design Studio (LDS) 235–46; assessment 243–4; course content 242; course readings 241; current and future challenges 244–6; defined 236; historical perspectives 236–7; in-class design activities 241–2; individual perspectives *238–9*; pedagogy 242–3; physical setting 237–40, 245; project work 242; student discussions 240, 241; weekly format 240
learning environment(s) 10, 13, 25, 30, 125, 128, 244, 251, 256, 261, 277, 278
learning outcomes 13, 16, 33, 67, 124, 235, 271
Learning Research and Development Center 138
Learning Sciences movement 138
learning styles 267
learning theories *see* Applied Theories of Instructional Design
learning values 29
lectures 5, 13, 63, 89
left brain/right brain struggle 103
legitimate peripheral participation (LPP) 49, 50
liberal professional education 232
life events 113
listening 112, 174, 229
Little, P. 274

McCluske, Marit 5, 8, 12, 13, 180–94
Macintosh computers 65
major projects 66–7, 69
The Man with the Dog 85–6
'Many Projects' studio 11
Massachusetts Institute of Technology (MIT) 251, 273

Master of Arts in Communications and
  Technology (MACT) 206–7, 208–19
mastery approach 224
'mathematics game' project 55
meaning-making 122
memorandums of understanding
  (MOU) 25
mental concepts 142
mentors/mentoring 47, 49, 82, 165,
  166, 175, 176, 252, 274
meta-discussions 252
meta-studio critique 26
metaphorical thinking 220
military ISD 138
mindmapping 211, *212*
Mindstorms 37
mini-lectures 82–3, 109, 115, 157
mistakes (instructor) 30, 31, 49, 70
mistakes (student) 42, 130, 158
Mitgang, L. 265
model-centredness 141
Moggridge, B. 46
Monson, C. 256
moral coherence 19
moral issues 18–20
motivation 31, 49, 51, 107, 243–4
multi-disciplinarity 148
multi-level studio environment 277
multi-tasking 178
multi-week projects 76, 83–4

N2K (need to know) 12, 170
NASAD Handbook (2014-15) 65
National Association of Schools of Art
  and Design (NASAD) 64–5
National Council for Interior Design
  Qualification (NCIDQ) 110
negotiated products 11
negotiated projects 10
Neilsen, Jacob 209
Nelson, Harold 225, 242
non profit agencies 31–2
normative commitments 261, 262

Ohio State University (OSU) 39
one-to-one mentoring 47
online courses: creative problem
  solving 192; instructional technology
  program 197–8; Learning Design
  Studio 244–5, *see also* virtual
  studio(s).
online discussion 32, 244
online environments *see* virtual studio(s)

online forum (RDSC) 80–1
online interaction 126–7, 132
online tutorials 95–6
openness 125, 176
originality 190
outcomes *see* learning outcomes
over-communication 84
overlapping projects 83–4

Pable, Jill B. 5, 11, 16, 17, 101–22
paint elevation 174
panel discussions 47
Papert, Seymour 37, 43, 49, 235
Parrish, P.E. 46
past knowledge: connecting with, and
  understanding of 12, 170
Pecha Kucha format 242
pedagogical activities 251–2, 256, 272,
  278–9
pedagogical control 254
pedagogy 257, 278; discouragement
  of particular learning styles 267;
  Learning Design Studio 242–3;
  product-based 177; rethinking and
  sequencing of content 14; scenic
  design course 169; and studio space
  15, 16; and subversion 207–8, *see
  also* critical pedagogy; signature
  pedagogy(ies)
peer assessment 28, 214
peer critique 63, 235, 276
peer feedback 62, 63, 75, 201, 243
peer mentoring 252
peer pressure 108
peer scaffolding 242
perfectionism 112, 113, 168
performance review 26, 48–9, 230
personal computers (PCs) 139
personal/individual discovery 202, 252
personas 48, 210
physical activity 9
physical settings 14–15; advanced design
  course (BYU) 147; interior design
  course (FSU) 108; interior design
  studio (Indiana University) 64–6; ISD
  course (BYU) 145; Krause Innovation
  Studio 237–40; scenic design course
  172; systems thinking and design
  course 228–9
'pin up' spaces 108
PLATO 139
Poetry Project 107
polytechnic schools (German) 249

positive stress 8
post-structuralists 206
power dynamics: critique culture 261
power relationships 82, 261, 262
pre-design discovery 105
precedents (design) 141, 142, 157
prescriptive theories 154
presentations: interior design course
(FSU) 111; interior design studio 63,
66; learning design studio 242; scenic
design course 167; systems thinking
and design course 228
pressure(s) 8, 10, 13, 15, 25, 32, 73,
74, 80, 93, 108, 134, 184, 192, 265
primary level systems design 231
problem-based learning 29, 256, 271,
274
problem-solving 109, 222, 225, 232,
253, 256, 277
process 13, 110, 177
process models 138, 141, 146, 278
process skills 14
product-based pedagogy 177
production classes: instructional design
course 90
professional experiences: sharing 70
professional identity(ies) 19, 202, 203,
205, 263, 276
professional journals 28
programming 38, 139
project management 29, 30–1, 35–6
project nights 51
project participants: RDSC course 76
project realism 80
project-based learning 5, 38, 213, 256,
271, 274
projects: advanced design course 147–8;
applied theories of instructional
design course 157; creative problem
solving course 192; educational
multimedia course (UGA) 43–4,
50, 54–9; emotional dimension 7;
instructional design course 31–2;
interior design course (FSU) 105–7,
111, 118; interior design studio
(Indiana University) 60–1, 66–8; lake
studio course 134, 135; Learning
Design Studio 242; RDSC course
74–5, 76–80; scenic design course
167–8, 173–4, 178; size and number
9–10; systems thinking and design
course 227–8, *see also* 'Big Project'
studio; 'Many Projects' studio

prototypes/prototyping 38, 78, 156,
186, 245, 253, 271
public critiques 157–8, 266–7
public premiere of products 13, 125–6
purpose of design 253

quasi-therapist role 16, 168

random word/image stimulation 185
Rapid Design for Slow Change (RDSC)
73–86; evolution 83–6; instructor
role 81–3; origins 73–4; projects
76–80; the reflective practitioner
80–1; students 74; studio mechanics
74–6; This I Believe 84–6
Rapid Interaction (Design) Practice
73–4
rapport 68, 110
Real World Instructional Design 196
real-world design 197, 275, 277, 278
real-world learning 29
reassurance 8
received understanding 5
reflection(s): instructional technology
program 198; interior design course
(FSU) 110; student-directed learning
274
reflection weeks (RDSC) 83, 84
reflection-in-action 251, 256
reflection-on-action 251, 256
reflective action 271
reflective activities 12–13
reflective journals 199, 202, 230, 231
reflective practice: industrial design
studio 253; in instructional systems
design 276–7; as a subversive goal,
in UCD course 214; theatrical scenic
design course 12, 13, 164–79
reflective practitioners 46, 80–1, 220
The Reflective Practitioner 260–1
Reimer, Y.J. 275, 276
reinterpret (concept learning) 115
rendering 174
Rensselaer Polytechnic Institute 273,
278
repetition 11, 116, 183
representation construction 275
representation presentation and
discussion 275
research: scenic design process 173
residential construction project 66
resource-intensive approaches 14–15,
264–5

resources: in the learning design studio 244; systems thinking and design course 227, 232
Revisit/Redo project 178
revolutionary phase: evolution of instructional design 137–9
rich learning environment 25
Rich, Peter 146, 147
Rieber, Lloyd P. 5, 7, 17, 37–59
right reasons 19–20
Roberts, A. 267
'role-playing game' projects 55, 56
Rook, Michael M. 12, 16, 235–46
Rowland, Gordon 5, 6–7, 7, 9, 11, 13, 14, 18, 222–33, 276

SAT (systems approach to training) 138
satisfaction 9, 108
scaffolding 29, 44, 198, 202, 211, 242, 245–6
SCALE-UP project 273–4
Schön, D.A. 142, 251, 256, 260–1, 275, 276
Schwier, Richard A. 10, 12, 15, 19, 21–36
Scott, Susan 84
script analysis: scenic design process 173
scrutiny (instructor) 17
second timers (UGA) 45–7; mentoring roles 47, 49; redesign of experience 52–3
self-assessment 214, *217*
self-directed design 32
self-directed learning 29, 38
self-learning 220
self-organization (student) 108–9
'sense of design as discovery' 9
sequencing 14, 166–7
SET (systems engineering of training) 138
Shaffer, D.W. 251, 252, 272
shared trust 28
sharing: between students 111, 124–5, 126, 128, 174, 227; with a broader audience 50, 125–6; experiences with students 70
showcase (UGA) 49–50, 51, 53
Shulman, L.S. 271
Siegel, Martin A. 11, 12, 73–86, 276
signature activities 12–13
signature pedagogy(ies) 5, 250, 252, 271
Simon, H. 142

single assignment course 92
situated cognition 49
situated learning 29, 49, 277
'six degrees of Kevin Bacon' 121
sketches: scenic design process 173
skills: of creativity 185–6; scenic design 169–70; separation of design and 169, 170, 174
Skype 22
Slack 84
slow change interaction design 74
slow change projects 76
small projects 10, 11
Smith, Kennon M. 5, 8, 9, 10, 13, 15, 16, 60–72, 91, 141, 142, 257, 260–8
social action 210, 220
social agency 19, 21, 29, 31
social climate 261
social cohesion 52
social engagement 11
social issues 18–20
social media 130, 240, *see also* blogs/ blogging
social sensitivity criterion (project selection) 31
social structures 64
social theory 261
social value: of projects 134
socialization: critique as a form of 276
software skills 44
space planning 68, 69, 102, 105, 114
Spector J.M. 201, 202, 203
standpoint theory 209, 210
STEM fields 271, 274
Stevens, G. 261
Stolterman, E. 242
Storyshare project 78
student advisory panel (UGA) 39
student consultants 50–1
student expectations 47–8, 61
'student' persona 48
student support 48–9, 130, 201, 202
student wellbeing 9, 261, 266
student workload 32, 35, 63, 178, 265
student-centeredness 125, 274
student-directed learning 274
student-teacher relationship 68–9, 125
student/teacher ratio 64–5, 265
students 256–7; activity-centric experience 9, 94; as co-learners 229; creative problem solving course 184; differential responses to 16–17; educational multimedia design

course 39; emotional dimension of studio 7, 8, 9, 34, 49; feedback to *see* feedback; instructional design course 21–2, 30; interactions *see* interactions; interior design course 61; learner role 261; learning *see* learning; RDSC course 74; sharing between 111, 124–5, 126, 128, 174, 227; sharing experiences with 70; Studio 1 interior design course 102–4; and studio culture 266

Studio 1 *see* interior design course (Florida State University)

studio/studio approach: as activity-centric 9–13; concerns regarding 263–7; courage and ingenuity in starting and maintaining 17–18; design cases *see* design cases; differential responses to students and variable goals 16–17; emergence of term 248; emergent views of 271–9; emotional dimension 7–9, 34, 49, 135; features 250–3; historical views of 249–50; instructors *see* instructors; interest in 1; moral and social issues 18–20; pacing, assignments and sequencing 13–14; as a personal complex enterprise 20; and practice communities 253–6; settings *see* physical settings; virtual studio(s); varieties of 142–3

studio bridge 263

studio culture(s) 250, 252, 256, 261, 262, 266–7, 276, 278

studio physics 273, 278

Studio Project Manager (UGA) 40

subjectivity 118, 119, 121, 175, 177, 190

subversive practice 206–20

success (student) 8, 131

summative feedback 243

support *see* design support; student support

surface structures/features 251, 255, 256, 257, 272, 274, 276, 278

syllabus: scenic design course 178–9

systematic approach 138–9, 141

systems modelling 227–8

Systems Thinking and Design 222–33; context 223; course specifics 225–9; design decisions 230–2; history of the course 223–5; next steps 232–3; teaching elements 229–30

Taylor, S.S. 272

teachers *see* instructors

teaching: creative problem solving course 193–4; expertise, acknowledging boundaries of 71; impact of functional-layer approach 144–5; instructional design (studio learning experience) 92–8; as iterative practice 159–62; lake studio course 125–6; philosophy, educational multimedia design course 49–51; systems thinking and design course 229–30

teaching assistants 118, 193–4

team assessment 214

team meetings 25–6

team work 11, 22, 51, 90, 255, 267

team-based design 32

team-based learning environments 277

team-teaching approach 39–40, 49

Technical Design course (Studio 1) 102, 103

technical proficiency 155

technology: blended groups 16; constructionism 37–8; interior design course (FSU) 110; keeping up with new 12; in the learning design studio 236

technology modules (LDS) 242

Temple University 164, 167, 172

Texas A&M University 39

theatrical scenic design course 12, 13, 164–79

theoretical features: lake studio course 132–3

theoretical influences: educational multimedia course 37–40

theoretical perspective: systems thinking and design course 231–2

theory(ies) 14; prescriptive 154, *see also* Applied Theories of Instructional Design; critical theory; social theory; standpoint theory

This I Believe 12, 84–6

TICCIT project 138–9, 140

time factor/pressures 10, 32, 80, 93, 134, 254

time management 109, 112–13, 171, 177

tool phase: evolution of instructional design 139–40

Torrance Test of Creative Thinking 182

Tracey, Monica W. 6–7, 9, 14, 15, 16, 195–205, 277

transdisciplinarity 232, 251, 274, 278
transformative learning 132, 229–30, 231
transformed practice 17–18
transforming curriculum 6
translation of ideas 101, 121
translations of studio (disciplinary) 272–8
transparency 8, 68
trust 8, 9, 13, 28, 130, 134
TUTOR 139–40

uncertainty(ies) 69–70, 135, 199, 200, 201, 204
Undisciplined and Out of Control 225
United States 249, 260, 267
University of Georgia (UGA): educational multimedia design 37–59; instructional systems design 276–8
University of North Carolina 273–4
University of Saskatchewan 7, 32
usability 253
user-centered design course 18, 208–19; assessment 217

values 19
values-based approaches 29, 210
verbal presentations 111
versioning 11
video conferencing 25, 34
video courses: software skills 44
video design 126, 127

video projects 10
video-based communication 15, 22
virtual studio(s) 15–16, 251, 276; instructional design course 22, 34, 36; lake studio course 126, *see also* online courses
visual communication 112
vulnerabilities 112
Vygotsky, L.S. 184

WebCT 207, 209
Webster, H. 261
West, Rick 146, 147
'What's Hot?' activity 12, 240
'where do we start' questions 32
white models: scenic design process 173
'wholist' learning styles 267
wicked problems 256, 271
'widow(er) maker' course 7–8
Willenbrock, L. 261, 262
Wilson, B.G. 46
Wilson, Jack 273
Wilson, Jay 5, 9, 10, 13, 123–36
Winograd, Terry 275, 276
workload (student) 32, 35, 63, 178, 265
workplace: connection to 226, 227, 232
workshops: educational multimedia course (UGA) 51; face-to-face (ETAD) 126, 127, 134; scenic design course 178–9

Yammer social media 240